George III

MANCHESTER
UNIVERSITY PRESS

George III

King and politicians
1760–1770

Peter D. G. Thomas

Manchester University Press
Manchester and New York

distributed exclusively in the USA by Palgrave

Copyright © Peter D. G. Thomas 2002

The right of Peter D. G. Thomas to be identified as the author of this work has been asserted by him in accordance with the Copyright, Designs and Patents Act 1988.

Published by Manchester University Press
Oxford Road, Manchester M13 9NR, UK
and Room 400, 175 Fifth Avenue, New York, NY 10010, USA
www.manchesteruniversitypress.co.uk

Distributed exclusively in the USA by
Palgrave, 175 Fifth Avenue, New York,
NY 10010, USA

Distributed exclusively in Canada by
UBC Press, University of British Columbia, 2029 West Mall,
Vancouver, BC, Canada V6T 1Z2

British Library Cataloguing-in-Publication Data
A catalogue record for this book is available from the British Library

Library of Congress Cataloging-in-Publication Data applied for

ISBN 0 7190 6428 7   *hardback*
      0 7190 6429 5   *paperback*

First published 2002

10 09 08 07 06 05 04 03 02   10 9 8 7 6 5 4 3 2 1

Typeset in Sabon
by Northern Phototypesetting Co. Ltd, Bolton
Printed in Great Britain
by Bookcraft (Bath) Ltd, Midsomer Norton

Contents

Preface

The eighteenth century was long deemed 'the classical age of the constitution' in Britain, with cabinet government based on a two-party system of Whigs and Tories in Parliament, and a monarchy whose powers had been emasculated by the Glorious Revolution of 1688–89. This simple picture was destroyed in 1929 when Sir Lewis Namier published his *The Structure of Politics at the Accession of George III*. He demonstrated that no such party system existed; that the monarchy was not a cypher; and that the correct political analysis of Parliament was of an administration side comprising factions of politicians currently in office, a Court Party of office-holders, and supportive independents, and an opposition side of other political factions and independent MPs. Namier reached this conclusion by a methodology that revolutionised the writing of political history. He broadened it to discuss not merely the leading politicians but also the rank and file, the so-called counting of heads; and he deepened it by the use of such techniques as prosopography, the study of social and family connections.

Namier, who became Professor of Modern History at the University of Manchester in 1931, was one of the most influential historians of the twentieth century, for imitators and disciples sought to apply his interpretation of how political history should be written to earlier and later periods of British history, and to foreign countries. 'We are almost all Namierites now', wrote his most recent biographer (Linda Colley, *Namier* (1989), p. 101). In due course there was a reaction against the enthusiastic application of his methodology. Critics were rightly convinced that ideas and ideals formed part of political history, but wrongly claimed that the counting of heads necessarily implied the discounting of such considerations. The illogicality of that contention has been demonstrated by much recent scholarship.

Namier's conclusions as to the absence of party politics in eighteenth-century Britain have been modified, though not refuted, by historians studying the beginning and end of the century, but his perception of the political system of mid-eighteenth-century Britain has retained general acceptance. The structure he depicted is the essential framework for a proper understanding of power politics and policy-making. This book, by Namier's last research student, is an attempt to apply that interpretation to the political story of the first decade of George III's reign, Namier's home territory. Factional politics was at its height in the 1760s, a circumstance that gave the King much more freedom of manoeuvre than if a party system had existed.

The role of George III has been the subject of frequent and ongoing debates among historians. This book provides detailed information from which readers may well draw conflicting conclusions, according to their prejudices. Much of it has come to light since a mid-twentieth-century controversy over interpretations of George III's political behaviour. There can be no doubt now that the King closely concerned himself with ministerial appointments. How far he was involved in policy decisions is less clear, for much of any such participation would have been in verbal discussions of which little record survives. Whether his behaviour was unconstitutional is, at bottom, a matter of interpretation. One factor can be subtracted from any argument about the King. Nothing is said here of the King's alleged insanity, the one 'fact' most people know about George III: for his illness of porphyria, which it really was, did not surface at this time.

This book is primarily a study of high politics, for the power structure was centred on the Crown and Parliament. One pioneer of the currently fashionable study of popular politics, John Brewer, in 1976 highlighted this decade as one of an alternative structure of politics to that depicted by Namier (*Party Ideology and Popular Politics at the Accession of George III*). His book, however, discussed not the events of the period but the wider political environment, drawing attention to the growing importance of public opinion, and especially to the press in its various manifestations. There can be no doubt that political matters were extensively discussed in newspapers, taverns, and coffee-houses. Demagogue John Wilkes did make a notable impact on the political scene, in the press and on the streets, as this author's biography of him has shown (*John Wilkes: A Friend to Liberty* (1996)). But when the furore had died down, the political world was still dominated by the King and the Parliamentary factions.

In the writing of this book I have, as ever, incurred many obligations. Above all I am grateful to the Leverhulme Trust for an Emeritus Fellowship that has made possible the research for and production of it. I thank Thomas Bartlett for the loan long ago of manuscript transcripts, and Karl Schweizer for the elucidation of some points concerning foreign policy. It is particularly pleasing to acknowledge the benefit I have derived from the published and unpublished work of twelve of my former research students: Huw Bowen, Heather Breeze, Nicola Davies, Margaret Escott, Dylan Jones, the late Philip Lawson, Jonathan Nicholas, Martyn Powell, David Prior, Anita Rees, Sian Rees, and Dale Williams.

For permission to use manuscripts I am indebted to the Duke of Grafton; the Marquess of Bute; the Earl of Malmesbury; the William L. Clements Library; and the Henry E. Huntingdon Library. I have received valuable assistance from the staff of the National Library of Wales; the British Library; the Public Record Office; the Institute of Historical Research; and the Library of the University of Wales, Aberystwyth. Mrs Dorothy Evans has patiently converted my manuscript into a text fit for the printer. I am grateful for the guidance and help of the staff of Manchester University Press in the final stage of production.

1

The parameters of politics

Britain has never had a written constitution. The closest approximation was the Revolution Settlement of William III's reign, as embodied especially in the 1689 Bill of Rights and the 1701 Act of Settlement. But the provisions were essentially negative, stipulating what the monarch could not do. The sovereign could not override the law of the land, and, in practice, for financial and other reasons, could not govern without an annual meeting of Parliament. By 'the Revolution', as it was denoted in the eighteenth century, politicians in Britain prevented the evolution of an autocratic monarchy. Yet the sovereign retained the executive power, and William III certainly exercised it; but under his successors the functions of policy-making and patronage fell increasingly into the hands of ministers who were Parliamentary politicians. Twice, moreover, in 1742 and 1744, George II was compelled by the politicians who controlled Parliament to part with Premiers he wished to retain: and for long historians were accustomed to portray him as a king held 'in chains' by his ministers.

How far the balance of power in the British constitution had already tilted from the Crown to the House of Commons was the issue underlying the controversy over the behaviour of George III when he inherited the throne in 1760. For the active role played by that new young monarch seemed to many contemporaries accustomed to envisaging Parliament as the power centre of their political world to be a reversion to pre-1689 practice. Was he subverting the constitution, as portrayed by the traditional interpretation long held by Whig or liberal historians? That view stemmed from the circumstance that the Hanoverian Succession of 1714 effectively deprived the monarchy of a choice between the two parties of Whig and Tory. All ministries between 1714 and 1760 were Whig, albeit opposed

often by malcontent Whigs as well as a dwindling number of Tories.
This seemingly permanent political alignment, with Sir Robert Walpole, Henry Pelham and his brother the Duke of Newcastle successive
leaders of the dominant 'old Whig corps', gave rise to terminology
appropriate to the 'court versus country' situation that had evolved.
That most commonly used in mid-century Parliamentary debate was
'administration' and 'opposition', and by 1770 the even more frank
designations of 'the majority' and 'the minority', previously deemed
irregular, had become 'the constant language'.[1]

This political dominance of 'the Whig oligarchy' led to the assumption, both contemporary and historical, that the reign of George II
witnessed a significant loss of power by the Crown. Recent reassess-
ments of the role of that monarch have largely undermined that interpretation, which forms the premiss for the consequent charge that
George III was somehow seeking to turn back the constitutional
clock.[2] George II certainly did make the famous complaint in 1744
that 'ministers are the Kings in this country'.[3] But his remark was less
a description of the British scene than an implicit comparison with his
own autocratic role in Hanover and that of monarchs in continental
Europe. George II was no William III, in that he did not initiate policies, but in the making of ministries the King played a positive role
even during his old age in the 1750s;[4] and the able but detested
William Pitt was kept out of cabinet office until the crisis of the Seven
Years War. His ministers had to pay heed to his wishes in every aspect
of politics. Foreign policy was distorted by the King's insistence on the
need to safeguard his beloved Electorate of Hanover. At election times
George II took an active part in approving the choice of candidates
and authorising royal expenditure. As for patronage, he exerted more
control over posts in the army and at Court than did George III, and
he kept a close eye on the bestowal of bishoprics, peerages, and honours generally. Incessant complaints by the Duke of Newcastle bear
ample testimony to this royal influence, and in 1755 George II even
told the Duke, then head of the ministry, that there was no first minister in Britain, and that his control over appointments was confined
to the Treasury.[5] In a reversal of historical tradition, George II, in the
exercise of a whole range of royal powers, compared favourably with
his grandson.

If there was scant loss of royal power under George II for his successor to recover after 1760, the old idea of Whig mythology that
George III had ambitions of autocratic monarchy is complete non-
sense. The myth that his mother Augusta, Dowager Princess of Wales,

urged her son, 'George, be a King', with the implication that she meant a monarch in the German tradition, has long been exploded. Historian Sir Lewis Namier joked that she was referring to his table manners. His mother's successful endeavour was to instil in her eldest son, though not his brothers, the virtues of religion and morality.[6] George III's concept of himself as an honest and moral man contributed to his strength of character, but that was the sole political consequence of his maternal upbringing. His tutor Lord Bute taught the young Prince to revere the constitution as established by the Revolution Settlement. Political liberty in Britain, that phenomenon so widely admired in Europe, was the result of a system of checks and balances between the executive, headed by the monarch, and the legislature, embodied in the two Houses of Parliament, with the added safeguard of an independent judicature.[7] By 1760 the Prince had began to think for himself, and perceived two royal threats to the balance of the constitution, the unfettered power of the Crown to create peers, and the existence of an army under royal control. That in an essay on the British constitution, written only a few months before his accession, George III privately showed this concern about the potential danger to liberty from the monarchy is an ironic contrast to much contemporary and historical portrayal of his behaviour as King.[8]

Bute's sound constitutional indoctrination of the future King was marred by prejudices he instilled about the contemporary political scene. The young Prince of Wales was led to condemn the Hanoverian propensities of his grandfather George II; to deplore the division into parties that prevented government by a coalition of the best men; and generally to regard the governing politicians in Britain and Ireland as corrupt and selfish. On 4 May 1760 he wrote to Bute, 'I look upon the majority of politicians as intent on their own private interests instead of that of the public'.[9] The consequence of all this was not only that the new young King would, with the naive idea of cleansing the political system, assert the Crown's power of appointing ministers, a right so lapsed that many Parliamentarians were to regard it as improper; but that he formulated the logical conclusion that Bute himself must be his political saviour. That had not been the intention of Bute, a man more suited to scholarship than to politics. But, hoist with his own petard, he was willing to forsake a quiet private life to become Prime Minister, a task he performed conscientiously and creditably, but quit within a year.

Although George III then had to fall back on Parliamentary politicians, men not always to his liking, he maintained the practice of allowing his ministers to govern. For, contrary to much historical interpretation, it was never his intention to impose measures as well as choose ministers. Often, as early on over America and India, he had no opinion on matters of policy. When he did, he often made his views known to individual ministers. But there was never any question of the King enforcing his opinions by the threat of removing recalcitrant ministers from office, except for one brief occasion in 1762 when Bute was encountering resistance over the peace terms. Horace Walpole understood from his friend Henry Conway, Secretary of State 1765–68, that 'whether hating or liking the persons he employed, he seemed to resign himself entirely to their conduct for the time'.[10] George III's practice was recalled in 1775 by Lord Hillsborough, who had sat in cabinet from 1768 to 1772 as American Secretary. 'The King ... always will leave his sentiments, and conform to his Ministers, though he will argue with them, and very sensibly; but if they adhere to their own opinion, he will say, "Well. Do you choose it should be so? Then let it be."'[11] It was the cabinet, albeit often influenced by royal opinions, that made decisions on policy

'There is in our constitution no such thing as a cabinet', MP Charles Jenkinson reminded the House of Commons on 12 February 1770, and the usual designation in government papers was 'meeting of the King's servants'.[12] But MP James Harris put matters in a practical perspective when he made this comment after similar assertions in Parliament a week earlier. 'Strange! As if all matters political were not to be discussed in the cabinet, and the ministers to come down to either House without knowing each other's minds.'[13] The cabinet may have been unofficial, but its existence was accepted in newspapers, correspondence and Parliamentary debate. Its informality was reflected in irregularity of meetings and variation of composition. It met as need arose, usually at least once a week save in the summer recess of Parliament, and almost always at the private houses of ministers, any one of whom might summon a meeting. The size of the cabinet varied considerably, but the first decade of George III's reign saw the final evolution of a small, efficient cabinet, a development not approved by the sovereign, who perceived therein a curtailment of his own political role.

At the head of the cabinet was the Prime Minister, not yet a term much in vogue nor one favoured by Lord North, who held the post for twelve years from 1770. Press references were often to 'the Premier', those in Parliament simply to 'the Minister'. George Grenville, who held the post from 1763 to 1765, later referred to having been 'First Minister'.[14] The post was usually but not invariably equated with the office of First Lord of the Treasury, for it was desirable for the Premier to control the main fount of patronage. If he was an MP and not a peer, though only two Premiers, Grenville and North, were during this period, the Prime Minister would also be Chancellor of the Exchequer, for the good reason that finance constituted the main government business in the Commons. Otherwise the Chancellor of the Exchequer did not sit regularly in cabinet until Charles Townshend secured that status late in 1766.[15] The other major executive officers were the two Secretaries of State, equal in rank. In theory each could handle any matter that arose, and in emergency might do so, but in practice they had a clear division of responsibility. The Southern Secretaryship was now deemed the more important, and Northern Secretaries sometimes moved to take a vacancy there, as in 1763 and 1768.[16] The Southern Secretary handled diplomatic relations with France, Spain, Portugal, and the Mediterranean countries: but he was also responsible for the American and other colonies, Ireland, and acted as unofficial Home Secretary. The Northern Secretary was concerned with the German states, Holland, Scandinavia, and Russia, and seemingly also with Scotland. In 1768 a third Secretaryship of State was created, for America, though its claim to equality of status was sometimes disputed by holders of the senior Secretaryships. If these busy executive posts constituted the heart of the cabinet, membership also included the three traditional great offices of state: the Lord Chancellor, head of the legal profession, who presided over the House of Lords; the Lord President of the Privy Council, that increasingly formal institution numbering around a hundred, that constituted the official advisory body for the Crown; and the Lord Privy Seal, responsible for the official signing of state documents. In 1768 this last post, when held by a political nonentity, was excluded from the cabinet in order to reduce its size, but soon afterwards was restored to membership. The other customary cabinet post was First Lord of the Admiralty, a tacit acknowledgement of the importance of the navy. The army was represented in wartime, but not always in peace, by the Commander-in-Chief or the Master-General of the Ordnance, never by the civilian Secretary at War. The President of the Board of Trade and Plantations was not a member, but always attended on American business until the creation of the American Department. The Lord-Lieutenant of Ireland took a seat when over in Britain, but that claim was to fade with his permanent residence in Dublin from 1767.

In 1760 membership of the cabinet was not confined to leading office-holders. It then included two political allies of Prime Minister

Newcastle, in the Duke of Devonshire and the Earl of Hardwicke, Lord Chancellor from 1737 to 1756, now without office but Newcastle's prop and confidant. Lord Mansfield, Lord Chief Justice of King's Bench, continued to sit through three ministries until the autumn of 1763. Bute sought to emulate Newcastle's practice by bringing in some of his friends when he took the Treasury in May 1762. Lord Melcombe attended only briefly, dying in July, and Lord Waldegrave refused, but another Bute man, Lord Egmont, though only Postmaster-General, sat in cabinet even before he took the Admiralty in September 1763. Lord Gower, holding merely the Royal Household post of Master of the Wardrobe, attended cabinet during the second half of Bute's ministry, October 1762 to April 1763, to represent his brother-in-law the Duke of Bedford, Lord Privy Seal but absent negotiating peace in Paris. So too then did Henry Fox, only Paymaster of the Forces but now also Leader of the Commons.

This anachronistic situation must have been anathema to the tidy mind of George Grenville. Soon after he became Prime Minister in 1763 the cabinet was virtually reduced to a small group of office-holders, although he did accept Lord Marchmont as a replacement lawyer for Lord Mansfield. Thereafter the cabinet had no more than a dozen members, and sometimes as few as six. Grenville also effectively put an end to what George III called 'the common cabinet' to distinguish it from 'the ministerial cabinet'.[17] This body, comprising numerous politicians, household officers, and such dignitaries as the Archbishop of Canterbury, and called by some historians 'the Nominal Cabinet', had been expanded beyond the limit of efficiency. Horace Walpole commented in 1761 that the rank of 'cabinet counsellor will soon become indistinct from Privy Counsellor by growing as numerous'.[18] It met occasionally in the early years of George III's reign, as to ratify the peace terms finally signed in 1763, but thereafter its political role was formal, notably the approval of royal speeches prior to their presentation to Parliament.

The cabinet proper was by contrast the genuine centre of decision-making, where the Prime Minister, though he presided, did not always get his way: Grenville was overruled on the American land settlement of 1763, and Grafton defeated over the American tea duty in 1769. The usual practice was for each item of business to be introduced by an appropriate departmental minister, with ensuing discussions customarily being commenced by the newer members, so that they would not be overawed by their seniors. If consensus could not be achieved, decisions were taken by majority votes. Policy disagreements seldom led to resignations. Those usually occurred only if a minister had been overruled in a matter concerning his own department, as when Southern Secretary Weymouth resigned in 1770 over the Falkland Islands Crisis, and American Secretary Hillsborough in 1772 over a proposed Ohio colony. Rather was acceptance of a majority decision the norm: of the three MPs who argued in cabinet on 13 January 1769 against the expulsion of John Wilkes from the House of Commons, two voted for expulsion and the other abstained when that business came before the House on 3 February. Cabinet decisions were recorded in minutes, which were, so Southern Secretary Shelburne wrote in 1767, 'according to the indispensable custom of those meetings, read over to the Lords present, to know whether it expressed their sentiments as they wished them to be laid before His Majesty'.[19] They were respectfully tendered to the King in form only as 'advice', and also formed a security for those ministers executing the decisions taken.[20] George III, often having put in his word beforehand, would accept the decisions of his 'ministerial cabinet': but they often also needed endorsement by Parliament.

There was by now a set pattern to the annual Parliamentary session. The important business would usually be done between the Christmas and Easter recesses, for attendance was otherwise poor. The session began in both Houses of Lords and Commons with the voting of an Address in reply to the King's Speech, which had stated the ministry's opinions and intentions. The ensuing debates set the political tone of the new session, and a failure of opposition to force a vote over an amendment usually betokened a quiet time for the administration. Taxation was routine and seldom controversial, though administrations were discomforted over a cider tax in 1763 and a window tax in 1766, and actually defeated in 1767 over the rate of land tax to be imposed. Levied on estate rents, that was the sole direct tax on income, but by now more revenue accrued from customs and excise duties. All measures of home policy, financial and otherwise, were enacted by legislation. This was now standardised into some dozen stages in each House, of which the second reading, to debate the principle, and the committee, to discuss the details, were the most significant. All MPs and peers were free at any time to propose motions and initiate legislation. Government might seek approval of policy measures. Opposition motions often took the form of requests for papers on current political issues or general resolutions of principle critical of ministerial behaviour. By now administration had an array of obstructive devices to block direct votes on awkward topics, often generically described as 'the previous question', which specifically was a counter that the motion be not put. Adjournments and amendments served the same purpose of avoiding embarrassment. Such were the weapons of Parliamentary warfare, deployed in the political arena of Westminster.[21]

Parliament, in the context of the political battle for power, meant the House of Commons. Contemporaries knew that contests between administration and opposition over policies and for office were decided there. The House of Lords as a political institution enjoyed prestige rather than power, and setbacks for ministers there were merely inconvenient and annoying. No ministry would be overthrown by defeat in the Lords, and its chief role was that of a political sounding-board. It did contain the bulk of the nation's political leadership, a majority of the cabinet and the heads of most opposition factions. Its debates were often of high quality, and widely reported in the press during the 1770s. Yet all this was rather a sham. At best the Lords was a forum for propaganda, as opposition peer Lord Temple acknowledged when in 1770 he announced he would not attend merely to 'talk to tapestry' after the Lords, to counter the onset of Parliamentary reporting, decided to prohibit public attendance.[22]

It was not merely that the Lords lacked a significant role in the body politic. There was in any case also the circumstance of a permanent majority for government there. That this ministerial hold on the Lords rested on a triple foundation of bishops, Scots, and courtiers was stated by radical journalist John Almon in 1770, when in the monthly *London Museum* he described 'the Court Lords' as 'consisting of the Scotch Lords, the Bishops, the Placed-Lords, etc.', and has long been received historical wisdom.[23] All the twenty-six bishops of England and Wales owed their appointment to a minister, and since their promotion and patronage prospects depended on support of the current administration most of them transferred their allegiance on any change of ministry. Newcastle, long responsible for ecclesiastical appointments under George II, was the first fallen minister of the new reign to suffer such desertions, with his famous joke that even the bishops forgot their Maker. The sixteen Scottish representative peers were chosen at the time of each general election, when the Scottish peerage, meeting in Edinburgh, tended to vote almost en bloc the government list sent from London. The third component of a government majority was a Court Party, comprising peers who held offices of honour or profit, often in the Royal Household itself, and about a dozen impecunious peers who had pensions. In 1774 Treasury

Secretary John Robinson listed sixty-five English and ten Scottish peers as holding office.[24] George III's youthful fear about the power of the Crown to create peers was irrelevant to the Parliamentary scene, but it was reflected in his reluctance to make new peers, until a logjam of promises was broken by ten creations on the same day, 20 May 1776. Ministerial control of the Lords was buttressed by a procedural device peculiar to that House, that of proxy voting, whereby peers expecting to be absent could entrust their votes to other peers. Since it was more respectable to support the King's government than to demonstrate hostility to it, ministers found it easier to collect proxies than their opponents. But proxies were not an essential weapon. When called for they served to increase a ministerial majority, but never in this period did they reverse a decision made by the peers actually present.

Since the membership of the House of Lords remained constant at around two hundred, the combined size of these groups of government supporters would appear to guarantee a safe majority for any ministry, and that was almost invariably the case. But in the 1760s two developments disrupted the customary pattern of political behaviour. The factionalisation of politics in that decade meant that about half the House of Lords owed allegiance to various political leaders and at some time voted against the King's government. This circumstance did not in itself threaten ministerial control of the Lords, for one or more of the factions were always with administration. But the Court Party was disrupted by the American question, as many peers deemed the policies of the Rockingham and Chatham ministries too conciliatory towards the colonies. Courtiers, Scottish peers and bishops all voted in some numbers over America against the Rockingham ministry, which in 1766 actually suffered two Lords defeats on relevant issues, by 63 to 60 and by 59 to 55, on 4 and 6 February respectively. They could rebel in safety because the King's favourite Lord Bute was at their head. Prime Minister Rockingham then put pressure on George III, and the key measure of repeal of the Stamp Act was carried by 73 votes to 61, the majority being raised by proxies to 105 to 71. That total of 176 was the largest at any Lords division during the century. This near-success of a challenge to ministerial policy was exceptional. The opposition attacks in the Lords during 1767 ran the Chatham ministry close, down to a majority of only three, 65 to 62, on 26 May; but they threatened only embarrassment over opposition motions, not defeat of government policy, and the conflict was different, comprising an alliance of factions against a court party whose unity was much tighter than in 1766. Nor, despite George III's belief in 'an intention to storm my closet',[25] did the opposition hope to bring down the ministry by defeat in the Lords: and the sole consequence was to frighten the cabinet into abortive coalition negotiations during the recess.[26]

Too much should not be read into these ministerial difficulties in the House of Lords during the mid-1760s. The Grafton and North ministries had no problems there as normality returned from 1768, and Chatham, on his return to opposition in 1770, found that his peerage had politically emasculated him, since the House of Lords lacked the significant body of independent opinion that as William Pitt he had made his power base in the Commons. In the four sessions from 1771 to 1774 the opposition did not even force a Lords vote on the Address, and the Rockinghamite party made the best of a bad job by exploiting the procedural device of printed *Protests* against Lords decisions, using them as a vehicle for press portrayals of opposition viewpoints. The House of Lords was again a mere sounding-board.

The contrasting independence of the House of Commons stemmed from the electoral system. The electorate was beyond the control of government, and not merely because of its size, for which 300,000 voters can be no more than an informed guess, in the absence of both electoral rolls and frequent polls.[27] Political power lay with the landed class, whose estates, prestige and other modes of influence created 'natural' political interests, on which government could make little impact. Most constituencies were controlled by the squires, the myth of an aristocratic oligarchy of a few great patrons having been destroyed long ago, in 1929, by Sir Lewis Namier, who calculated that in the English boroughs 55 peers influenced the election of only 111 MPs.[28] Subsequent research, and the inclusion of county seats, has raised that total to around 150 MPs, and the greatest patron, the Duke of Newcastle, is now credited with ten rather than seven seats.[29]

There were 314 constituencies returning 558 MPs, forty-five of them for small Scottish electorates mostly under the control of 'friends of government', whoever was minister. By contrast, the forty English counties were the most obvious bastions of independence. Here wide interpretations of the forty-shilling freehold franchise produced an average electorate of 4,000, too great a number for Scottish peer Lord Denbigh, who informed the House of Lords in 1773 that 'he was for raising the qualification of all the electors of England':[30] his was a lone voice when most commentators on the electoral system advocated its expansion and reform. If tiny Rutland had only 800

voters, giant Yorkshire had 20,000, being by far the largest constituency in the country. Over three-quarters of the eighty county MPs
were squires, the remainder being sprigs of the aristocracy. Often one
seat out of the two for a shire might by convention or calculation be
conceded to a local aristocrat, as to the Duke of Devonshire in
Derbyshire. The county representation was usually decided at public
meetings, for the gentry could only lead and not dictate to the freeholders. Since contests were fearsomely expensive, few counties
actually went to the poll.

The squirearchy also sat for the twenty-four Welsh seats, county
and borough alike, and for most of the 405 seats of the 203 English
boroughs, whose great varieties of franchises bestowed by separate
charters are conventionally classified into five categories: twelve pot-
walloper or householder boroughs; ninety-two freeman or burgess
boroughs; thirty-seven 'scot and lot' or ratepayer boroughs; twenty-
seven corporation boroughs; and thirty-five burgage and freeholder
boroughs, where the franchise simply appertained to a piece of property. A wide franchise did not necessarily mean a large electorate, but
there was some correlation. Twenty-eight freeman boroughs had over
1,000 voters, whereas the largest corporation borough, Bath, had
only sixty. Small electorates were usually easy to control, and fifteen
corporation boroughs were now the pocket boroughs of local squires
or peers. So were nineteen of the burgage and freeholder boroughs,
since the purchase of a majority of relevant properties in a borough
was simple, though often expensive. Such pocket boroughs should be
distinguished from the 'rotten' or venal boroughs. Numerous voters
perceived elections as opportunities for material gain. Bribery implies
freedom of choice, and the thrust of some modern research is to
demonstrate that candidates had far less command of constituencies
than was formerly assumed.[31] Too much should not be made of this
independence of the electorate. That the average length of an MP's
service in Parliament was over twenty years underlines the point that
the basic problem confronting a ministry there was the power of
the gentry, not the behaviour of the mass electorate, though any
constituency pressures from counties and large boroughs were likely
to be against the government of the day.

After each general election a ministry was therefore confronted
with a House of Commons over the membership of which it had had
very limited influence. At the general election of 1761 the ministry
directly controlled only thirty seats, the so-called Treasury and Admiralty boroughs where those two departments had many voters on

their payroll.[32] A ministry otherwise spent on average only £50,000
at a general election to assist a few favoured candidates, when the
purchase of one seat in 1761 cost £2,000, and considerably more
by 1768.[33]

A typical House of Commons would thus comprise 500 self-
returning MPs, as against 50 elected under government influence. The
problem of ministerial control can be perceived in the circumstance
that some 300 MPs would be independent, with about 100 belonging
to the hard core of political factions, and some 150 to a Court Party
of office-holders. This tripartite analysis of MPs and peers into placemen, politicians and independents is that portrayed by Sir Lewis
Namier in his seminal work *The Structure of Politics at the Accession
of George III*, wherein he destroyed the prevailing notion of a two-
party framework of Whigs and Tories. The political alignment he
substituted comprised an administration side of politicians, placemen,
and independents, challenged by an opposition of other politicians
and independents.

It is time to put some flesh on these bare bones of analysis. The
smallest of the three political segments of Parliament comprised the
party factions. These were the men ambitious for the power and
emoluments of office, and often with opinions on policy-making,
from whom all ministries were constructed. They competed for, and
filled the high offices of state, such lesser posts as membership of the
Boards of Treasury, Admiralty, and Trade, and other executive offices
of government, together with numerous household and court posts,
and a few sinecures, some of which were clearly reserved for men
whose role was to give debating support to government. The factions
were temporary phenomena, meteors in the political firmament,
often ending on the death of their leader, or perhaps then merging
into the general body of supporters or opponents of government.
Contemporaries disagreed, as do historians, as to the precise composition of these groupings, and with good reason, for many attach-
ments were fluctuating and uncertain. Historian John Brooke in 1956
essayed an examination of factional politics at its height in 1767,
identifying four main groups: but even his careful calculations have
been subjected to subsequent corrections.[34]

Lord Chatham, then head of the ministry, had never as William Pitt
sought to be a party leader, and his following of a score of MPs and a
handful of peers was hardly worthy of that name. Without the efforts
of his chief lieutenant Lord Shelburne the group might well have broken up after 1770, when Chatham absented himself from Parliament

for some years, and it was often denoted 'the Shelburne party' even before his death in 1778. Shelburne returned to Parliament lawyer John Dunning and firebrand Colonel Isaac Barré to give the party a vocal presence in the Commons, while he and Lord Camden spoke in the Lords on behalf of their frequently absent leader.

In 1767 the other three factions were all in opposition. Chatham's brother-in-law George Grenville had while Prime Minister from 1763 to 1765 acquired a personal following: this numbered about forty in 1767, but was reduced to thirty at the general election of 1768.[35] The Bedfordites were often equated with the Grenvillites, and sometimes listed with them, because they had together formed the ministry of 1763–65. That was a mistake, to become apparent when the groups parted company at the end of 1767. The tightly organised Bedford faction dated from the 1740s, headed by a group of peers, Bedford, Gower, Sandwich and Weymouth. Their real weight was in the House of Lords, where this formidable debating team headed a band of fifteen peers, but their electoral influence also provided a useful twenty votes in the Commons, where Richard Rigby was a robust speaker. The Bedford faction was notorious for its naked desire for the financial and other benefits of office. Dismissed in July 1765, they contrived to return to government before the end of 1767, for being in opposition was anathema to the Bedford group, an attitude signified in the response of Rigby when congratulated in 1765 on having won a debate though not the vote. 'No! Damme! A minority never was in the right from the beginning of the world to this day; a minority is always absurd.'[36]

In contrast with the transitory nature of those factions dependent on the career of their leader was the party headed in 1767 by the Marquess of Rockingham. Claiming to be 'the Whig party', with a political lineage from 'the old Whig corps' headed successively in office by Sir Robert Walpole, Henry Pelham and the Duke of Newcastle – and according to journalist John Almon known as 'the Pelhams' as late as 1766[37] – this group has traditionally been seen by historians as the link with the future Whig party subsequently headed on Rockingham's death in 1782 by Charles James Fox and his nineteenth-century successors.[38] A recent alternative interpretation portrays the Rockinghamites as 'a country party', heir to the opponents of that Whig monopoly of power in the earlier eighteenth century.[39] This apparent conflict of opinion is rather a difference in emphasis: for both views are served by the Rockinghamite claim to be defending 'liberty' against the power of the Crown.

The size and continuity of the party would seem to represent a strong case for the traditional interpretation, but analysis of the constantly changing party personnel weakens that line of argument. For a significant proportion of the 'old Whig corps' men and families of George II's reign were supporters of Lord North's ministry in the 1770s, and not in opposition with Lord Rockingham. Most of them were lost in 1762 and 1766. In November 1762 Newcastle, no longer at the Treasury, drastically reduced the estimated size of his Commons support from 238 to 142. Even that was optimistic, for a modern assessment puts this at 69 MPs in December. The party had recovered somewhat by the time of the formation of the Rockingham ministry, to number 105 MPs in 1765, and 111 at its dismissal in 1766. But there occurred then the loss of those who preferred office to the prospect of permanent opposition. Over 40 MPs deserted Rockingham when Chatham replaced him as Prime Minister, including his Commons Leader Henry Conway. Newcastle's papers at the time contain a list of 26 MPs optimistically headed 'friends of ours who remain with the present administration'.[40] But even the old Duke soon realised that they were lost for ever: in January 1767 he listed only 79 MPs and 44 peers as 'particular friends'.[41] At the general election of 1768 the Rockingham party had 54 MPs and 34 peers. Deaths and desertions further weakened the party, which reached its nadir at 43 MPs after the 1774 general election.[42]

The Rockinghamite party was in structure a larger and looser version of the Bedfordite group, with a nucleus of aristocratic families. The personal following of the Marquess numbered a dozen, half from his native Yorkshire. The Duke of Portland and Lord Albemarle each returned four MPs, the Duke of Richmond two. By 1768 Newcastle was down to six seats, and on his death later that year his nephew heir proved to be an adherent of government. The death in 1764 of the fourth Duke of Devonshire left the Cavendish family without an active aristocratic head, but Lord John Cavendish was prominent in the Commons. The death that same year of Newcastle's old friend the Earl of Hardwicke loosened the ties of the Yorke family with the party, even though Charles Yorke acted as Rockingham's Attorney-General and his brother the second earl was offered cabinet office: the Yorke family deserted in 1770. By then the two leading Rockinghamites in the Commons were men without aristocratic connections. Irish orator Edmund Burke, Rockingham's private secretary as Prime Minister, was the star performer, but William Dowdeswell carried more weight. Once deemed a Tory by Newcastle, this independent

MP for Worcestershire had been recruited as Chancellor of the Exchequer in 1765, and from 1766 to 1774 led the party in the Commons. Burke and Dowdeswell made a formidable pair, and the Rockinghamites altogether had a good array of speakers there. But lack of debating talent in the Lords was an obvious party weakness: only Richmond spoke effectively, for Rockingham was inarticulate and the other grandees like Portland virtually silent.

The Court Party outnumbered the political factions in the Commons. A snapshot of it is provided by a list compiled by or for Treasury Secretary John Robinson of MPs holding office in the summer of 1774. It yields a total of 135 for the Court Party, after 25 politicians in office have been excluded. They comprised 24 MPs in administrative posts; 46 holders of court offices; 39 soldiers and 2 naval men; 14 lawyers on the government payroll, useful in debate; 7 merchants holding government contracts; and 3 absent ambassadors.[43] Robinson did not include the few MPs who held simple pensions. These were often retainers until they were found a post, for to the actual Court Party there must be added the MPs and peers anxious to join it. Many of these posts, especially those at Court, involved little or no work. The duties of the eight-man Board of Green Cloth did not justify their £1,000 salaries, nor did the 12 Lords and 12 Grooms of the Royal Bedchamber have more than formal tasks to earn their respective salaries of £1,000 and £500 each. The Royal Household contained many such posts, for no office was abolished when its usefulness had passed. But the Court Party was not mere lobby-fodder, and several officials were hardworking. George Rice was one. Scion of an old Whig family but also son-in-law of Lord Talbot, a Bute man who became Steward of the Household on George's accession, Rice sat at the Board of Trade from 1761 to 1770, through all the ministerial vicissitudes of that decade: under Lord North he doubled his salary by moving in 1770 to the court office of Treasurer of the Chamber, but remained a government spokesman on colonial matters. The administrator-politician par excellence was Lord Barrington, who perceived it his duty to serve the King's government, whoever was Prime Minister. He was an office-holder continuously from 1746 to 1778, under a long succession of ministries, conduct often attributed to venality by contemporaries. He served nineteen years as an able Secretary at War, and his debating role in Parliament was not then confined to military matters. The Court Party altogether was a hybrid of sinecurists, administrators, and debaters.[44]

Since the Court Party and the politicians in government would never, despite some alarmist predictions about the power of the Crown, constitute a majority of any reasonably full House of Commons, the key to political power lay with the 300 or so independent MPs. In practice some independents would always vote for the King's minister. That Lord North in the 1770s enjoyed the invariable support of such 'old Tories' as Sir Roger Newdigate helps to explain the Tory label once fixed on that minister. A good number of independents were loosely attached to one or other of the factions. Many others followed the old Parliamentary tradition of opposition to the Crown. That attitude remained an important factor in the overall political situation, and since it usually prevailed among those MPs who seldom attended, the fuller the House was of MPs the greater the danger to ministers. Fortunately for government the presence of as many as 400 of the 558 MPs was rare. In the first decade of George III's reign the highest attendance at a vote was 455, on both 17 February 1764 and 12 February 1770. A mere 389 voted on 9 December 1762 over the Peace of Paris, and only 447 on 21 February 1766 over the repeal of the American Stamp Act. Apathy was one reason for the customary majority for government.

But there still remained the need for ministers, by argument in debate, to win the support of a proportion of the independents. It could never be taken for granted, and any failure to present the government case in debate would incur criticism. Hence the desirability for the Prime Minister to be in the House of Commons, since MPs did not relish being governed by proxy. Ministries headed by peers were short-lived and often in difficulty. That very predicament was the reason reputedly given by the Duke of Grafton to George III, for his resignation in 1770. 'As he found the great strength of the increasing minority was in the Lower House, he thought it most natural as well as advisable, to nominate a Premier there, in the scene of action; as he found by daily experience, that that was the fittest place for a Prime Minister, and that there was no doing any thing without it, as in the cases of Walpole, Pelham and Pitt.'[45]

Crown, Lords and Commons formed the three 'estates of the realm'. The third quarter of the eighteenth century saw the full flowering of what later became known as 'the fourth estate', as the press was greatly expanded and increasingly politicised, notably by the commencement of newspaper Parliamentary reporting from 1768. In 1760 London had four daily newspapers and five thrice-weekly ones. Boasting the largest daily sale then at over 2,000 was the *Public Advertiser*, owned by Henry Woodfall. It was to be the vehicle for the publication of the controversial anonymous letters of 'Junius' between 1769 and 1772, which put the circulation up to 5,000, but the paper never ventured into the field of Parliamentary reporting. Henry Woodfall left that to his brother William, in the daily *Morning Chronicle*, founded in 1769. His great circulation rival was the *Gazetteer*, with a sale of about 5,000 in the early 1770s.[46] The two other daily papers, the *Public Ledger* and the *Daily Advertiser*, were of no political account. The thrice-weekly papers were usually published on the post-days, Tuesday, Thursday and Saturday, for delivery to provincial towns as well as the metropolitan market. Most overtly political was the *London Evening Post*, anti-government since its foundation in 1734. The others were the *General Evening Post* and the *Whitehall Evening Post*, and two papers both started in 1757, the *London Chronicle* and *Lloyds Evening Post*. The *St. James's Chronicle* began in 1761, and the heightened political interest of the Middlesex Election case of 1768–69 led to a further press expansion, two more thrice-weeklies appearing in 1769, the *Middlesex Journal* and the *London Packet*. By 1770 five daily and eight thrice-weekly newspapers were being published in London.[47] The circulation of individual papers was only a few thousand at best, but stamp tax returns show the average total daily sale of newspapers throughout Britain was nearly 25,000, a total that includes about forty provincial and about a dozen other weekly papers. Since it was the practice of taverns and coffee-houses to take in newspapers for the benefit of their customers, the average readership per copy may have been as high as twenty, or up to a half a million a day nationwide.[48] Even the illiterate would have spicy items read out aloud to them over a drink of ale, tea or coffee. Contemporary cartoons mocked such 'coffee-house politicians', shopkeepers, artisans and others who worked for their living debating the issues of the day as if they were gentlemen, a phenomenon that astonished visiting foreigners.

The preponderance of political information and comment, much relating to Europe and America, is a feature of the eighteenth-century press. There was a great deal of 'blood and sex' crime coverage, but the bulk of the news and gossip was clearly directed to an audience interested in politics for its own sake. Much political comment was in the form of pseudonymous articles, sometimes written in-house but usually submitted by outside contributors. Such was their sales value that, like news items in general, they were widely reprinted in papers of varying political hues. Some newspapers indeed, adopted a neutral political stance altogether. They included the two Woodfall papers of the *Morning Chronicle* and the *Public Advertiser*, the *General Evening Post*, and the *London Packet*. *Lloyds Evening Post* was generally

pro-government, and the *London Chronicle*, hitherto neutral, became
so during the North ministry. The *St James's Chronicle* favoured the
opposition, but the real criticism of government, regardless of minister, came from three radical papers. The *London Evening Post* soon
came out in support of John Wilkes. Its printer John Miller had personal links with both Wilkes and John Almon, the pioneer of Parliamentary newspaper reporting, who in the early 1760s worked on the
Gazetteer, also an anti-establishment paper under successive editors
Charles Say and Roger Thompson. A third in the same vein was the
Middlesex Journal or Chronicle of Liberty, to give the flavour of its full
title, founded in 1769 by radical MP William Beckford. It was no
coincidence that these three newspapers led the 1771 fight to establish Parliamentary reporting.

If such newspapers presaged the future of the press, a heritage from
past political practice was the weekly essay paper, still a significant
part of the British scene. The most important in 1760 was the *Monitor*, which flourished as a Tory and then Pittite paper from 1755 to
1765.[49] It was respectable as well as influential, and some too outrageous pieces were sent on to the *North Briton*, founded by John
Wilkes in 1762 to counter such ministerial papers as the *Briton* during the Bute ministry of 1762–63: attaining a circulation of nearly
2,000 as against 250 for its rival, the *North Briton* was a spectacular
journalistic success.[50] The political excitement of 1768–69 led to a
new flood of weeklies, including a revived *North Briton*, not now
edited by Wilkes, and merged in May 1771 with *Bingley's Journal*,
which was founded in June 1770 and appeared under variant titles
over several years. Two scurrilous weeklies had a briefer existence.
The *Parliamentary Spy* lasted only from November 1769 to May
1770, and the *Whisperer* from February 1770 to January 1772: the
press hit a new low in these two papers, compared with which, so
Horace Walpole wrote in March 1770, the *North Briton* of John
Wilkes had been 'milk and honey'.[51]

Little part in the political game was now played by monthly magazines. A new one was indeed launched at this time with a political
purpose: but the *Political Register*, founded in 1767 to support
Grenville, virtually foundered in 1769. The long-established *Gentleman's Magazine* and *London Magazine* vainly sought to compete in
Parliamentary reporting from 1770, but their accounts were brief and
belated. Also unsuccessful, presumably for the same reasons, were
two others established to specialise in the same field, the *London
Museum*, begun in 1770, and the *Parliamentary Register*, started in

1774, each associated with John Almon: both seem to have expired in their second year.[52]

Heavyweight public political debate was conducted not in the periodical press but in pamphlets, an old political weapon. Often they were instigated, subsidised and even written by Parliamentary politicians, and a new phenomenon in George III's reign was the appearance in this form of Parliamentary speeches, genuine or otherwise, in order to put a point of view. A standard print-run for a pamphlet was 500, but the sale of popular pamphlets would rise to many more. That of Israel Mauduit's *Considerations on the Present German War* in 1760, probably the most influential pamphlet of the period, was 5,750 copies, significantly more than the 3,250 of Edmund Burke's more famous 1770 treatise on party, *Thoughts on the Cause of the Present Discontent*.[53] The influence of pamphlets was far greater than their circulation, limited by production problems and price, would suggest; for summaries promptly and widely appeared in the periodical press, including the *Gentleman's Magazine*, whose monthly sale of 10,000 copies was mostly to the rural squirearchy.

In contrast to this serious political literature was the flood of ephemeral publications designed to appeal to a wider public. These ranged from one-sheet handbills, produced in their thousands, often with an election or a riot in mind, to ballads, presumably sung in taverns and at street corners. By 1760 cartoons were probably more important than ballads as an influence on and reflection of popular opinion. They were published separately, not as part of a printed periodical, for they were expensive to produce. A print cost 6*d*, or 1*s* if coloured, as compared with 2½*d* for a newspaper. A run would be about 500, until the soft copper plates wore out. Despite their price cartoons had a widespread impact, for, like newspapers, they were available for perusal in taverns and other places of public resort. Specialist print-shops were a feature of the London scene, some with portfolios for hire, while the poor could have a free look at window displays. With their appeal also to the illiterate, cartoons could reach a wide public.

This metropolitan picture was replicated on a lesser scale throughout Britain. Towns small and large had coffee-houses and taverns that took in London and provincial papers. The forty or so newspapers published weekly in old towns like York and Chester and new industrial centres such as Birmingham and Leeds had distributional networks covering large areas. The *Newcastle Journal* was sold from coast to coast across northern England, while Wales, without any papers of its own, was comprehensively served by those in the border towns of Chester, Hereford and Gloucester. The press was now a pervasive influence throughout Britain.[54]

By the 1760s the press was an important part of the political world. It brought 'the people' into politics, but that term did not include the lower orders of society. This practical definition was made by a *Gazetteer* correspondent in 1763. 'By the people I understand not the mob, but those who are to make any judgement of public affairs. Among those I reckon the Nobility and Gentry, the Professions ... and the trading part of the Kingdom.'[55] But that same year the Wilkite movement seemingly broke the rules of the political game. Prime Minister George Grenville perceived that 'the clamour of the people' then was not for a change of ministry, another reshuffle of Parliamentary politicians, but against the political establishment as a whole.[56] The Wilkite mobs of 1768 shouted 'Damn the King! Damn the Government!' The ruling élite at Westminster closed ranks, with opposition politicians criticising the ministry not for deploying soldiers against the crowd but for failing nevertheless to maintain order.[57] The Wilkite phenomenon added a new dimension to politics, but one that should not be misunderstood. The occasional and violent street mobs alarmed contemporaries, but the power base that Wilkes created in London came from men of some substance, the freemen of the City and the freeholders of Middlesex, the lower middle class of the day, not the proletariat.[58]

Wilkism was an exception, for otherwise popular politics made no significant impact on the government of Britain. There was much public interest in political matters, as reflected in the development of the press. The century was punctuated by manifestations of great popular excitement; but, apart from the Wilkite movement, they were short-lived phenomena, with little permanent significance. Popular politics was the politics of impotence, unless a cause was taken up at Westminster.[59]

A Parliamentary system of government was susceptible not only to public opinion but also to private lobbying; it has indeed often been surmised that the word 'lobby' in this sense derives from the lobby outside the old House of Commons. By the eighteenth century such activity was part of the British political scene. Chartered trading companies, like the Africa Company and the Levant Company, had long brought their influence to bear on government policy. The East India Company was the greatest of them all, but in the reign of George III became the subject of political intervention, and its role was essentially defensive. Other parts of the empire brought pressure to bear in Whitehall and Westminster as need arose. Oldest and best organised was the West India Interest. By 1760 there existed a Society of West India Merchants. Numerous sugar plantation owners were resident in Britain, some of them MPs. Most of the islands appointed their own paid agents. There were occasions when the interests of planters and merchants did not coincide, as in 1766, but in 1775 they worked together under the American threat to their economy.[60] The North American colonies also had paid agents to safeguard their interests, and by the 1760s there was a Committee of North American Merchants. These London-based organisations in times of trouble sought and obtained support from ports and industrial towns throughout Britain, as by thirty circular letters from the American Merchants Committee in December 1765 concerning the Stamp Act Crisis. Bristol's Society of Merchant Venturers and the manufacturers of the English Midlands and North were also wont to act on their own initiative. This lobbying must however be put into perspective, for the attitude of government was the decisive factor. The petitioning campaign of 1766 over America succeeded because the aim accorded with ministerial thinking: that of 1775 failed because it ran counter to administration policy. For in Parliament the predominance of the landed interest meant that commerce, industry, and colonial interests commanded few votes and carried little weight. Emphasis on them is a distorting mirror of political reality, and equally so is undue attention to popular opinion. The political system was not yet markedly susceptible to outside pressure. The key centres of power were the Crown, the cabinet, and the House of Commons. The political story of the first decade of George III's reign is the uncertain balance between them.

Notes

1 *Cavendish Debates*, I, 444. William Dowdeswell is the MP quoted.
2 J.B. Owen, 'George II Reconsidered', in Whiteman, *et al.* (eds), *Statesmen, Scholars and Merchants*, pp. 113–34. Newman, *The World Turned Inside Out*.
3 Yorke, *Hardwicke*, I, 382.
4 Clark, *Dynamics of Change*.
5 Yorke, *Hardwicke*, II, 224–5.
6 Bullion, 'George, Be a King! ... ', in Taylor, *et al.* (eds), *Hanoverian Britain and Empire*, pp. 177–97.
7 Brooke, *King George III*, pp. 55–8.

 8 Thomas, *BIHR,* 60 (1987), pp. 361–3.
 9 *Bute Letters*, pp. 45–6.
10 Walpole, *Memoirs*, III, 66.
11 *Hutchinson Diary*, I, 378.
12 *Cavendish Debates*, I, 447.
13 *Malmesbury Letters*, I, 191–2.
14 Malmesbury MSS. Photocopies B913.
15 *Grafton Autobiography*, pp. 92, 103.
16 *Chesterfield Letters*, VI, 2,543. Grafton MSS. no. 799.
17 Bute MSS (Cardiff), no. 301.
18 *Corr. of George III*, II, 73. Walpole, *Memoirs*, III, 219.
19 *CHOP*, II, 212.
20 Much writing on the eighteenth-century cabinet is confused and contra-
    dictory, and outdated by new sources of information. The most useful
    accounts are Williams, *History*, 22 (1937–38), 240–52; Pares, *George III
    and the Politicians*, pp. 142–81; Namier, *Crossroads of Power*, pp. 93–
    123; and Christie, *Myth and Reality*, pp. 55–108.
21 For more information on the practice and procedure of Parliament see
    Thomas, *House of Commons*, and, for the Lords, A.J. Rees, Thesis.
22 Malmesbury MSS. Photocopies B33.
23 *London Museum*, June 1770, p. 391. Pares, *George III and the Politicians*,
    pp. 39–43. Recent caveats to this analysis are critically discussed by Can-
    non, *Aristocratic Century*, pp. 94–104.
24 *Parliamentary Papers of John Robinson*, pp. 12–14. I have omitted from
    the list holders of such posts as county lieutenancies, who included oppo-
    sition leader Rockingham: cf. Cannon, *Aristocratic Century*, p. 97.
25 *Corr. of George III*, I, 480.
26 Thomas, *British Politics and the Stamp Act Crisis*, pp. 199–205, 241–6,
    315–17, 330–5. McCahill, 'The House of Lords in the 1760s', in Jones,
    ed., *Pillar of the Constitution*, pp. 165–98.
27 O'Gorman, *Voters, Patrons and Parties*, p. 179 raises the traditional esti-
    mate of 280,000 to 340,000.
28 Namier, *Structure of Politics*, pp. 144–6.
29 Cannon, *Aristocratic Century*, pp. 104–10.
30 *Chatham Papers*, IV, 280.
31 This is an argument in O'Gorman, *Voters, Patrons and Parties*.
32 Namier, *Structure of Politics*, pp. 139–42.
33 *Chesterfield Letters*, VI, 2,621, 2,832.
34 Brooke, *Chatham Administration*, pp. 248–94.
35 Lawson, *George Grenville*, pp. 221–3, 263, 269.
36 Hoffman, *Edmund Burke*. p. 325.

37 *Chatham Anecdotes*, II, 35.
38 This interpretation is reaffirmed in O'Gorman, *Rise of Party*.
39 Elofson, *Rockingham Connection*.
40 BL Add. MSS. 33001, fo. 368.
41 BL Add. MSS. 33001, fos 344–9.
42 O'Gorman, *Rise of Party*, pp. 44, 219–20, 319–20, 563.
43 *Parliamentary Papers of John Robinson*, pp. 14–17. This is my own analysis of the information. MPs holding two posts, as court and military
   offices, have been counted only once. I have excluded ten MPs listed: six
   holders of county lieutenancies, two of them opposition MPs; three other
   opposition MPs; and the Speaker.
44 For a full study of Barrington's career see Jones, Thesis.
45 *London Evening Post*, 27 Jan. 1770.
46 Haig, *The Gazetteer*, p. 79.
47 Thomas, *EHR*, 74 (1959), 623–5.
48 Brewer, *Party Ideology and Popular Politics*, pp. 141–3. The calculation
   is mine. A contemporary readership estimate of only ten per paper is cited
   by Barker, *Newspapers, Politics and Public Opinion*, p. 23.
49 Peters, *EHR*, 86 (1971), 206–27.
50 Thomas, *John Wilkes*, pp. 19–26.
51 Walpole, *Letters*, VII, 369. Even radical journalist John Almon commented in 1770 that the *Whisperer* was 'detestable in the highest degree'.
   London Museum, May 1770, p. 267.
52 Thomas, *EHR*, 74 (1959), 626–32. Simmons and Thomas, *Proceedings
   and Debates*, V, vii–viii.
53 Brewer, *Party Ideology and Popular Politics*, p. 146.
54 For general surveys of the press at this time see Thomas, Thesis, pp. 8–31;
   Rea, *The English Press in Politics*; and Brewer, *Party Ideology and Popular Politics*, pp. 139–60.
55 *Gazetteer*, 11 Feb. 1763, quoted in Brewer, *Party Ideology and Popular
   Politics*, p. 236.
56 *Grenville Papers*, II, 239.
57 Thomas, *John Wilkes*, pp. 83–4.
58 This was established by Rudé, *Wilkes and Liberty*.
59 The period from 1760 to 1775 is virtually by-passed by Rogers, *Crowd,
   Culture and Politics in Georgian Britain*; and, apart from Wilkism, by Wilson, *The Sense of the People*.
60 Thomas, *British Politics and the Stamp Act Crisis*, pp. 256–7, 261;
   Thomas, *Tea Party to Independence*, p. 182. For the West India Interest
   see Penson, *EHR*, 36, (1921), 373–92.

2

The political scenario in 1760

Party terminology in eighteenth-century Britain is a minefield of myth, prejudice, and contradiction. Not since the 1720s had the line between administration and opposition been one between Whig and Tory parties. Outside the main Whig government party, headed since 1754 by the Duke of Newcastle, there existed smaller Whig factions, varyingly in and out of office. In the 1750s only two were of real significance. One was a small talented family group in which the leading figures were the foremost Commons orator William Pitt and his two Grenville brothers-in-law, George and the wealthy Lord Temple. This group went into opposition in 1755. The other, in opposition since 1751, was the clique of peers headed by the Duke of Bedford.

Whigs in opposition naturally allied for tactical reasons with the dwindling rump of MPs, down to about 100 in the 1750s, whom many called Tory, because of their political ancestry and attitude of unvarying opposition. That pejorative designation was especially fixed on them by Whig ministers, to ensure that George I and George II excluded them from office, and there was some historical justification. Their championship of the privileged position of the Church of England, and resentment at Britain's involvement in Europe, both had roots in Tory attitudes before 1714. But the seventeenth-century Tory party had also supported the Stuart monarchy, and Whig propaganda therefore sought to affix to Tories the stigmata of support of absolutism and also of Jacobitism, that movement to restore the exiled Stuarts to the throne. Hence developed the myth that the Glorious Revolution of 1688 had been solely a Whig achievement, a claim unfair to Tories past and present. In 1770 'Sir William Bagot, a country gentleman of ancient family ... gave the most plausible and pleasing picture of a Tory that you can imagine', wrote Parliamentary diarist James Harris. 'He called them lovers of the Episcopal Church, but friends to toleration and the principles of the Revolution.'[1]

There was therefore good reason for this standing opposition of Tory lineage to prefer the more respectable designation of 'the country interest'. The main thrust of their political stance was concern to curb the power of the Crown. For although the Revolution Settlement of William III's reign had prevented the emergence of an autocratic sovereign ruling in disregard of the law and without a Parliament, the subsequent growth of government power, civil and military, led to a different fear, that Parliament would be corrupted into compliance with the monarchy. Hence 'the country programme', designed to curb Crown influence over Parliament, comprising such ideas as Place Bills, to exclude office-holders from Parliament, some of which were enacted, and unsuccessful efforts to repeal the 1716 Septennial Act, on the ground that frequent elections would render MPs more responsible to their constituents.

This court-country dialogue was one chief political battleground of the earlier Hanoverian period. Foreign policy was the other. That was dominated by the concept of 'the Old System', the need for a European alliance against Britain's eternal foe France, antipathy towards this traditional enemy being reinforced in mid-century by increasing colonial and commercial rivalry. The concept was part of the Whig tradition, in contrast to the more isolationist one of a blue-water strategy, avoiding continental entanglements, associated with Tory ideas. This clash was in part merely a difference over tactics, as is apparent from this Whig view of Newcastle in 1749. 'France will outdo us at sea when they have nothing to lose by land ... Our alliances upon the continent, ... by diverting the expense of France, enable us to maintain our superiority at sea.'[2] Apart from this Whig perception that it was in Britain's long-term interest to prevent French hegemony of western Europe, there had been since 1714 a second reason for the Old System, the concern of George I and George II, both born and bred in Hanover, for the safety of their beloved Electorate, which in effect deprived Britain of the advantage of being an island state. Since 1689 the Old System had been a triple alliance of Britain with two other states both fearful of French power, Austria, and Holland.

The seemingly eternal verities of home politics and foreign policy were suddenly ended by the coincidence of a political crisis consequent on the death of Prime Minister Henry Pelham in 1754 with a catastrophic start to another French war: hostilities began that year in North America, though not in Europe until 1756. The Duke of Newcastle could and did replace his brother at the Treasury, but he had to find a House of Commons Leader.[3] William Pitt, the obvious candidate, would be an awkward colleague, for he was an advocate of maritime rather than continental warfare, and George II disliked him for his anti-Hanoverian stance. So Newcastle preferred Henry Fox, currently Secretary at War, a man reckoned by many to be a better debater than Pitt and one who would not quarrel with the Duke on policy. He was acceptable to the King as a friend of his son the Duke of Cumberland. But this arrangement lasted only until 1756, a year of disasters, notably the loss of Minorca, Britain's naval base in the western Mediterranean, and the failure of Newcastle's diplomacy. Britain thereby lost the traditional alliance with Austria, and therefore Russia also, Holland being now neutral, in exchange for the supposedly weaker help of Prussia. Newcastle resigned, but after an abortive attempt by Pitt to run the war without the Duke's Parliamentary majority, the two men formed a coalition ministry in June 1757 that reunited the whole Whig party in office for the first time in George II's reign: this arrangement Lord Temple famously later described as Pitt being 'minister of measures' and Newcastle as 'minister of numbers'.[4] Pitt became Southern Secretary, with Temple in the cabinet as Lord Privy Seal; but Pitt failed to secure for Grenville the post he coveted of Chancellor of the Exchequer, in place of the incumbent, Henry Legge. Newcastle took the Treasury, but since his long-term confidant Lord Hardwicke refused to be Lord Chancellor again, Sir Robert Henley, created Lord Henley in 1760, became Lord Keeper of the Great Seal, a less prestigious version of the same post. Lord Holderness, a tame Secretary of State since 1751, remained as Northern Secretary. Also a fixture in the cabinet since 1751, as Lord President of the Council, was Lord Granville: formerly the Lord Carteret who had opposed and briefly succeeded Sir Robert Walpole, this now-mellowed statesman was to retain that post until his death in 1763. Henry Fox was content to be without high office, making a notorious fortune as Paymaster of the Forces. The Duke of Bedford was recalled from opposition, being tactfully and tactically given the post of Lord-Lieutenant of Ireland. More remarkable even than the unification of all Whig groups in government was the attitude of the Tories or 'country party'. In 1762 Pitt recalled that during the war he had enjoyed the support of 'many gentlemen who had been of the denomination of Tories':[5] and on 21 April 1760, playing to the Tory gallery, this undoubted Whig even told the House of Commons that he was 'neither Whig nor Tory'.[6] The Tories rallied to support Pitt as a minister whose professed strategy of maritime warfare accorded with their own idea of how to fight France. Both he and they were in that respect soon to learn wisdom from experience.

The political significance of George III's accession in 1760 has been reassessed in the light of these perceptions of the 1750s. No longer can any credence be given to the old tradition of a new King destroying a Whig oligarchy to put a Tory party in power. The era of political instability had already begun with the death of Henry Pelham in 1754, and was not caused by the positive role of the young sovereign. That circumstance was disguised, and its consequence postponed, by the temporary wartime coalition of all the Whig factions in the Newcastle-Pitt ministry. There was no monolithic Whig party in power for the King to displace. Nor was there any semblance of a Tory party by which he could replace it. The political battles of the new reign were fought by men and factions who all called themselves Whig. In this party context George III's initiative was merely to remove his grandfather's proscription from honours and offices of those deemed Tory. They were now made welcome at the royal court, and five 'old Tories', headed by Lord Oxford, were soon appointed to the King's Bedchamber. All this aroused alarm and indignation among the 'old Whigs', especially Newcastle himself, but the Tories at Westminster did not constitute a positive factor in the political game. The picture has been confused by Sir Lewis Namier himself, the historian who destroyed the notion of a two-party system for this period. Namier constructed a much-cited but misleading list of 113 Tory MPs returned at the general election of 1761.[7] But this was put together from Parliamentary lists compiled by or for Newcastle between 1754 and 1766, and for the Duke 'Tory' was a generic term for politicians who always opposed him. Scrutiny of the list shows that at least twenty were Whig by any test, followers of Bedford or Leicester House or simply new MPs who sided against the Duke from 1761. One such was Sir Herbert Lloyd, whose family had been Whig since Anne's reign, and whose own father and brother had been Newcastle men under George II. Lloyd, who entered the Commons in 1761, obtained a baronetcy from Bute and voted against the Rockingham ministry's repeal of the Stamp Act, enough for Newcastle to label him a Tory.[8]

The 'old Tory' MPs numbered under a hundred in the 1760s, and they followed varying political paths.[9] Each 'Whig' faction gained the support of some, and others became courtiers, but most merged into the loose body of independents. In Newcastle's 1767 Commons list, indeed, all independents were designated Tory.[10] Others, like diarist James Harris, did distinguish 'old Tories', men like Sir Roger Newdigate, by the test of their championship of the Church of England.[11] A broad focus of Tory unity was still provided by the Cocoa Tree coffeehouse in Pall Mall, which had been the London meeting-place of Tory squires in George II's reign. The phrase 'Cocoa Tree' continued to be a common political term to denote the supposedly collective behaviour of independent squires, usually of Tory stock. It was in this sense that Whig Sir James Lowther wrote in January 1770 to courtier Charles Jenkinson, 'I think we shall see the Tories unite in a body as much as ever, though perhaps under a different appellation, for … the few who took places have now lost all interest at the Cocoa Tree.'[12] That forecast was erroneous, for the then incoming ministry of Lord North was perceived by many 'old Tories' like Newdigate to be so different from the Whig-led administrations of the 1760s as to merit their support. By George III's reign the Cocoa Tree was a club for like-minded men, not a political power base for a non-existent Tory Party.

The European alignment in what became known, but obviously not in America, as the Seven Years War saw Britain and Prussia overmatched by France, Austria and Russia. Against the odds the Anglo-Prussian partnership held out in North Germany. While Frederick the Great beat off the Austrians and the Russians, being rarely confronted by the two together, Prussia's western flank was protected against French attack by an army financed rather than contributed by Britain, and based in Hanover. Led by a German commander, Ferdinand of Brunswick, it achieved a notable victory at Minden on 1 August 1759, but the failure of the British cavalry under Lord George Sackville to press home an attack that might have converted a success into a rout led to a court-martial conviction that ended his military career: the disgrace did not put paid to his political prospects, and he was to become American Secretary in 1775 as Lord George Germain. From 1758 Britain also paid Prussia an annual subsidy of four million crowns, equivalent to £670,000, but no formal treaty of alliance was ever made. Early in 1760 the survival of Prussia still remained uncertain.

Overseas, by contrast, the war was proving a glorious triumph for Britain with success against France in America, Africa, and Asia. In 1760 the final conquest of Canada was imminent, and Britain's mastery of the sea had been confirmed by Admiral Sir Edward Hawke's defeat of the French navy at Quiberon Bay late in 1759: this ensured that France would not save the rest of her West Indies or recover her losses there, in West Africa, and in India. Pitt's achievement had been magnificent, and won him contemporary adulation. His reputation as the triumphant war minister secured him enduring popularity that he was to exploit as a politician. Nowadays he is no longer seen as the great war minister of legend, with a master plan for victory. His boast to Parliament on 13 November 1759 that America had been conquered in Germany was a retrospective rationalisation of a series of ad hoc decisions.[13] Superior resources had been at his disposal, notably Britain's control of the high seas from the onset of hostilities. France had been defeated overseas because of her heavy European commitments, whereas until 1760 the German war had been cheap for Britain. Luck had played its part, in French incompetence and Spanish neutrality, but those advantages were now to end. In 1758 there came to power in France the Duke of Choiseul, who for the next twelve years strove to reverse the recent tide of disasters that had befallen his country. Aware that the overseas war was lost, Choiseul thought first of a direct invasion of Britain, and then sought territorial gains in western Germany as bargaining counters at the peace negotiations. His long-term aim was a war of revenge on Britain. He would have the support of Charles III of Spain, who from his accession in 1759 adopted an anti-British stance, fearful that Britain would next have designs on Spain's American Empire, and also bearing a personal grudge about British naval bullying in 1742 when he had been King of Naples, a threat of bombardment to coerce him into neutrality in the previous French war.

In 1760 the military situation in Germany was of more immediate concern to the British government than this latent Spanish threat. Prussia was in evident danger of defeat by Russia and Austria, and had lost her Rhineland territories to France. In 1760 Newcastle and Pitt, equally aware that America could still be lost in Europe, concurred in a change of strategy, pouring British soldiers into western Germany until in August the British commander there, Lord Granby, had to be told that no more men could be spared. Ferdinand of Brunswick, deploying 65,000 foreign troops in British pay as well as this British army, held off the still formidable French army in western Germany, but without a battlefield victory. Pitt knew it was a creditable performance, but one seemingly not good value for the £14 million the war cost Britain in 1760, and he rightly feared a political backlash at home. Even the long awaited news in September of the final conquest of Canada did not seem adequate compensation for the national effort in money and manpower, and Pitt therefore hit upon the idea of a maritime exploit that would satisfy national pride, the seizure of Belleisle, a fortified island off the west coast of France. It could serve as a naval base, and then as an exchange for Minorca. But Pitt failed to persuade the cabinet into agreeing to this expedition before the death of George II.[14]

That event had long posed a threat to the ministry of Newcastle and Pitt, both of whom had incurred the hostility of the Court of the Prince of Wales at Leicester House.[15] Newcastle for the young Prince symbolised everything that was wrong with his grandfather's reign: indulgence in expensive wars; corruption in government; and what he deemed to be the bridling of royal power. Pitt by contrast had once been high in favour at Leicester House, cultivating the Prince's tutor and mentor, Lord Bute, when in opposition in the mid-1750s, and in so doing aligning in a royal family quarrel with the Princess Dowager of Wales against her brother-in-law the Duke of Cumberland. As the war progressed this friendship had been transformed into hostility. Pitt had more important matters on his mind than the petty demands of Leicester House concerning patronage and information; and Leicester House disapproved of the military campaign in Germany that had soon formed an integral part of his war policy. At the end of 1758 the Prince wrote about Pitt to Bute that 'he seems to forget that the day will come when he must expect to be treated according to his desserts': and on 4 May 1760 he commented to Bute that he would not have 'the blackest of hearts' in his government.[16]

1760 was once deemed a watershed in British history because of the supposed political and constitutional intentions of the new King. Another emphasis on its significance now derives from the emergence of Britain as an imperial power. Empire replaced Europe as the chief focus of attention, for a period of peace after a generation of wars and international crises enabled attention to be given to imperial issues, old and new. There were long-standing problems in North America and Ireland, while new ones were posed by the acquisition of territories in India and North America.

But this historical perspective should not overshadow the contemporary obsession with the motivation and behaviour of George III that dominated the domestic political scene for much of the 1760s and beyond. The old party terminology was revived, but to denote attitudes not men. Toryism was support for the new proactive role of the Crown, whereas Whiggism was the defence of liberty: this was the language of opposition, for it would be several decades before government politicians, as distinct from a few country squires, adopted the designation of Tory. The Duke of Newcastle in 1765 referred to 'this Tory reign', and the next year claimed that all his life he had served 'the Whig cause, which I will ever look upon, as the cause of liberty'.[17] William Pitt as early as 1762 expressed 'his apprehension that the distinction of Whig and Tory was rising as high as ever ... that he would die a Whig'.[18] In 1768 George Grenville, by then a former Prime Minister, defined Toryism as support of 'the power and authority of the Crown against the rights of the people'.[19]

Parliament was the chief safeguard of liberty against the Crown, and if it was to fulfil this role, party organisation there was a necessary ingredient. That was why the royal intention to rule in disregard of party so alarmed Parliamentary politicians. Grenville said in 1769 that 'Twas on the worst of principles of politics that the measure had been pursued of breaking all connections and partys'.[20] The Rockingham group always held party to be the essence of politics, and the most famous contemporary defence of party came from Edmund Burke in his 1770 pamphlet *Thoughts on the Present Discontents*. 'Party is a body of men united, for promoting by their joint endeavours the national interest, upon some particular principle in which they are all agreed.' When in a Commons debate of 13 May 1768 Henry Conway attacked 'factious connections', he was answered by his former fellow Rockinghamites Lord John Cavendish and Edmund Burke, who both asserted that 'connections among persons of principle were right'.[21] More remarkable was the endorsement of party, albeit qualified, by Camden, Lord Chancellor in the Chatham ministry that had been an avowed attack on such connections: in November 1768 Camden stated that 'twas right every man should follow his connections and act agreeably to them. That the man, who acted merely from his own sentiment, had no weight and could do little good – only a man should be careful not to go too far in following his friends – there were times and measures, when twas fitting to leave them'.[22]

Unconstitutional implications magnified the offence, in opposition eyes, of the King's conception of his political role. Lord Bute, whom at his accession he intended to make his Prime Minister, was a royal favourite, not even in Parliament until returned to the Lords in 1761 as a Scottish representative peer. Even after that reluctant Premier resigned in 1763, suspicion of his secret influence was a major political issue of the 1760s, and long survived in popular mythology even after Parliamentary politicians realised that it no longer had any validity. Grenville,

his successor as Prime Minister, quarrelled with the King over the issue.
George III stopped consulting Bute on political matters in March 1765.[23]
Realisation of his loss of influence gradually dawned on contemporary
perception. Parliamentary lists from 1767 ceased to include 'the Butes'
as a separate party: and a note in Mrs Grenville's diary for 1768 demonstrated final awareness of the change. 'That the Earl's favour was over,
and his credit gone, this is the language held universally.'[24]

When by the late 1760s it was obvious that Bute's political influence was over, there developed the notion of 'a double cabinet', with
the real power being in the hands not of the ministerial cabinet, itself
an unofficial body in theory, but of a group of Bute's former followers, men like Sir Gilbert Elliot and Charles Jenkinson, at the head of
a party of 'King's Friends'. Radical journalist John Almon wrote that
'there were about thirty persons who arrogantly assumed this appellation'.[25] There was some foundation for the belief that certain politicians not in important offices were high in favour at the royal court.
But the existence of a secret cabinet was pure fiction, and can hardly
have been given credence by any politicians with knowledge of the
inner workings of government. Yet it remained a point of popular
propaganda into the American War, and John Almon expounded it as
historical fact in his account of the period. 'It is necessary to observe,
for the reader's information, that the system of the British Cabinet,
since the accession of the present King, has been to maintain <u>two</u> Cabinets, one <u>official</u>, the other <u>efficient</u>.'[26]

Opposition could hint at such suspicions of constitutional malpractice in Parliamentary debates, and they were widely voiced in the
contemporary press; but such matters were too vague and too delicate
to be raised directly by formal motions. Suspicion of corruption was
another matter, and George III had an Achilles heel in the King's Civil
List. Ironically the deficit was due not to the bribery of politicians, but
to a naively high-minded decision of Bute and George III. Bute
adopted a pledge of Frederick Prince of Wales in 1747 to a fixed Civil
List of £800,000, and the Civil List Act of 1760 surrendered in lieu
the royal revenues, then £877,000 and steadily rising. It was a disastrous bargain for the new young King, who apart from heavy initial
expenditure, had far more family commitments than his grandfather
– not merely his mother and uncle, but also a wife, children and adult
siblings. George III's expenditure in the 1760s averaged over
£900,000 a year, wiping out a nest-egg left by George II, and in 1769
he asked Parliament to pay off a debt of £513,000. Since there was
general realisation of the true state of affairs, opposition attempts to

exploit the situation in Parliament failed dismally.[27] The Civil List debt was a poorly chosen topic over which to attack the Crown, but for the moment there was no other: not until the 1770s was there again a country programme of proposals to limit government power. Political attention was diverted to the more urgent problems of empire, while the King's ministers found foreign policy more difficult than might have been expected after a successful war.

Foreign policy attracted more Parliamentary attention than the role of the Crown in the new reign, but no longer was it in the fore-front of political attention. One reason was that George III's accession removed the Hanover factor. His antipathy towards his grandfather embraced detestation of what only a year earlier he described as 'that horrid Electorate which has always lived on the very vitals of this poor country'.[28] George III's famous declaration to Parliament on 18 November 1760, 'Born and educated in this country, I glory in the name of Britain', was therefore of especial significance for the con-duct of foreign policy.[29] He never visited Hanover, and though British cabinets remained vaguely aware that the Electorate still represented a hostage to fortune, the King's lack of concern was so notorious that France made no attempt to seize it during the American War.

The absence of the Hanoverian complication paled into insignifi-cance by comparison with the basic problem of finding an ally to combat the evident intention of Choiseul to seek revenge for France's defeat in the Seven Years War. In this respect George III was one of many British politicians who failed to perceive reality. In 1771 he still han-kered after a return to the Old Alliance of the 1740s. 'England in conjunction with the House of Austria and the [Dutch] Republic seems the most secure barrier, ... and if Russia could be added to this, I think the Court of Versailles would not be in a hurry to commence hostili-ties.'[30] But Austrian Chancellor Kaunitz, in control of his country's foreign policy from 1753 to the French Revolution, found the French alliance he had contrived in 1756 highly advantageous: it secured peace in western Europe, so that Austria could safely pursue her ambitions in the east. No help on the European mainland, by contrast, could be expected from an insular and isolationist Britain, an opinion reinforced by the constant British ministerial changes of the 1760s, that led Kau-nitz to believe that a Parliamentary government could not be a stable ally. But he wished to prevent Britain finding another ally, and so encouraged false hopes that the 'Old System' might yet be revived.

The King's misapprehension about the prospect of an Austrian alliance was shared by many British politicians, notably the Duke of

Newcastle. Equally impracticable was the Pitt idea of reviving the wartime alliance with Prussia. Frederick II was well satisfied with the Russian partnership he achieved in 1764. That the other four Great Powers were paired off in alliances left Britain in isolation. The post-war situation, too, had changed in other ways to Britain's disadvantage from that before the Seven Years War. Her very success in that conflict meant that no longer could Britain seek to procure allies by the argument of a French threat to a European balance of power. It was anachronistic and obtuse of Northern Secretary Conway to write in 1767 that 'the liberties of Europe' were left 'at the mercy of the House of Bourbon'.[31] For Choiseul had no ambition of continental hegemony, while Britain's deployment of her navy both to control neutral trade during the war and as a coercive diplomatic weapon afterwards served only to enhance the image of Britain, rather than France, as the bully of Europe. There had in any case been a shift in European perspectives. No longer did the other Great Powers regard the Anglo-French rivalry as the dominant factor in continental politics. The attention of Austria, Prussia and Russia was focused on Eastern Europe, the prospect of territorial plunder from the perceived weaknesses of Poland and the Ottoman Empire.

The failure of the traditional Whig policy of seeking anti-French allies in Europe led British politicians to adopt a Tory-style isolationist stance, behind the shield of the navy's 'wooden walls'. By 1767 the then First Lord of the Treasury Grafton could reflect that British policy was 'constantly to have a fleet in forwardness equal to what both houses of Bourbon could bring forth'.[32] Financial economies introduced by that parsimonious Premier Grenville in fact denied the navy adequate funding. During the 1760s most of the fleet of 150 ships of the line were laid up, only a basic squadron of twenty guardships being kept in active service. This strategy sufficed to maintain British naval supremacy, since all Choiseul's efforts to rebuild the French navy foundered on lack of materials, manpower, and money, and so did the Spanish attempt. At the time of the Falkland Islands Crisis of 1770 some eighty British ships were soon fit for action, and there was every confidence Britain could defeat the combined enemy fleets.[33]

If the conduct of British foreign policy posed more problems than could be anticipated in 1760, the attention of both government and Parliament was increasingly taken up by imperial matters. One early issue was whether Britain should retain Quebec or the rich West Indies sugar island of Guadeloupe, also captured in 1759. A vigorous press debate was conducted in pamphlets rather than newspapers.

Voices were raised that correctly anticipated the future course of events, putting the view that the older colonies would become more difficult to control if the French threat to them was removed. An additional argument for returning Quebec and keeping Guadeloupe was that the British sugar islands would not be able to supply the enlarged American market. Since the main motive for the war had been the conquest of Canada in order to remove the French menace, the matter was not one for serious argument at Whitehall or Westminster. But Grenville was among those who favoured acquiring Guadeloupe and not Canada, and Lord Bute seemingly proposed that idea to Pitt, only to be rebuffed. 'Fy, Fy, My Lord. No, No.'[34]

In 1763 Britain ended the war in possession of all North America east of the Mississippi River, buttressing the fifteen old colonies along the Atlantic seaboard from Newfoundland to Georgia. The problem of how to organise and control the new territory loomed large in the public mind, but a preliminary settlement was to be promptly enacted by a Royal Proclamation of 1763. Three new colonies were created, one of Quebec from the old French colony and restricted to the St Lawrence valley, and two from territory ceded by Spain. These were East Florida, roughly equivalent to the modern state of Florida, and West Florida, a coastal strip along the Gulf of Mexico to the mouth of the Mississippi. Since nearly all the new European inhabitants were French or Spanish, no elected assemblies were permitted, such as existed in the older British colonies. The remainder of the new territory, north and south of the Great Lakes and in the Mississippi valley, was to be a vast Indian reservation, where trade was permitted but settlement forbidden, a veto avowedly temporary and designed to avert Indian troubles. The British army in North America, the financing of which was to cause so much trouble, was almost entirely stationed in the new colonies and the Indian reservation, as much to control the inhabitants there as to defend them.

The British government's attempt to raise money for army costs was the immediate occasion of the quarrel with the older colonies; but officials in both America and London had long been aware of the defiant attitude of the colonists. Demonstrated pragmatically by contravention of such trade laws as did not suit them, it had been shown more directly in the weakening of royal government, as the elected assemblies deployed the power of the purse and other weapons to encroach on the authority of governors and their subordinates. During little more than a decade from 1763 this negative and empirical defiance would become a positive denial of the right of the

British Parliament to tax and legislate for colonies which had their own assemblies.

The other major new acquisition was in India, where Robert Clive's victory at Plassey in 1757 over the Nawab of Bengal trans-ferred to the East India Company effective control of that province, albeit under the nominal rule of puppet Nawabs. But a trading com-pany was unsuited to be a territorial ruler, and as early as 1759 Clive himself, Governor there from 1758 to 1760, wrote to Pitt on that very point. 'So large a sovereignty may possibly be an object too extensive for a Mercantile Company, and it is to be feared they are not of them-selves able, without the nation's assistance, to maintain so wide a dominion.'[35] For the democratic constitution of the Company offered ample scope to those who sought to exploit the prospects of great wealth, together with considerable patronage and political power. The final word lay with the 2,000 or more shareholders who pos-sessed the voting qualification of £500 stock. Meeting as the General Court of Proprietors, they decided the biannual dividend, and every April chose by secret ballot the twenty-four Directors responsible for the management of the Company. The immediate result of the news of Plassey was a successful coup at the 1758 election of Directors. Laurence Sulivan, a former Company servant, became Chairman after winning a majority of fourteen to ten Directors. He was to hold power for six years, but among those offended by his reforming meas-ures was Clive himself, who returned to Britain in 1760 with a for-tune estimated at £300,000, and with a recent grant to him by the Nawab of Bengal of an annual *jagir* or land rent of £27,000, payable through the Company. Conflict between Clive and Sulivan was post-poned because Sulivan was anxious to avoid a quarrel with the return-ing hero. Clive indeed had no desire to run the Company, but circumstances soon drew him into Company politics.

One way or another, India was destined to become a major politi-cal issue of the new reign. The problems of ruling a province of twenty million inhabitants could not be left to the East India Com-pany. There was soon growing concern over both misgovernment in Bengal and the return to Britain of wealthy 'nabobs', company ser-vants who were commonly believed to have made their money at the expense of both Company and India. That the Company seemed now to be a financial honey pot attracted the attention of government and speculators alike, and its management became part of the political scene. The General Court began to meet frequently, nearly once a fortnight by the early 1770s, with over a hundred MPs sitting as proprietors and dominating its debates.[36] Chatham in 1769 referred to its meetings as 'little Parliaments'.[37]

If India was a new problem, Ireland was an old one: but in the mid-eighteenth century the challenge to British control came not from the downtrodden Catholics, but from the Protestant Ascendancy, even though this ruling Anglican minority numbered only one-tenth of the population. The somewhat larger minority of Presbyterians, mostly resident in Ulster, were still effectively excluded from power-sharing. As for the Catholic majority, about three-quarters of the Irish people, among the numerous restrictions imposed on them by the Penal Code of 1690 to 1730 was exclusion not only from Parliament, but also from the franchise and all offices, local and national. Legal sanctions were reinforced by military coercion: an Irish army of 12,000 men was mostly deployed in small, scattered units to act as a police force rather than for its ostensible purpose of national defence: the Whiteboy peasant riots of the 1760s were suppressed without difficulty. The Ascendancy was very much a Protestant garrison, and the Irish political system, very similar in structure to that of Britain, was an Anglican preserve.

Ireland was perceived in Britain as an imperial problem, but it was one complicated by many political and personal links that spanned the Irish Sea. Ireland was ruled by a Lord-Lieutenant, always a British peer, in the name of George III, who therefore took a personal interest in appointments. The Viceroy formed part of the ministry in London, and a change there almost always entailed a replacement in Dublin. The Lord-Lieutenant would take over with him a Chief Secretary of his own choice, a key figure with responsibility for management of the Irish House of Commons: the young Henry Grattan referred to the 1770 incumbent as 'the Macaroni Prime Minister', a snide reference to his manners and inferior status.[38]

The chief political task of the Lord-Lieutenant was management of the Irish Parliament, which met only in alternate years. It could not vote him out of office, but there was the need to obtain some finance, for the Irish Hereditary Revenue did not meet the full cost of government. The British government, moreover, always wanted to avoid the public embarrassments of hostile resolutions and awkward legislation. But, for a variety of reasons, the Irish Parliament was often more difficult to control than that at Westminster. As in Britain, the House of Lords, small in size, was easier to manage. Of 140 lay peers in 1775, about a third were absentee, mostly British politicians given Irish titles. The four archbishops and eighteen bishops of the Anglican Church of Ireland were usually as amenable to government influence as their fellows at Westminster, and most peers also felt the pull of offices and honours. The hard core of opposition lords was usually under a dozen.[39] But the Irish House of Commons was often trouble-some to Dublin Castle.

The 300 Irish MPs were, as in Britain, mainly landowners who secured their own elections, for there were few patrons who con-trolled more than one constituency. They all sat for two-member constituencies, 32 counties and 118 boroughs, whose electoral fran-chises were similar to those in Britain. The forty-shilling freehold county qualification produced altogether 50,000 voters. Dublin headed the boroughs with 4,000, but 75 boroughs had 13 voters or less, including nearly all the 55 corporation boroughs. The Irish Com-mons therefore comprised country gentlemen and relatives of peers, few of whom owed any thanks to government for their elections.[40]

It was a more difficult problem of management than British minis-ters faced at Westminster. There was little sense of loyalty to an absent sovereign. On the contrary, opponents of government could adopt a 'Patriot' stance by voicing Irish grievances, for Ireland had not obtained many of the British safeguards of liberty. There was no Habeas Corpus Act, and no security of tenure for judges. A Parlia-mentary general election need take place only on the death of a sov-ereign, since Ireland had no equivalent to a Septennial Act, and the election of 1728 had been the only one of George II's reign. By 1760 there was mounting Irish pressure to remedy these constitutional defects. But above all there was the grievance of the so-called Poyn-ings Law of 1494, whereby all Irish legislation had to be approved by the British Privy Council, by now in effect the ministry, which had the right to accept, refuse or modify it. Other parts of Poynings Law had been modified in practice over the course of time. The Irish Parlia-ment was now allowed to introduce legislation, 'by a liberal interpre-tation of the law', so Prime Minister Lord North told the British House of Commons on 3 May 1770.[41] Whether initiation of financial business was still the preserve of the Irish Privy Council remained, however, a point of dispute. More recently a Declaratory Act of 1720 had asserted the right of the Westminster Parliament to legislate for Ireland 'in all cases whatsoever'. That power had seldom been exer-cised, apart from economic legislation concerned with the whole British Empire. Many of these Irish grievances existed more in theory than in practice, but they signified the inferior status of Ireland, and discussion of them became a regular feature of Irish Parliamentary debates after 1760.

The crux of the Irish problem facing Britain was not the potentially recalcitrant behaviour of the Dublin Parliament. It lay in the circumstance that British Lord-Lieutenants had in effect sold the pass, by conceding too much power to Irish politicians. Since the Irish Parliament met only every other year, it had become the practice for the Viceroy to reside in Ireland for little more than the Parliamentary sessions, on average some eight months every two years. Otherwise Ireland was ruled by Irish magnates appointed Lords Justices. This habit of merely intermittent direct British control inevitably resulted in power being transferred to the Irish aristocracy. Opposition peer Lord Charlemont penned this sardonic account of the state of affairs in the early 1760s. 'A certain set of men, whose only principle was the lust of power and emolument, and whose only ability was the art of party management, had then such influence in Parliament, an influence as ill-directed as it was undue, that the Lord Lieutenant was wholly in their power and could confer no favour but at their recommendation. They were styled "undertakers"'.[42]

Their final takeover of power came when the Duke of Bedford was Lord-Lieutenant from 1757 to 1761. He began, indeed, by trying to govern without the aid of the faction leaders who had dominated the Irish political scene for decades, albeit often as rivals: Lord Shannon, who as Henry Boyle had been Irish Speaker from 1733 to 1756, and possessed an electoral power base in the Cork region; George Stone, who was Primate of Ireland as Archbishop of Armagh, and well-connected in British politics; and John Ponsonby, whose family was intermarried with the Cavendishs, had been Speaker since 1756, and was First Commissioner of the Revenue Board, a post that gave him more patronage than the Viceroy. Abandoning confrontation, Bedford appointed them Lords Justices during his absence of 1758–59. Self-interest led the three men to form an alliance that dominated Irish politics for the next six years. Bedford, under pressure from a ministry that did not want a wartime Irish crisis, had sold out to the Undertakers, and his 1761 resignation was born of frustration, a compound of anger and despair.[43] 'That country was come to such a pass that no man that was at ease or had another character to lose would care to go among them.' So did the Duke of Devonshire, himself a former viceroy, explain to Lord Bute the Duke of Bedford's refusal 'to go any more' to Ireland as Lord-Lieutenant.[44] His legacy was an Irish problem to be added to others that arose more directly out of the Seven Years War. The high moral tone adopted by George III ensured that the Irish Undertakers would be included among the bad men whose day of reckoning had come.

Notes

1 *Malmesbury Letters*, I, 202.
2 BL Add. MSS. 35410, fo. 140.
3 The political crisis of 1754–57 is discussed in detail in Clark, *Dynamics of Change*.
4 *Grenville Papers*, I, 405.
5 BL Add. MSS. 32945, fos 1–2.
6 BL Add. MSS. 32905, fo. 14.
7 Namier, *Age*, pp. 419–21.
8 BL Add. MSS. 32974, fo. 170.
9 Christie, *PH*, 6 (1987), 47–68.
10 BL Add. MSS. 33001, fos 357–63.
11 Malmesbury MSS. Photocopies A883.
12 BL Add. MSS. 38206, fo. 20.
13 BL Add. MSS. 32898, fos 223–4. For the modern reappraisal of Pitt as a war minister see Middleton, *Bells of Victory*, *passim*.
14 Middleton, *Bells of Victory*, pp. 150–69.
15 On this see McKelvey, *George III and Lord Bute: The Leicester House Years*.
16 *Bute Letters*, pp. 18, 45.
17 BL Add. MSS. 32972, fos 193–4; 32973, fo. 84.
18 BL Add. MSS. 32945, fos 1–2.
19 Grenville Letter-Books, II. G. Grenville to T. Pitt, 22 Oct. 1768.
20 Malmesbury MSS. Photocopies B925.
21 BL Add. MSS. 32990, fos 61–2.
22 Malmesbury MSS. Photocopies B902. Camden had just broken with Chatham to stay on in office.
23 BL Add. MSS. 51379, fos 175–6.
24 *Grenville Papers*, IV, 407.
25 *Chatham Anecdotes*, I, 418 n.
26 *Chatham Anecdotes*, II, 213–17. For opposition belief in 'secret influence' at this time see Hamer, Thesis, pp. 244–65.
27 Reitan, *BIHR*, 47 (1974), 186–201. For the complete Civil List expenditure between 1752 and 1769 see *Commons Journals*, XXXII, 466–603, 626–7, 729–30.
28 *Bute Letters*, p. 28.
29 Brooke, *King George III*, pp. 88, 390–1.
30 *Corr. of George III*, II, 204.
31 Scott, *British Foreign Policy*, p. 89 n.
32 *Grafton Autobiography*, p. 168.

33 Tracy, *Navies*, pp. 8–31.
34 Malmesbury MSS. Photocopies B885. For accounts of this controversy see Grant, *AHR*, 17 (1911–12), 735–43, and Namier, *Age*, pp. 273–82.
35 *Chatham Papers*, I, 389–90.
36 Bowen, *HJ*, 34 (1991), 857–72.
37 *Grafton Autobiography*, p. 237. For the East India Company see Sutherland, *East India Company*, esp. pp. 49–269, and Bowen, *Revenue and Reform*.
38 *Macartney Papers*, p. xxxii, n. 82.
39 Johnston, *Great Britain and Ireland*, pp. 256–69.
40 Johnston, *Great Britain and Ireland*, pp. 120–78, 321–30.
41 BL Egerton MSS, 222, fo. 70.
42 *HMC Charlemont*, I, 144–5.
43 For the Bedford Viceroyalty see Powell, Thesis, pp. 57–82.
44 *Devonshire Diary*, p. 78.

3

Pitt and Newcastle (1760–1762): war and peace

George II died suddenly on 25 October 1760, at the age of seventy-seven. His ministers were taken unawares. Paymaster Henry Fox wrote caustically afterwards of the Privy Council that day: 'I am of opinion they were as much unprepared as if the late King had been only 25, and seemed to have determined nothing'.[1] Bute, by contrast, had prepared a Proclamation for the young King, making a reference to the 'bloody and expensive war', which Pitt insisted on altering before publication to 'expensive but just and necessary war'. Lord Egmont, a Leicester House man, commented that this converted a declaration 'implying a disposition to peace, into one which imported … a strong adoption of the war'.[2] During the day George III suggested to Bute that he should take ministerial office, seemingly as Northern Secretary in place of Lord Holderness, but Bute declined, so the King recalled on 6 March 1761, 'as not chusing to throw himself into so much business and not knowing what the other ministers might think of it'.[3] That discussion presumably preceded one that Bute had with Pitt in the evening, when he announced that his aim was to be 'a private man at the side of the King'. Pitt made it clear he would not accept Bute as head of the ministry, and he threatened resignation if there was any change in war policy.[4] Pitt knew he had the whip hand, as Lord Egmont noted. 'Pitt seems not serene, but bears it higher from the natural turn of his insolent temper, and from a supposition that his popular interest with the mob and the Tories, will force him to be continued in his office, at least during the continuance of the war'. But the Duke of Newcastle looked 'as if he was quite sunk, … agitated in his mind. All his adherents confounded.'[5] Pitt's refusal to serve under Bute ensured the Duke's continuance at the Treasury. The offer was made through Bute on 27 October. Newcastle consulted his friends, lamenting that he had 'lost the best King, the best Master, and the best friend that ever subject had. God knows what consequences it may have.'[6] The Duke of Devonshire told him 'he owed it to his friends and the Whig Party who would be broke to pieces and turned adrift'.[7] Mansfield and Bedford were among others with similar advice, and Pitt let Newcastle know that he wanted the Duke at the Treasury. Only Hardwicke thought he would be wiser to retire. On 31 October, having been assured he would have 'the choice of the new Parliament', Newcastle decided to retain the Treasury.[8] Pitt from the first suspected that Bute's intention was 'to be *the* Minister behind the curtain'.[9] For the moment Bute took only a household post as Groom of the Stole, but with a seat in the cabinet. This was so as to report back to the King, as Bute told Pitt on 27 October. 'The King would have no meetings held at which he [Bute] was not present.'[10]

Politicians who had sought the mere acquiescence of George II found themselves with a King eager to play a positive role in government. Instead of a septuagenarian there was a young man of twenty-two on the throne, one with a mind of his own. Lord Egmont soon noticed the new monarch's distinctive stance. 'The King is advised to keep every body at a distance but with shew of great civility and courtesy but to endeavour to fix a character of being immoveable in his determination.'[11] George III was a busy politician, keenly interested in day to day events, with opinions on policies and personalities. It is impossible to ascertain how many of the ideas and suggestions to be found in his correspondence had been put into his head either by way of conversation or by letters that no longer survive. He soon shook off his early emotional dependence on Bute, and it became his frequent but not invariable habit to pre-empt cabinet meetings by making his opinions known in advance. The new King already had clear views on foreign policy and on Ireland, and later formulated others on such matters as America and India. Yet his personal feelings towards individual politicians sometimes caused him to appoint or dismiss ministers regardless of his opinion of their policies. He developed a strong antipathy to the Duke of Bedford and to George Grenville, whose views respectively on international peace and imperial organisation accorded closely with his own. In 1765 he dismissed them from office on personal as much as constitutional grounds, ironically replacing them with the political heirs of 'the Whig oligarchy' whose removal from power had been his guiding political principle on his accession. For George III then sought peace not only because of his abhorrence of bloodshed, but also to have the opportunity to

deal with the wicked and corrupt men whom he thought had sub-
verted the working of the excellent British constitution.

There was at first no dichotomy between men and measures. George
III began his reign with the simple plan of making Bute his Prime
Minister, as the key to the implementation of his political ideas. His
former tutor was genuinely reluctant to play the part, because of a well-
founded diffidence about his aptitude for the post, and because of his
distaste for the rough and tumble of politics, which for a Scottish royal
favourite proved to be very rough indeed. Unfounded rumours of a
scandalous liaison with the King's mother, the Dowager Princess of
Wales, increased the unpopularity of a man whose haughty demeanour
did nothing for his public image. Already in November 1760 Lord
Egmont noted the popular reaction. 'Strange talk of B—e and the
P—ss, verses and indecent prints published, even in the avenues to the
Play house the mob crying out no Scotch Government, No Petticoat
Government, in the very hearing of the King as he passes along.'[12]

That presaged the future. Pitt's veto on Bute, reflecting his own
current indispensability as war minister, prevented his immediate elevation to the head of the administration, even though many politicians flocked to his standard to win favour with the new young King.
War and peace dominated the immediate political agenda. How to
negotiate a peace that would convert temporary acquisitions into
permanent gains was the immediate problem, one thrown into sharp
relief by the intransigent attitude of Britain's own hard-pressed ally.
Frederick II of Prussia was stubbornly refusing to yield any territory
by treaty, however much was occupied by his enemies. France, if now
reinforced by Spain, would hold out for better terms than the course
of the war so far might seem to warrant. Choiseul was known to be
planning another Rhineland campaign for 1761. The German war
therefore had to be continued to preserve Britain's overseas gains.[13]

Just at this very moment Pitt's military strategy came under attack
with the publication in November 1760 of a famous and influential
pamphlet by woollen-draper Israel Mauduit, *Considerations on the
Present German War*. The whole concept of a continental campaign
was condemned as contrary to British interests, a diversion from the
contest with France, a contention reinforced by the claim that Britain
was paying Frederick to fight only his own enemies. Instead of a military defence of Hanover Britain should simply demand its return at
the end of the war, after conquering the entire French overseas
empire. The cost and seeming futility of the German war during the
next year or so seemed to provide confirmation of this argument,

which was echoed in Parliament and cabinet as well as the press. 'After having twice had honourable mention made of me in the House of Lords; and after having twenty times heard myself speaking through other men's mouths in the House of Commons', Mauduit recalled the significance of his pamphlet when writing to claim his reward from Bute on 27 December 1762, after all was over.[14]

That the King held the same opinion was demonstrated by his speech to Parliament on 18 November and by his later intimation to his ministers that Hanover need not be defended from French attack. But for the moment Pitt's direction of war policy was not challenged, and Bute sided with him against Newcastle when the Belleisle expedition was approved at a cabinet meeting on 11 November.[15] Before the end of the year lack of success in Germany led Newcastle to concur with Pitt's wish for a 'proper and timely operation' elsewhere to boost national morale.[16] The Duke accepted that 'if we cant make peace, we must try our fate with expeditions … and beat France into a peace'.[17] At a cabinet meeting of 31 December 1760 to plan future campaigns two major new initiatives were agreed. The army in Canada would be redeployed to the West Indies, primarily to attack Martinique, France's chief naval base there. The other project was the capture of the Île de France (Mauritius), a French island in the Indian Ocean that provided support for campaigns in India. Nor could the German war be neglected, since the French would seek to trade off any gains there against colonial losses, and early in 1761 sufficient reinforcements were sent there to produce the strategic aim of a stalemate.[18]

Harmony on war strategy failed to conceal divisions within the ministry. Newcastle was discovering that he was often not being consulted on patronage, the traditional prerogative of the Treasury. He was also concerned about the anomalous position of Bute, who was wielding political power without the responsibility of office. Above all the Duke was anxious to ensure that he would have the management of the general election due by March 1761. He had retained the Treasury on such a promise, and told Lord Chesterfield on 29 November 1760 that 'the securing of a good Parliament is my great and first object'.[19]

Both Pitt and Bute, from different motives, were content to allow Newcastle to manage the election campaign. Electioneering was not Pitt's kind of politics, and he had told Hardwicke on 29 October that 'for his part, he did not desire the chusing of a new Parliament, but only to have some of his friends taken care of'.[20] Bute was aware that he lacked the Duke's expertise and experience, and knew that management of the election was a point of no consequence. 'The new

Parliament would be the King's, let who will choose it', he thought, and that veteran politician Lord Bath, the former William Pulteney who had led the Commons opposition to Sir Robert Walpole, opined that Newcastle would 'soon find that his supposed friends were only the friends of his power, and will continue firm to him no longer than while he has the possession of the means of gratifying them'.[21] Newcastle missed the warning signs, that during the election campaign there were numerous individual desertions of the old minister for the young King and his favourite. Bute himself gave the Duke the names of only three candidates, at a meeting on 4 February 1761, having shed his earlier vague and exaggerated ideas about the number of seats to which the Crown could nominate. Newcastle's lists of the new House of Commons, gradually elected over several weeks after the dissolution of the old one on 20 March 1761, which gave him great satisfaction at the time, bore little relation to political alignments in the subsequent Parliament. That was indeed 'the King's', giving majorities to five successive ministries, three of which the Duke opposed. Most of those whom he deemed 'friends' in 1761 proved to be government men not Pelhamites, personal followers of the Duke, a distinction he would indeed not then have recognised.

By the time of the general election Bute had become Northern Secretary, the post he had refused from George III at his accession and again when pressed by his friends in November; but he had since changed his mind, after membership of the cabinet. The initiative came from Newcastle. 'We all thought, that considering his known might and influence, it was better for the public, and for us, that he should be in a responsible office, rather than do everything and answer for nothing.'[22] Holderness was willing to quit the post, but Pitt objected that favourites should not become ministers. Not until Pitt suffered a two-month illness could the proposal be implemented, Bute being formally appointed on 25 March. Pitt subsequently complained to Newcastle on 9 April that this had been done 'without concert with him; that he would overlook it and would go on with good humour'.[23]

Bute had already been acting as virtual Premier with regard to cabinet appointments. It was he who in January 1761 arranged the elevation of Lord Henley from Lord Keeper to Lord Chancellor, a post entailing membership of the cabinet.[24] And it was Bute who on 12 February offered Pitt's ally Lord Temple, then Lord Privy Seal, the Viceroyalty of Ireland. The following conversation was reputed to have ensued. 'I suppose your Lordship does not mean to look upon me as a bare Groom of the Stole. The King will have it otherwise.' To which Lord Temple replied, 'Certainly so. I look upon you as a Minister and desire to act with you as such'.[25] Bute suggested 'a permanent system' of 'harmony and union with him and Mr. Pitt'.[26] Such an alliance, the prospect of which made Newcastle tremble, was never on the cards. Temple was critical of Newcastle for having allowed Bute to undermine his authority as Premier, so he told Devonshire. 'After having been the Minister of the Country, to continue when the whole power was taken from him.' Temple himself had been insulted by the offer. 'If they had a proper consideration for him, why did they not offer him First Lord of the Treasury, or Secretary of State. He believed he should not have accepted either. But to make him that was Privy Seal, Knight of the Garter and so popular in this country such an offer, it was an affront.' Temple, who owed all his consequence to his brother-in-law Pitt, thought in his conceit that the two of them were the essential political fulcrum of any ministry, whether they were allied to Bute, Newcastle or the King's uncle the Duke of Cumberland.[27] When Temple eventually declined Ireland, the post of Lord-Lieutenant went to Lord Halifax, President of the Board of Trade since 1748, who asked Bute for it on 2 March.[28]

Contrary to appearances and expectations, however, it was not Bute who dismissed Henry Legge as Chancellor of the Exchequer without compensation of honour, office or pension. That step, Bute told Newcastle on 4 February, was insisted upon by the King himself. Legge had offended George III by personally and successfully opposing Bute's intended candidate in a 1759 Hampshire by-election. Legge had compounded his offence by failing to join the stampede of those who flocked to pay homage to the favourite in 1760. Instead he asked for 'marks of respect', having a high opinion of his own ability and seemingly a low one of Pitt, for he spoke disparagingly of wild men 'with great powers of speech and no *real* knowledge of business'.[29] Bute thought highly of him, and in a letter to Newcastle disclaimed all responsibility for Legge's dismissal, which took place in March 1761. 'That it was the King's own disgust and dislike to the man, that it was not his (Lord B's) doing. That his own real opinion was that it was most advisable to let him stay in till the end of the war'.[30]

It was an awkward time to fill such an important post. Newcastle had earlier thought George Grenville the only other possible candidate, but Pitt now declined to push his brother-in-law's application, a rebuff that widened their estrangement. Grenville had already offended Pitt by successfully sounding Bute and Newcastle about the

vacant Commons Speakership, held throughout George II's reign
by Arthur Onslow.[31] Legge was replaced by Secretary at War Lord
Barrington, always willing to turn his hand to anything. The highly
talented but unreliable Charles Townshend moved from a court post
to the War Office. These appointments both put square pegs in round
holes. Barrington lacked financial skills, and Townshend the steady
application required for his onerous task.

The ministry was now more openly a triumvirate. Newcastle had
wanted Bute to balance Pitt as co-Secretary, and promised his support
'in case Mr Pitt ... and he should differ'.[32] Matters did not work out
as he anticipated. Bute was content to allow Pitt the conduct of the
war, but increasingly encroached on Newcastle's control of patronage. The Duke found himself often being ignored or simply told what
to do.[33] When he unburdened his grievances on Hardwicke, he
received the unhelpful reply from his old friend on 8 August that the
time for him to resign had been at the change of sovereign. 'If your
Grace quits now, it must be either upon reasons of *personal usage* or
of *public* measures.'[34] By contrast Bute developed a confidential and
even supportive relationship with Pitt, who now decided to cancel the
proposed expedition to the Île de France. Eyre Coote's victory at
Wandewash in January 1760 had ended French power in southern
India and removed the worry about the French base in the Indian
Ocean. Another consideration, so Pitt told Bute on 13 March, was the
danger of a war with Spain. 'We may want our great ships.'[35] No such
objection applied to the Belleisle expedition, which should yield a dividend for the peace negotiations now proposed by France and agreed
to by Britain on 7 April.[36]

Throughout these negotiations of April to September 1761 the
British cabinet remained divided as to what terms should be demanded.
Pitt announced that his minimum stipulation was for North America
and the entire Newfoundland cod fishery, and that he would continue
the war rather than make colonial concessions to save or regain
Hanover. When Newcastle replied that France would certainly demand
a share in the fishery, Pitt threatened to make it a resignation issue.[37]
That Pitt also wished to retain the French slave trade ports of Senegal
and Gorée in West Africa, taken in 1758, and to regain Minorca in the
Mediterranean, was less a matter of concern to the Duke. Pitt's basic
aim was to weaken France as much as possible, to guard against a future
war of revenge. His desire for a monopoly of the cod fishery was to
deprive France of a famous 'nursery of seamen' as much as from economic motives. Since Choiseul was already planning such a war of

revenge, based on the reconstruction of the French navy, even before the peace was agreed, Pitt displayed sounder judgement than the Duke of Bedford. That Duke feared that France would be alienated by too severe terms, and objected to Pitt's apparent idea of retaining every conquest. Bedford displayed more shrewdness in his expectation of trouble from Britain's American colonies if the French threat from Canada was removed, and pointed out that French planters would be difficult to control in any conquered West Indies islands. Bedford also voiced fears that British monopolies of the West Africa slave trade ports and of the Newfoundland fishery would equally lead to widespread resentment in western Europe.[38] Bedford soon had the reputation of wanting a bad peace after a good war. Bute on the other hand took the view that George III dare not begin his reign with a treaty that failed to reflect the wartime triumphs. Bute sympathised far more than tradition has it with Pitt's desire to make worthwhile gains, and even sided with him at first over the fishery. Despite George III's public desire for peace the King's prestige had to be safeguarded.

Choiseul began the peace negotiations with a genuine desire to cut France's losses in the disastrous war, albeit with the long-term objective of revenge. But his ally Austria was not interested, being by 1761 confident of victory over Prussia, while Spain's increasingly evident willingness to support France in the current conflict meant that Choiseul was soon involved in simultaneous negotiations for making peace and continuing the war. He began with the realistic proposal for a treaty based on the status quo at specified dates in the future. The chief negotiations took place in Paris between Choiseul and British envoy Hans Stanley, whose hand was soon strengthened by news of the capture of Belleisle on 8 June. Choiseul was prepared to cede Canada, except for the retention of Cape Breton Island as an unfortified fishing base, and this concession ended the lingering Canada-Guadeloupe argument in Britain. The exchange of Belleisle for Minorca was suggested by Britain, who offered to restore Guadeloupe if France would evacuate the Rhineland. But the British cabinet, at a meeting on 24 June, split on the fishery question. Newcastle and Bedford were not prepared to continue the war for that reason, with Bedford warning that the German campaign might collapse during the haggle over that issue. Pitt and Temple were supported by Bute, who was afraid that Pitt would engross all popularity by his stand, but also was himself genuinely concerned that concession of the fishery and the sugar islands of the West Indies would mean that Britain gained little economically.[39] On 5 August Choiseul stated his final terms, some fishing rights with a base other than Cape Breton Island, and a refusal to evacuate the Prussian Rhineland.[40] On 19 August the British cabinet did concede a fishery, as Pitt gave way after Bute had changed his opinion, but it was too late. For on 15 August France and Spain signed a so-called Bourbon Family Compact, whereby Spain secretly promised France military and naval assistance if the peace negotiations failed. Choiseul promptly lost interest in them, for increasingly he had merely been flying a kite to see what terms Britain would offer.

The British government faced up to reality on 15 September by recalling peace envoy Stanley from Paris, but Pitt's colleagues refused to accept his demand for an immediate declaration of war on Spain, who was obviously arming but not yet ready. Anson said there were not enough ships, while Bedford and Newcastle raised financial objections.[41] Two further cabinet meetings of 18 and 21 September failed to resolve this deadlock, and it was agreed to await the return from Paris of Stanley, since he might have more information on the Family Compact. Meanwhile, on 24 September the cabinet members opposed to Pitt each informed George III of their opinions.[42] Stanley, when interviewed by the King on 30 September, gave it as his opinion that Spain would declare war, but George III thought he had been 'tutored' or awed by Pitt.[43]

The decisive cabinet meeting was on 2 October. Pitt argued that Britain was ready for war whereas Spain was not, and that her underhand behaviour had forfeited any claim to diplomatic courtesy. Of the other nine present, only Temple supported him. Newcastle warned of the vast cost. Bute said it was folly to assume Spanish hostility. Anson again stressed his lack of ships, implying that Pitt's idea of a pre-emptive strike was impractical. Pitt then declared that as Southern Secretary he dealt with Anglo-Spanish relations, and 'would be responsible for nothing but what he directed'.[44] Pitt formally resigned on 5 October, when he assured the King that he would not oppose the ministry 'unless he was attacked', an easy and ominous qualification.[45] Pitt accepted an annuity of £3,000, together with a peerage for his wife as Lady Chatham, because he was short of money. Grenville had told Bute so, but George III, far from adopting a cunning plan to ruin Pitt's reputation, was reluctant to bestow these rewards.[46] The episode led to rumours that the great war minister had been bribed to resign, to clear the path to power for Bute. Pitt therefore issued a public statement, in the form of a letter of 15 October to London MP William Beckford that was sent to the newspapers, pointing out that he had resigned on a difference of policy and that only afterwards was he offered rewards by his sovereign.[47]

Pitt's colleagues deemed a Spanish war too high a price to pay for his continuance in office, but Newcastle for one soon expressed awareness of the loss of the successful war minister, commenting to Hardwicke on 15 November. 'With all his faults we shall want Mr Pitt, if such a complicated, such an extensive war is to be carried on; I know nobody who can plan, or push the execution of any plan agreed upon, in the manner Mr Pitt did.'[48] For the same reason, Bute had sought to prevent rather than provoke Pitt's resignation, frankly admitting the motive to Newcastle. 'If we had any views of peace, he should be less solicitous what part Mr Pitt took, but that as a continuance of the war seemed unavoidable ... we should do what we could to hinder Mr Pitt from going out and thereby leaving the impracticability of his own war upon us.'[49] When Lord Melcombe congratulated Bute on the removal of 'a most impracticable colleague ... and a most dangerous minister', Bute replied that he was 'far from thinking' the change 'favourable', explaining that 'the change of a Minister cannot at present make any remarkable change in measures'.[50] The old view that Bute was now determined to make peace at any price is as erroneous as the one that Bute deliberately engineered Pitt's fall.[51]

Bute and Newcastle faced the problem of replacing Pitt, whose resignation had deprived the administration of both its war minister and Commons Leader. Bute, believing in the need to match Pitt in debate, proposed Paymaster Henry Fox. Newcastle said he was too unpopular, and suggested Grenville. Bute at first rejected this idea, since Grenville 'had not a manner of speaking which would do against Mr Pitt'.[52] Bute soon changed his mind, and with Newcastle's concurrence asked Grenville to fill the double vacancy left by Pitt. Grenville, though now finally breaking with Pitt, for obvious reasons of personal delicacy declined to succeed his brother-in-law as Southern Secretary; but he was persuaded by George III to become Commons Leader, with a seat in the cabinet, while retaining his old post as Treasurer of the Navy.[53]

The new Southern Secretary was a surprise appointment, the Earl of Egremont, a man who at the age of fifty-one was devoid of administrative experience and had played little part in politics. He was recommended, possibly through Lord Mansfield, by Grenville, who had married his sister. When Bute mentioned him to the Duke of Devonshire, the latter replied that he was 'a very good and proper man', but warned that the Duke of Bedford would be offended, in view of his experience as Southern Secretary from 1748 to 1751, and also at the Admiralty (1744–48) and in Ireland (1757–61). Bute replied that he suspected a 'league' between Bedford and Newcastle, which Devonshire denied. Bute then made the point that 'if a man who was thought ready to make any peace was to have Mr Pitt's place, it would be very unpopular'. Despite this apprehension of Bute that the bestowal of office on the Duke of Bedford would give the ministry too pacifist an image, he was given the cabinet post of Lord Privy Seal vacated by Lord Temple on his resignation with Pitt.[54]

The reconstructed ministry had inherited Pitt's war. Newcastle had no doubt as to what ought to be done. The Duke had always been the foremost advocate of a continental campaign, and in November he endorsed Pitt's famous boast about winning America in Germany by contending that America would now have to be defended there, to prevent colonial conquests being exchanged for territorial losses in Europe.[55] He was faced by colleagues who took a different view. At once he was deprived of the support in cabinet of such friends as Hardwicke and Devonshire by a Bute proposal that all policy matters should first be discussed by 'a cabinet council' of four, Newcastle, Grenville, Egremont and himself.[56] Newcastle told Hardwicke on 8 October that while he approved 'the narrowing the council … I can never think it reasonable, that the first concoction should be confined to us four, where I am sure to have three against one'.[57] By the end of the month he believed he was being excluded altogether, writing to Devonshire on 31 October that 'every day convinces me more and more that my Lord Bute intends to confine the first *concoctions* of affairs to himself, Lord Egremont and Mr G. Grenville. With them he is conferring every moment, and Lord Egremont has already got the *cant – he had received the King's orders.* For Your Grace knows, it is the King who does everything'.[58] Newcastle's sarcasm could not conceal his chagrin that he felt increasingly a 'cypher'.[59]

Cabinet newcomers Egremont and Grenville were soon uneasily aware of the mutual jealousy between Bute and Newcastle, 'the one saying you are minister for you have got the both Houses of Parliament, the other you have the King'.[60] Bute, confident that Newcastle would retire at the end of the war, saw no need for a showdown, and privately told Grenville that 'he thought it better to let the old man tide over a year or two more of his political life'.[61] Devonshire, also anxious to avoid a ministerial rift, assured the King on 18 November that Newcastle could easily be managed with the appearance of power, summarised by George III to Bute as 'a little seeming good humour from me and your telling him things before he hears them from others, ... for nothing is so hateful to him as the thoughts of retiring'.[62] Retaining Newcastle at the Treasury enabled Bute to use the Duke 'as a screen between him and the people', both popular opinion and the Parliamentary politicians. Pitt and Temple were soon attempting to frighten Newcastle into resignation, thinking Bute alone would be an easy target. During November they changed their tactics and approached Newcastle and Hardwicke for an alliance, being rebuffed by both. Temple thereupon warned Newcastle that 'Bute meant to get rid of him apace, as he had done of them', a myth soon to pass into historical legend.[63]

Newcastle may have begun to feel his isolation when the remodelled cabinet undertook its first task, the formulation of a reply to a paper of 28 August from the Spanish minister Richard Wall to the British ambassador in Madrid, Lord Bristol. It had raised such issues as an audacious Spanish claim to participate in the Newfoundland fishery, and the proposed eviction from Honduras of a long-established British settlement of logwood cutters. Newcastle, failing to perceive that these were merely diversions to clog any negotiation, would have favoured a less strongly worded reply than the letter of 28 October to Lord Bristol. This conventionally stated a wish to settle all disputes with Spain amicably, but with the proviso that 'there was nothing offensive contained in the late Treaty with France'.[64]

Ministerial minds were now turning to the first meeting of the new Parliament, elected over six months earlier. The session was due to open on 13 November, only a few weeks after Pitt's resignation. Grenville, his successor as Commons Leader, was confident that event would not jeopardise the ministerial majority, as Hardwicke told Newcastle. 'His main dependence seemed to be on your Grace's friends, the Whig party, which was the sheet anchor. He did not imagine that Mr Pitt would have any great following of the Tories ... The soberer part of them were sick of Mr Pitt's measures of war, more especially continental, and of the immense expense'.[65] This forecast of the forthcoming session proved sound. Pitt's numerical weakness in Parliament was to be starkly revealed as, in his own words, he found himself 'out-Toried by Lord Bute and out-Whigged by the Duke of Newcastle'.[66]

Such apprehension as Grenville had about the meeting of Parliament was the personal fear that as Commons Leader he would be outshone as a speaker by Henry Fox.[67] Bute undertook to dissuade Fox from undue participation in debate, the brilliant young Lord Shelburne being sent to convey this intimation. Fox, already promised by Bute a peerage for his wife, to maintain parity with Pitt, gave the assurance in a handsome manner, so Devonshire recorded under the date of 10 November. 'He said, for his part, he did not intend to be always answering Mr Pitt, that he should be glad to sit still. At the same time, if ever the Crown was attacked and administration wanted his assistance, he should be glad to give it.'[68]

No sooner had this point been settled to Grenville's satisfaction than he found himself overruled in cabinet, on 10 November, over a matter concerning the Commons. He was anxious to have the correspondence with Spain laid before the House, perhaps seeking to preempt a demand by Pitt. But Hardwicke opposed this as improper and offensive to Spain while negotiations were still in progress, and his objection was carried by the support of Bute, Newcastle, Mansfield and Devonshire. Next day Mansfield sought to mollify the indignant Grenville by suggesting a meeting of leading ministerialist MPs to consider the point. This aroused the ire of Hardwicke, who said he would not attend cabinet again if its decisions could be thus queried. A confrontation was avoided when Grenville dropped the idea. Such care not to offend Spanish susceptibilities soon seemed unnecessary. On 14 November a dispatch arrived from Lord Bristol, reporting that when he had asked the Spanish minister Richard Wall whether the Family Compact Treaty contained any hostile intent towards Britain, Wall had angrily adopted a warlike tone. This time Newcastle agreed with Bute's suggestion that 'a strong and spirited answer' should be sent.[69]

When the new Parliament met on 13 November, the debate on war policy was transferred from the cabinet to the House of Commons. Pittites defied their lack of numbers to launch a series of debates in support of their leader, and Pitt himself took several opportunities to explain his behaviour. In the debate of 13 November on the Address John Wilkes, not yet a radical, declared that Pitt was right to expect a Spanish war and threatened to move for the relevant papers. William Beckford reminded MPs that there was now no important officeholder in the House, depicting Grenville and others as mere subalterns. Beckford criticised the cession of any part of the cod fishery, and defended the German war as tying down French resources, a view supported by a third Pittite, Middlesex MP George Cooke. Pitt later rose to inform the House that he had resigned because he would not be responsible for the policy of others. 'America had been conquered in Germany', Pitt declared, when urging the need for the German war to continue. As for the fishery monopoly, he had yielded to a cabinet majority. The Address passed unanimously, as Pitt himself had urged.[70]

That the ministry accepted the need for the continental campaign was demonstrated on 9 December, when Secretary at War Charles Townshend proposed finance for an army of nearly 90,000 men in Germany. He declared that 'Mr Pitt's divine plan' should be continued to obtain a good peace. Bedfordite Richard Rigby thought the Prussian subsidy should be discontinued. Grenville equivocated, accepting the obligations of treaty and honour but not the strategic argument, contending that France was being defeated because of her naval weakness and not the German war. Pitt pointed out that the German war had been decided upon by Newcastle and Fox, before he came to office in 1756, and argued that Hanover was now a millstone around the French neck, not that of Britain. As for subsidies, it was usual to give them to our allies, as to Austria and Russia in the previous war.[71] The debate on the report was resumed the next day, when Lord George Sackville, the anti-hero of Minden, attacked the argument that the German war was a drain on French resources. But the highlight of the day was gross abuse of the absent Pitt by a new MP Colonel Isaac Barré, whose savage invective was to be a feature of Commons debates for the next two decades. He had served in Canada, and thought himself ill-rewarded by Pitt. Brought into Parliament by Buteite Lord Shelburne, he was instigated to attack Pitt by his patron and by Henry Fox.[72]

Next day, 11 December, two Pittite MPs, George Cooke and William Beckford, moved for the Spanish papers. Grenville promptly opposed this as improper, both because international diplomacy appertained to the Crown, and because negotiations were still in progress: the same arguments of impropriety had been used against him in cabinet when he himself had made the same proposal! Pitt supported the motion in a rather off-hand manner, and did not force a vote after a mere dozen yeas were answered by 'a clamorous No'. Diarist Harris deemed the motion to have been unwise as revealing Pitt's 'want of weight and influence'.[73] The Pittite group by itself clearly represented no threat in Parliament to the ministry, which now had to adjust its war policy to meet the Spanish threat.

The official professions to Parliament about continuing negotiations with Madrid had belied preparations for a Spanish war. An attack on Portugal, Britain's traditional ally, was to be expected, and a decision to send 6,000 soldiers there was taken on 26 December. War was formally declared on 2 January 1762, three months after Pitt's resignation on that point, after Spain had rejected a demand for information on the Family Compact Treaty. The best way to attack

Spain, so a cabinet on 6 January decided, was an assault on her strongest fortress in the New World, Havana in Cuba. That expedition should then attack New Orleans in Louisiana, while another force from India should attack Manila in the Philippines.[74] But the Spanish war provided another reason to end the German campaign, as Newcastle soon discovered: hence this lament to Hardwicke.

> My Lord Bute's schemes for foreign affairs are very different from ours. Popular maritime expeditions in war and a total dislike of all continental measures, are the basis of his politics. These differences of opinion in essentials make it impossible for us to draw together, even less than with Mr Pitt; for although he had all that popular nonsense about him, he mixed it with real system and backed it with a continental support which had sense in it.[75]

Bute had in fact set about ending the German entanglement soon after Pitt left office. On 20 November, as Northern Secretary, he told the Prussian envoy of a cabinet decision to remove from any renewal of the subsidy treaty, due to expire in December, the clause, stipulated by Pitt in 1758, that neither party could make a separate peace. The annual payment of four million crowns, or £670,000, would be continued. Frederick II was dismayed, since at the end of 1761 his military position seemed hopeless, with much of his territory under enemy occupation. But he did not dare to alienate Britain, hoping for diplomatic assistance as well as financial support. His response, received by Bute on 30 December, comprised two demands: that Britain should secure French neutrality in the German war, including evacuation of his Rhineland provinces, a British request that Choiseul had already rejected in the summer; and that Britain should pay him six million crowns a year, equivalent to £1 million, until the end of his war against the Austro-Russian coalition. In a sense this reply merely sought insurance, for Frederick expected a Spanish war would prevent any peace and oblige Britain to continue her German campaign.[76]

The Prussian King misread the political situation in Britain. Bute perceived the new commitments against Spain to be an argument to give up the British campaign in western Germany. He suggested this at the cabinet of 6 January, but not an end to the Prussian subsidy. Newcastle argued that such a decision would disastrously reverse the successful war strategy. France would then be able to concentrate on the overseas war, in alliance with Spain, and could take Hanover to bargain against losses elsewhere. Devonshire supported him with the arguments that Britain would be exposed to invasion, and that no state would trust her as an ally in future. Grenville backed Bute, and the others were silent, with no decision being taken.[77] George III approved Bute's idea, commenting that even though his Hanoverian subjects might suffer from a French invasion, 'I cannot help wishing that an end was put to that enormous expense by ordering our troops home'.[78]

The Duke of Bedford, absent from the cabinet, was dissatisfied with such indecision, and made known his intention to propose in the Lords a motion to end the German war. Newcastle failed to dissuade him on 14 January, when Bedford said that *'the King told him, he was determined to give up the German war*. That was news', Newcastle wrote to Hardwicke, 'and more than Lord Bute will say, or admit I am sure'.[79] Bedford put his motion on 5 February, when, to avoid publicising the ministerial split on the subject, Newcastle allowed Bute to defeat it indirectly by a previous question, thereby avoiding a vote on the motion itself, the division being 105 to 16. Buteite Shelburne was among those who sided with Bedford, who was angry at what he deemed Bute's deceptive behaviour.[80]

The European war scene was now transformed, miraculously for Frederick the Great, by the death of Czarina Elizabeth of Russia on 5 January, for she was succeeded by the Prussophile Peter III. He withdrew the Russian army from the war, and evacuated Pomerania and East Prussia. Newcastle was delighted, commenting to Hardwicke on 28 January, 'So much for Russia. This must make our peace in Germany, and I think with France and Spain if we manage right'.[81] George III more shrewdly and correctly feared that Frederick would not be satisfied with survival, observing to Bute on 5 February, 'I look on the so sudden retreat of the Russian forces, as liable to encourage that *too ambitious Monarch* to breath still stronger revenge against the Court of Vienna, on finding himself freed from one formidable foe, therefore 'tis our business to force him to peace'.[82] That was indeed exactly how Frederick II reacted, and he requested immediate payment of the British subsidy, obviously to attack Austria. He did not intend to stop fighting just when his luck had changed! Within the British government opinion was divided as to how the new situation could best be exploited. Grenville and Egremont argued that Britain herself should now press for better peace terms from France. Bute was always aware that he dare not risk unpopularity for the King by making an unsatisfactory peace, and the continued tide of war success paradoxically made his task all the more difficult. That Martinique had been taken became known on 21 March. Yet obviously Frederick II's improved military position reopened the arguments over both the British campaign in western

Germany and the direct subsidy payment to him. At a cabinet of 26 March Grenville revived the idea of abandoning the German war, so that Britain could concentrate her resources on the overseas struggle with France and Spain: but Newcastle, despite his own January hopes of peace, strongly and successfully opposed the suggestion.[83]

That was the Duke's last triumph in cabinet. Opposition to the German war was strengthened by a calculation by Chancellor of the Exchequer Lord Barrington on 31 March that a £2 million vote of credit would be needed to cover the war costs in both Germany and Portugal, not the £1 million originally envisaged.[84] Newcastle informed the cabinet on 8 April, when Grenville questioned the need for the extra money. Bute took the opportunity to attack Frederick II for not disclosing his war plans, and 'hinted' at stopping the Prussian subsidy. No decision was taken on either subject.[85] The heart of the matter was a genuine difference of opinion over policy. Newcastle thought it absurd folly to end the German campaign without a general peace, and therefore deemed the £2 million essential. His critics adopted one or, like Grenville, both of two counter-arguments: that the German war was not now necessary, and that Britain could not afford to fight in both Portugal and Germany. At a cabinet on 30 April Newcastle and his allies were outvoted on the £2 million credit by Bute, Grenville, Egremont, Henley, Granville and army commander Ligonier.[86] This explicit decision was followed by an equally important implicit one. 'We had afterwards some talking on the Prussian subsidy, from which the Dukes of Newcastle and Devonshire, and Lord Hardwicke, would not depart', Bute wrote to Bedford. 'The other Lords ... thought it highly improper to continue it, and the load of evidence we have, of the most determined emnity of that Prince, and under our own most necessitous circumstances; I should therefore suppose the King will not consent to it; and the vote of credit will be asked for without it.'[87] Newcastle drew the same inference, commenting to Hardwicke about 'refusing the Prussian subsidy which I take to be now decided'.[88] Grenville did not regard the financial dispute as settled, and saw the King on both 5 and 6 May to argue that if Newcastle secured the second million 'it would be making him master'. George III told Bute that he had replied that 'the whole affair is the most unpleasant one I have had before me since I have mounted the throne', for he was receiving contradictory expert advice as to how much extra money was needed.[89] But Newcastle now gave up the point, since he had decided to resign.

That idea had been in his mind for some time: on 10 April he had told Hardwicke, 'I am determined not to engage another year'.[90] Now he thought the war strategy in ruins, believing, wrongly, as events turned out, that the decision to vote only an extra £1 million would end Britain's German campaign. This conviction may have strengthened his reluctance to take ministerial responsibility for a peace that could never fulfil expectations aroused by the great success of the war.[91] Pique also entered into his decision. Others shared the opinion of Henry Legge that the Duke was being pressurised into resignation 'by taking away from him all powers'.[92] Newcastle had also long been aware that since early in March Treasury Secretary Samuel Martin had been secretly priming Bute with financial information, to the effect that the extra million was not needed; and he had been openly challenged at the Treasury Board by Gilbert Elliot and James Oswald, both Scotsmen.[93] Such behaviour hurt him. Nor was the Duke's suspicion of a plot to replace him by Bute unfounded. Later, on 1 September, Lord Mansfield told Newcastle that driving the Duke out of office 'was not my Lord Bute's own inclination: but that his Lordship had been forced to it; or advised to it, by the Princess Dowager of Wales, Mr George Grenville and Mr Elliot, by representing to my Lord Bute, that he was nothing, while I had the Treasury'.[94] There does not appear to be any strictly contemporary evidence of this scheming:[95] but the recollection accords with the known reluctance of Bute to become Premier, and the intention of George III to make him so. In mid-April the King wrote to Bute this forecast of what would happen in the event of Newcastle's resignation. 'Are not those who now appear attached to him men of the most mercenary views, men who will ever follow him that pays them; in my conscience I dont believe he would have ten followers if out of place.'[96] This attempt to allay the fears of Bute about Newcastle's Parliamentary strength was a shrewd prediction, even if it did cynically underestimate the pull of party and personal loyalties. Soon afterwards the King directly stated to Bute what could hardly have been news, that he was 'the successor I have long had in my eye to the Duke of Newcastle'.[97]

The change of ministry began on 7 May, when Newcastle informed Bute that he would give way on the second million, but that he intended to resign. Bute neither sought to dissuade him nor voiced any regret, omissions the Duke deemed incivility. The Duke gave assurances, as he did to the King later, that he would not go into opposition, reporting to Devonshire, 'I said also smiling. I extremely approve your peace; I wish, I could approve so much your war; meaning his ridiculous maritime war'. Newcastle next went to the King, and said that he was yielding on the financial argument but would resign the Treasury as soon as George III could make proper arrangements. The King asked him to reconsider the decision, since the financial controversy was over.[98] That was a mere courtesy, for when reporting the conversation to Bute George III estimated it would be a fortnight before he could take over the Treasury.[99]

The conduct of the war was meanwhile raised in Parliament by the Pittite group, when on 11 May Chancellor of the Exchequer Lord Barrington moved the vote of credit for £1 million.[100] John Wilkes and William Beckford expressed a preference for the German war. Grenville replied that on the contrary peace should be sought, since the National Debt had grown by £50 million during the previous four years. The debate was dominated by one of Pitt's great speeches, in which he ranged over matters domestic and foreign. He began by saying that although out of office he would not 'stoop to that little hackneyed practice of party, opposing whatever was the measure of the adversary. He had stood forth for general war, and for reduction of the House of Bourbon. To advise still longer war was constancy to the same plan.' Pitt deplored the idea that there was a choice between Portugal and Germany. He supported both campaigns, agreeing therefore, he said with the two parts of the ministry, and claimed that the German war cost France more than Britain. A continental alliance had always been the key to British success, as in the days of Elizabeth I and William III. 'He wished to move that the continuation of the subsidy to Prussia might be added to the vote of credit: but it did not become him to move for more than was asked by the King's servants; yet he wished the vote of credit had been greater, and he knew the Duke of Newcastle wished so too'. Diarist James Harris confirmed those views recorded by Walpole, and then noted how Pitt 'threw out the plan of an alliance with Russia, Prussia, Hesse, Brunswick, and Sweden ... (Mr Pitt I call an Inigo Jones in politics, a man of great ideas, a projector of noble and magnificent plans – but architects, though they find the plan, never consider themselves as concerned to find the means).' George III suspected Pitt's speech to be 'a lure', to draw him and Newcastle together.[101] The £1 million credit was voted without dissent, and when on 14 May Lord Barrington proposed taxes to raise the money he mentioned that £700,000 had been saved by non-payment of the Prussian subsidy.[102]

Before his formal resignation Newcastle retracted his promise not to oppose. Offended that he was not pressed to stay on at the Treasury,

he reacted accordingly, on 14 May informing the young Lord Rockingham that 'I shall take care that his Majesty shall know when I resign
that I am at liberty to act, as I shall think proper, upon every occasion
that may happen'.[103] Five days later George III informed Bute that 'the
Duke of Newcastle has quite altered his language, he says he hopes I
will look on him as at liberty to act as his conscience shall guide him, I
reply'd that this is the language every man that opposes uses.'[104] That
Newcastle was still an active player in the political game caused the
King and Bute to revise a strategy based on the assumption that Bute
would inherit the Duke's Parliamentary following. The Bute ministry
would face the opposition of two distinct factions, the Pitt group and
the Newcastle party. To prevent an alliance between them became an
immediate concern.

This political problem would be complicated by difficult policy
decisions. There was a peace to be made, and consequential problems
arising out of Britain's greatly extended empire: arrangements would
have to be made concerning North America, and Britain's acquisitions
elsewhere, notably India. Ireland was in a sense another wartime
legacy, a problem postponed again by the Viceroyalty of Lord Halifax. He had opted for that poisoned chalice in March 1761, confident
that he could manage the three leading Undertakers, Lord Shannon,
Archbishop Stone of Armagh, and Irish Commons Speaker John Ponsonby, who was also head of the Revenue Board, the main centre of
Irish patronage. 'He has heard of combinations … to handcuff and
fetter him', Lord Chesterfield told the Bishop of Waterford on 12 September 1761, 'but he seems not in the least apprehensive of them'.[105]
Halifax's intention was merely to ride the Undertaker tiger, not to
tame it. Edmund Burke, who went back to Ireland as an aide to the
new Chief Secretary, William Hamilton, commented that Halifax and
Hamilton had 'no notion of dividing in order to govern, they only
propose not to be absolutely governed'.[106] Like his predecessors,
Halifax soon found that a nominal majority was no insurance against
Parliamentary defeat on a popular question. On 2 November 1761 an
opposition motion complaining of the financial cost of pensions was
carried by 82 votes to 80 in the Irish Commons. The Viceroy thereupon threatened the Undertakers with loss of their patronage if they
could not manage Parliament better, and secured a money bill, with
the assistance of Speaker Ponsonby and Lord Shannon, by 147 votes
to 37.[107] Halifax further showed his mettle over a demand for an
absentee tax on official salaries. He suggested to a meeting of office-
holders that the idea be extended to all salaries, thereby ensuring the

Castle Party would kill the proposal.[108] But Halifax deemed it unwise
to resist an Irish Septennial Bill voted by a 108 to 43 majority in the
Commons. Many MPs, under constituency pressure, had supported a
measure that was contrary to their own personal interests, since regular elections would make life more difficult for MPs and Undertakers alike. The British Privy Council rejected the measure only after a
difference of opinion; Lord Hardwicke was one who thought British
power in Ireland would be strengthened by it.[109] Control of Ireland
was rising to the top of the British political agenda as European peace
beckoned, and rumours that Halifax would be residing permanently
in Ireland anticipated the overt policy change later in the decade. In
Dublin Sir Henry Cavendish heard that 'Lord Halifax is to make a
long stay with us ... Whatever may be thought expedient now, sometime or other residence will be found necessary'. In London Henry
Fox believed that the original intention was for Halifax to stay for two
biennial Parliamentary sessions and the long intervening recess, a
period of nearly three years.[110] Evidence that the British government
had some permanent change in mind was an increase in the Lord-
Lieutenant's salary from £12,000 to £16,000, for Southern Secretary
Egremont told Halifax on 20 March 1762 that the reason was
'the King's intention that for the future the residence of the Lord-
Lieutenants in Ireland shall be longer than has hitherto been customary'.[111] Halifax, aware of the prospect of a cabinet post at home, was
unwilling to play any such role, and left Ireland on 1 May. He nevertheless retained the office of Lord-Lieutenant throughout the Bute
ministry, for the Irish Parliament was enjoying a biennial recess.

Notes

1 BL Add. MSS. 51406, fo. 57.
2 He recorded both the original and the altered wording. *Leicester House
   Politics*, pp. 214–15.
3 *Devonshire Diary*, p. 89.
4 Namier, *Age*, pp. 120–1.
5 *Leicester House Politics*, p. 216.
6 BL Add. MSS. 32913, fo. 399.
7 *Devonshire Diary*, p. 43.
8 Namier, *Age*, pp. 122–6.
9 BL Add. MSS. 32913, fos 426–9.
10 *Devonshire Diary*, pp. 42–3.
11 *Leicester House Politics*, p. 227.

12 *Leicester House Politics*, p. 227.
13 Middleton, *Bells of Victory*, pp. 158–9, 177.
14 Bute MSS (Cardiff), unnumbered. For a detailed study of the impact of the pamphlet see Schweizer, 'Israel Mauduit ... ', in Taylor, *et al.* (eds), *Hanoverian Britain and Empire*, pp. 198–209.
15 *Devonshire Diary*, pp. 56–7. Middleton, *Bells of Victory*, pp. 172–3.
16 BL Add. MSS. 32916, fo. 369.
17 BL Add. MSS. 32916, fos 385–6.
18 Middleton, *Bells of Victory*, pp. 176–8.
19 BL Add. MSS. 32915, fo. 168.
20 BL Add. MSS. 32913, fos 426–9.
21 Namier, *Age*, p. 156.
22 BL Add. MSS. 32921, fo. 60.
23 BL Add. MSS. 32920, fos 64–8. *Dodington Diary*, pp. 402–3. *Devonshire Diary*, pp. 72–3, 75, 88–9, 93.
24 *Dodington Diary*, p. 414.
25 BL Add. MSS. 32919, fo. 287.
26 *Devonshire Diary*, pp. 81–2.
27 *Devonshire Diary*, pp. 82–3.
28 *Devonshire Diary*, p. 78 n.
29 Malmesbury MSS. Photocopies A168.
30 BL Add. MSS. 32919, fo. 42.
31 *Chatham Anecdotes*, I, 304–5.
32 BL Add. MSS. 32920, fos 64–71; 36797, fos 48–50.
33 Namier, *Age*, pp. 284–6.
34 BL Add. MSS. 32826, fo. 311.
35 *Devonshire Diary*, pp. 90–1.
36 For these negotiations see Rashed, *Peace of Paris*, pp. 70–114, and Schweizer, 'Lord Bute, William Pitt ... ', in Schweizer, ed., *Lord Bute*, pp. 41–55.
37 *Devonshire Diary*, pp. 92–3. Middleton, *Bells of Victory*, pp. 182–4.
38 BL Add. MSS. 32922, fos 5–6, 449–51. Namier, *Age*, pp. 275–6.
39 *Devonshire Diary*, pp. 102, 109.
40 *Grenville Papers*, I, 381–2.
41 *Devonshire Diary*, pp. 120–5. Middleton, *Bells of Victory*, pp. 192–3.
42 *Devonshire Diary*, pp. 130–6.
43 *Bute Letters*, p. 65.
44 *Devonshire Diary*, pp. 137–9. Middleton, *Bells of Victory*, pp. 196–7.
45 *Devonshire Diary*, p. 140.
46 *Grenville Papers*, I, 412–13. *Bute Letters*, pp. 47, 50, 63.
47 *Chatham Papers*, II, 158–9. For the public controversy see Peters, *Pitt and Popularity*, pp. 204–11.

48 BL Add. MSS. 32931, fos 45–9. Quoted by Namier, *Age*, pp. 306–7, but misquoted by Middleton, *Bells of Victory*, p. 197.
49 Yorke, *Hardwicke*, III, 323. For a reassessment of Bute's attitude see Schweizer, *CJH*, 8 (1973), 111–25.
50 *Dodington Diary*, p. 425.
51 Rashed, *Peace of Paris*, p. 118, repeats the traditional view.
52 BL Add. MSS. 32928, fos 362–5.
53 BL Add. MSS. 32930, fo. 104. Malmesbury MSS. Photocopies B691. *Grenville Papers*, I, 401–2. *Devonshire Diary*, p. 140. *Dodington Diary*, pp. 425–6.
54 *Grenville Papers*, I, 411. *Devonshire Diary*, pp. 141, 148–51.
55 BL Add. MSS. 32919, fo. 133; 32931, fos 46–7.
56 *Devonshire Diary*, p. 142.
57 BL Add. MSS. 32929, fos 115–16.
58 BL Add. MSS. 32930, fo. 221.
59 BL Add. MSS. 32932, fo. 363.
60 *Devonshire Diary*, p. 145.
61 *Grenville Papers*, I, 396.
62 *Bute Letters*, p. 70. *Devonshire Diary*, p. 150.
63 *Devonshire Diary*, pp. 146, 149–50.
64 *Devonshire Diary*, pp. 121, 126, 144–5.
65 BL Add. MSS. 32929, fo. 332.
66 Yorke, *Hardwicke*, III, 430.
67 BL Add. MSS. 32930, fo. 226.
68 *Devonshire Diary*, p. 148.
69 *Devonshire Diary*, pp 148–9.
70 Malmesbury MSS. Harris Diary, 13 Nov. 1761. Walpole, *Memoirs*, I, 71–7.
71 Malmesbury MSS. Harris Diary, 9 Dec. 1761. Walpole, *Memoirs*, I, 78–83.
72 Walpole, *Memoirs*, I, 85–8.
73 Malmesbury MSS. Harris Diary, 11 Dec. 1761.
74 PRO 30/47/21 (cabinet minute of 6 Jan. 1762). *Bute Letters*, p. 78. *Devonshire Diary*, p. 154. Middleton, *Bells of Victory*, pp. 200–5.
75 Yorke, *Hardwicke*, III, 357.
76 Schweizer, *CJH*, 13 (1978), 383–95.
77 BL Add. MSS. 32933, fos 178–82. *Devonshire Diary*, pp. 154–5.
78 *Bute Letters*, p. 78.
79 BL Add. MSS. 32933, fo. 320.
80 *Devonshire Diary*, pp. 155–7. On this episode see Schweizer, *PH*, 5 (1986), 107–23.
81 BL Add. MSS. 32934, fo. 45.
82 *Bute Letters*, p. 81.

83 *Devonshire Diary*, pp. 158–62.
84 Middleton, *Bells of Victory*, p. 207, citing BL Add. MSS. 33040, fos 317–19.
85 *Devonshire Diary*, p. 166. PRO 30/47/21 (cabinet minute).
86 Nicholas, Thesis, p. 44, citing PRO/30/47/21 (cabinet minute).
87 *Bedford Papers*, III, 76–7.
88 BL Add. MSS. 32938, ff. 20–1.
89 *Bute Letters*, p. 100.
90 BL Add. MSS. 32937, fo. 14.
91 Namier, *Age*, p. 336, quoting a memorandum of 12 May.
92 Malmesbury MSS. Photocopies A171.
93 Nicholas, Thesis, p. 47. Namier, *Age*, p. 313 N.
94 BL Add. MSS. 32942, fo. 114
95 As is noted by Nicholas, Thesis, p. 49, who states 'the case remains unproven'.
96 *Bute Letters*, p. 91.
97 *Bute Letters*, pp. 92–3.
98 BL Add. MSS. 32938, fos 105–11.
99 *Bute Letters*, p. 101.
100 For this debate see Malmesbury MSS. Harris Diary, 11 May 1762; Walpole, *Memoirs*, I, 127–32; and Almon, *Debates*, VI, 146–9.
101 *Bute Letters*, p. 103.
102 Malmesbury MSS. Harris Diary, 14 May 1762.
103 BL Add. MSS. 32938, fos 262–4.
104 *Bute Letters*, p. 107.
105 *Chesterfield Letters*, V, 2,382.
106 Hoffman, *Edmund Burke*, p. 279.
107 Grafton MSS. no. 539. *CHOP*, I, 79.
108 Powell, Thesis, pp. 87–9.
109 Walpole, *Memoirs*, I, 111. Powell, Thesis, pp. 89–91.
110 Powell, Thesis, pp. 91. Powell has discussed the background to the resident Viceroyalty in *IHS*, 31 (1998), 19–36.
111 *CHOP*, I, 167.

4

The Bute ministry (1762–1763): peace and cider

'It was over with [the] Duke of Newcastle – that they should have all the speakers in the House of Commons, and Lord Bute would be strong enough to carry all before him.'[1] So did that robust Bedfordite Richard Rigby realistically pronounce on the new political system. Lord Bute himself took a lot of convincing that such was the case. Even after Newcastle intimated his intention to resign the Treasury Bute was resisting pressure to succeed him, from above by the King and from below by men like James Oswald and Gilbert Elliot. Under 'anecdotes' on 9 May the Duke of Devonshire recorded that Bute 'hesitated and was afraid'.[2] Bute's personal distaste for politics was strengthened by awareness of his own limitations, as spelt out in June by the hostile Henry Legge: 'proud, cunning but not wise, and ignorant of men and business'.[3] Bute was a good Parliamentary speaker and a conscientious administrator, faring better as Premier than many contemporaries anticipated and most historians have judged. But his heart was not in it. Bute was to accept office only out of a sense of duty to his young sovereign, and made it clear to George III that he was doing so only on a temporary basis. 'The end of my labours was solemnly determined, even before I undertook them', Bute was to tell Henry Fox on 2 March 1763.[4] It was a well-kept secret, though his young acolyte Lord Shelburne claimed to have known it, informing diarist James Harris on 7 April 1763, the day after Bute's resignation was announced. 'It had been his intention to retire (as he, Lord Shelburne, knew) for more than a twelve-month', once he had settled the peace terms.[5] Bute's opponents naturally assumed that he intended to be Premier for as long as possible, and conducted the political battle accordingly. When he did resign many thought he had been forced out of office.

The formation of Bute's ministry was protracted because he refused to take the Treasury unless he had a competent Chancellor of the Exchequer, for the incumbent Lord Barrington evidently would not do. Bute's first choice was Commons Leader George Grenville, who refused that onerous and non-cabinet post, holding out for the Northern Secretaryship that Bute himself would be vacating. Bute then asked Charles Townshend, but the Secretary at War also refused.[6] Such was the growing desperation that there were rumours of recourse being made to former Chancellor Henry Legge, though a man much out of favour with both George III and Bute.[7] On 19 May the impatient King told Bute that 'the thoughts of his not accepting the Treasury or of his retiring chill my blood'. If Bute could not find 'a good Chancellor of the Exchequer, he should seek for an honest quiet man'. In such an eventuality James Oswald, presumably disqualified as a Scot, could do the financial business.[8] Bute accordingly fell back on one of his own supporters, Sir Francis Dashwood, to take responsibility for the nation's finances, to his own amused astonishment. John Wilkes, a Buckinghamshire friend, later made a public jest of the appointment by depicting Dashwood as a man 'puzzling all his life over tavern bills'.[9]

The other major problem concerned the King's objections to Grenville's appointment as Northern Secretary. George III thought him unfit 'for a post where either decision or activity are necessary',[10] and he disliked the prospect of the two Secretaryships of State being held by brothers-in-law, both opposed to a soft peace. Bute saw no impropriety in that, and after Lord Halifax declined the post he prevailed on the King to accept Grenville.[11] Otherwise, as in most ministerial changes of the period, there was much continuity of personnel under a new Prime Minister. Lord Granville, over seventy, remained as Lord President of the Council, until his death on 2 January 1763. Lord Henley continued as Lord Chancellor, Lord Egremont as Southern Secretary, the Duke of Bedford as Lord Privy Seal, and Lord Ligonier, though now eighty-two, as army Commander-in-Chief and Master-General of the Ordnance. When Lord Anson, retained at the Admiralty, died on 6 June, Lord Melcombe refused the post on grounds of ill health, but though without office was now summoned to attend cabinet, as Hardwicke and Devonshire had been under Newcastle, since Bute could count on his support: but he died on 28 July. Lord Halifax was appointed, being permitted to retain his absentee high-salary Lord-Lieutenancy of Ireland both then and when he became Northern Secretary from October. This pluralism both symbolised the lack of

attention paid to Ireland in the alternate years when the Dublin Parliament was not in session, and reflected the reluctance of the ministry
to curb the Undertakers, for the chief of them, Primate Stone, was high
in favour with the Bute party.[12] It was the behaviour of Chief Secretary
Hamilton that foreshadowed the future, the creation of a Castle Party.
He saw his Irish posting as a career move, and sought to create his own
faction in the Irish Parliament by recruiting from independent MPs. He
stayed on as Chief Secretary when Halifax finally resigned at the
beginning of Grenville's ministry.

Outside the cabinet there was also little change. Lord Barrington
thankfully vacated the Exchequer to become Treasurer of the Navy,
Grenville's old post. Henry Fox, unambitious for the high office befit-
ting a man of his ability, retained the lucrative Pay Office. Charles
Yorke and Sir Fletcher Norton remained as Attorney-General and
Solicitor-General, and Charles Townshend as Secretary at War. The
Bute ministry was not a group of sycophants, nor based on Scots and
Tories, as later Whig legends had it, but a coalition of experienced
politicians, drawn from the former Leicester House group, the
Bedford faction, and above all from 'the old Whig corps', men like
Halifax, Barrington, Yorke, and others like Lord North at the Treasury Board, who had deserted Newcastle with varying degrees of awk-
wardness and embarrassment. Bute's levees were crowded,
significantly with many previously deemed Newcastle's friends.[13] Such
men were mindful of their own futures, and the continuous but
unavailing pressure on the Duke to retire altogether from politics was
not disinterested. Hardwicke feared for the careers of his sons, others
for their own.

Newcastle formally resigned the Treasury on 26 May, and refused
the King's offer of a pension, even though his personal finances had
suffered greatly in the service of the state.[14] The Duke, disorientated
at being out of office and disgruntled at his lack of influence, sought
to adjust to an unfamiliar role after over forty years in government, a
record thirty-seven in the cabinet. It was symptomatic of his confusion that he should have requested friends to stay on in office, while
still expecting their political support. The Duke even thought that he
would still receive cabinet papers, until Hardwicke convinced him
that that was an unrealistic expectation.[15]

On his resignation Newcastle promptly contacted the King's uncle,
the Duke of Cumberland, who remained hostile to his old foes of
Leicester House, the Princess Dowager of Wales and Lord Bute. Hardwicke warned him that this conduct would be construed as planning

an opposition, which would be both factious, unless the peace terms were clearly unsatisfactory, and futile, without Pitt. The Bute ministry was indeed alarmed at the prospect of an alliance between Newcastle and Pitt, whose followers shunned the royal court. So did those personally associated with the Duke of Devonshire, who now ceased to attend cabinet even though he was still summoned. He and Hardwicke were both widely held to have retired from politics. During the summer of 1762 Newcastle therefore received several ministerial approaches, including the offer of Lord President of the Council, all of which he refused, fearing that he would incur a share of the odium for the forthcoming peace treaty without any say in its final formulation. These feelers stopped when it became clear that Pitt would not cooperate in Parliament with the Duke.[16]

Much of the peace settlement had already been agreed while Newcastle was at the Treasury, and he risked the charge of factious behaviour by opposing it. Discussions with France had resumed in December 1761, and Britain had soon conceded a French share in the Newfoundland fishery with two small island bases to support it. After news came of the capture of Martinique, the cabinet met on 27 April to decide on new terms in the light of this success: in the absence of an unwell Grenville, it resolved to demand all French North America east of the Mississippi, in exchange for the return of Martinique and Guadeloupe, and to retain the other captured West Indies islands.[17] Bute was pushing for gains France might be expected to concede. The Newcastle cabinet had also agreed to demand Minorca back in exchange for Belleisle, and, in West Africa, to restore Gorée and keep Senegal.[18]

These terms broadly satisfied Choiseul, who was fearful of Austrian defection in face of the Russian turnabout, for Prussia continued her war without the British subsidy. But Spain was unwilling to make peace. Her Portuguese campaign had started well, and she also hoped to gain Gibraltar. So in June Choiseul actually urged Britain to prevent the Spanish capture of Lisbon, a feat largely achieved by the British expeditionary force.[19] Meanwhile the Anglo-French negotiation stumbled over the insistence of Choiseul on retaining St Lucia in the West Indies and New Orleans at the mouth of the Mississippi, even though it was on the east side of that river, the agreed boundary. Deadlock threatened when the Bute cabinet at meetings on 21 and 24 June unanimously insisted on the previous terms.[20] For a French response of 2 July repeated both these demands and a refusal to evacuate the Rhineland until peace was made. The situation was resolved by Egremont, who privately informed George III that he was willing to concede St Lucia if the other gains were agreed, while insisting that the hard-line Grenville should not be told: so much for the King's earlier fear of the two of them conspiring together! Bute and Egremont, without informing the cabinet, then secretly told France of this proposed concession. News of Choiseul's acceptance of this offer came on 8 July, leaving Bute and Egremont with the problem of persuading the cabinet to change its mind.[21]

This task was rendered more difficult by news that the Duke of Brunswick had won another victory over the French in Germany, with Lord Granby the British hero: Newcastle's pessimism about the German war had proved unfounded. On 1 July Horace Walpole summarised the basic ministerial dilemma. 'Lord Bute's situation is unpleasant: misfortunes would remind us of Mr Pitt's glory; advantages will stiffen us against accepting even such a peace as he rejected'.[22] Egremont was now privately urging Choiseul to make St Lucia a condition of peace at the very time when his brother-in-law Grenville led the ministerial refusal to concede that point. Yet at a cabinet of 26 July Egremont failed to support a proposal of Bute that the French terms be accepted, and no decision was made.[23] An angry King told Bute that he was 'thunderstruck', and declared that if the opportunity for peace was missed 'I must insist on most of the cabinet of this day being then dismissed'.[24] In a rare display of the royal pressure once deemed characteristic of his reign George III then closeted several ministers individually, presumably deploying this threat.[25] Two days later, on 28 July, the cabinet agreed to give up St Lucia and New Orleans.[26]

At that cabinet the Duke of Bedford was appointed to go to Paris as negotiator with both France and Spain, a poor choice. George III commented to Bute later in the year that 'a man of more coolness and less jealousy of temper would have done the business in half the time', and, more succinctly, on 16 January 1763 that his 'warmth of temper turns hillocks into mountains'.[27] This temperament got in the way of a pacifism so notorious that the ministry deemed it prudent to restrict his discretion, for there were widespread fears that he would concede too much, as voiced by Newcastle to Hardwicke on 31 July. 'I doubt there is scarce any peace his Grace would reject.'[28] After the usual summer break a cabinet of 3 September gave Bedford precise instructions on key points: the Mississippi was to be the colonial boundary between Britain and France, with free navigation for both nations; the Prussian Rhineland was to be evacuated, and both countries were to be neutral in any continuing war between Prussia and Austria; France was not to help Spain in Portugal.

Bedford was in any case instructed not to sign anything without prior royal approval.[29]

Southern Secretary Egremont soon became concerned about what 'that headstrong silly wretch' was conceding, mostly minor points but also the return of Cuba, if it was taken, without compensation.[30] The mutual antipathy of Bedford and Egremont was to outlast the peace negotiations, during which Egremont was the link between envoy and cabinet, magnifying small concessions by the envoy and passing on to him instructions he disliked. George Grenville was the real obstacle to an early peace. On 29 September Rigby warned Bedford that he 'governs Lord Egremont like a child and ... his Lordship has a cordial hatred for you. This I beg you to depend upon, and to have constantly in your thoughts when you write to him. He will lie and make mischief for the sake of doing so, you know of old'.[31]

Havana was reputed to be the strongest fortress in the New World, and Spaniards had scorned the possibility of its capture. On 29 September news of its fall arrived in London, and this precipitated a political crisis in Whitehall, as Grenville and Egremont demanded adequate compensation for its return.[32] Earlier George III had actually told Bute that he was 'much hurt' at the prospect of this success, fearing it would delay the peace.[33] But he now promptly accepted the principle of compensation, mentioning Florida himself the next day.[34] The conduct of the 'two rascally Secretaries of State', as Rigby designated them to Bedford, nevertheless so exasperated the King that on 2 October he even accepted Bute's suggestion of making Newcastle and Henry Fox Secretaries in their stead, confident that they would never unite against Bute.[35] The outcome was that Grenville found himself replaced by Henry Fox as Commons Leader and by Halifax as Northern Secretary. The dispute over Havana was merely the excuse for Grenville's removal as Commons Leader. Fox had already been thought of on 27 September, before the Cuba news arrived.[36] Bute had decided he did not want there to carry the peace a man who still objected to some of the terms, notably the cession of Guadeloupe and St Lucia.[37] On 6 October Bute told Fox that 'Mr Grenville (half unable, half unwilling) could go on no longer. His Majesty was in great concern lest a good peace in a good House of Commons should be lost, and his authority disgraced, for want of a proper person to support his honest measures, and keep his closet from that force with which it was so threatened'. Fox declined to succeed Grenville as Northern Secretary, but agreed to be Commons Leader with a cabinet place. He warned Bute that his promotion would add 'unpopularity to unpopularity', and, so he told Bedford, that 'my name might frighten Tories away'.[38]

For Henry Fox, unlike Pitt and Grenville, had been a prominent member of the 'old Whig corps', holding various posts under Walpole, Pelham and Newcastle. His acceptance of office under Bute was therefore seen by the Whig grandees as desertion in a way that the behaviour of men like Grenville was not. In a conversation of 31 July with the Duke of Devonshire Fox had answered such a reproach for siding with Bute over the peace terms: 'It was not supporting my Lord Bute, but acting according to his opinions'. Fox had also then disagreed with Devonshire's aristocratic resentment at Bute's assumption of power: 'that the nobility would not be governed in that manner'. Fox had replied that, on the contrary, 'it was hard indeed, if nothing would do but tearing the King's Favourite from his Majesty's person'. Conscious that he might be accused of desertion, Fox then 'affected to say, that Whig and Tory no longer subsisted, in order to prove, that he was not acting against the Whigs'.[39] Fox's 'Court Whig' record and cynical personality made him an eminently suitable choice for converting into firm Parliamentary support those former administration men who had opted for Bute rather than Newcastle during the summer recess.

On 9 October Bute sent his private secretary Charles Jenkinson, later a man reputed to be close to George III, to inform Grenville that Fox would be taking over the lead in the Commons. Bute himself then informed Grenville that he must exchange offices with Lord Halifax, the First Lord of the Admiralty, a post inferior in status and salary, a blow to the purse of a man without private means as well as to his pride.[40] Naturally anxious not to alienate the King, Grenville had little choice but to accept his demotion, but he warned Bute and, later, the King that Fox was unpopular: to which George III replied, 'We must call in bad men to govern bad men'.[41]

That Grenville's insistence on compensation for Havana had little to do with his demotion was underlined by the decision of the reshuffled cabinet on 22 October to demand either Florida or Puerto Rico. That was a unanimous view, except that Grenville and Egremont pressed for both.[42] Bedford, who feared the peace would be jeopardised by this demand, was specifically instructed that Spanish non-acceptance would mean continuation of the war. Spain must also concede the Honduras logwood settlements, and give up her outrageous claim to a share in the Newfoundland fishery. Choiseul, anxious both for peace and maintenance of Spanish goodwill, had, on news of the fall of Havana, already offered Spain that part of Louisiana west of the Mississippi. Before the end of October the Spanish government decided to cede Florida and accept western Louisiana. The peace preliminaries were agreed by the British cabinet on 10 November.[43]

The Bute administration had achieved its timetable objective of securing peace before the Parliamentary session: financial complications and possible criticism were thereby avoided. Ministerial concern over Parliamentary acceptance of the peace terms was to prove groundless. But in the autumn of 1762 that fear should be seen against a background of both press hostility to Bute and the manifest intention of Pitt and Newcastle to oppose the peace.

Bute's accession to office sparked off a hitherto unprecedented propaganda campaign against him. At one level there was a barrage of cartoons, totalling some four hundred during the ministry. At another there was a press attack, mainly in the weekly political essay papers that were a feature of the period.[44] Bute had anticipated the need for a press campaign and had mobilised an array of writers; but all were outgunned by John Wilkes in 'the war of the weeklies'. The first issue of the *Briton*, founded by Bute and written by Tobias Smollett, appeared on 29 May. It was countered a week later by the *North Briton*, launched by Wilkes, who also contributed to the Pittite *Monitor*. The ministry retaliated on 12 June with the *Auditor*. The controversy centred on the peace terms and on Bute himself, as Wilkes exploited anti-Scottish prejudice and used historical precedents about royal favourites, notably Roger Mortimer, the favourite of young Edward III and lover of that King's mother, a parallel applied to Bute by press innuendo and unfounded popular rumour. The audience was much wider than the limited circulation of these papers, for extracts from the weeklies were reprinted in the daily and thrice-weekly newspapers and in the monthly magazines. This broader newspaper press also entered the fray on its own account, by no means always against Bute. As the peace negotiations came to a head, opposition papers, led by the *London Evening Post* and the *Gazetteer*, criticised any concessions to Britain's enemies, but the ministry was defended by the *London Chronicle* and several sponsored pamphlets.[45]

By the late summer of 1762 the Duke of Newcastle had adapted to the role of opposition, and sought to avoid the slur of 'faction' by claiming that on foreign policy he differed in principle from the ministry. Russia's complete withdrawal from the war after Catherine II deposed her husband in July strengthened, in Newcastle's opinion, the case for support of Prussia, a line of argument showing him to be yesterday's man. More convincing was the contention that Britain's war successes in 1762 justified demands for better peace terms than the Duke himself had earlier accepted. George III, at a private interview on 3 September, failed to persuade Newcastle to drop his opposition to the peace. So, a few days later, did Devonshire and Hardwicke, even though the latter warned him that only Pitt would be the beneficiary of any political success against Bute.[46]

Grenville now suggested an alternative ministerial tactic, that Newcastle, Hardwicke and Devonshire be summoned to attend cabinet, to compel them to share responsibility for the peace. Bute replied that the first two were no longer in office, but Devonshire had retained his court post of Lord Chamberlain and could still be deemed a cabinet member, though he had ignored all summonses since Newcastle's resignation.[47] A letter to Devonshire, then at Bath, was answered by a refusal on 3 October. The King was highly indignant, commenting to Bute on 5 October that 'this is a personal affront ... I have no doubt that the Duke of Devonshire is too timid to have taken such a step had he not known that the Dukes of Cumberland and Newcastle would approve of it. We must therefore turn our eyes some other way and see whether ... the House of Commons cant be managed without these proud Dukes.'[48]

There followed the successful approach to Henry Fox, but Bute nevertheless made one last attempt to secure the support of Newcastle and Hardwicke, Halifax being sent to visit the Duke on 16 October. Newcastle and his friends remained unwilling to share the responsibility. '*Coalition* is the favourite word of the administration at present', wrote Cumberland to Newcastle on 17 October, 'but when pressed, it is always dribbled down more than a share of the odium, and hardly any power to serve the country'.[49] Six days later Hardwicke was even more frank in his assessment of the offer. 'No office hinted at, no particular proposition made; only *pray come to Court and Council*, and help to support those who had demolished you.'[50] The leadership of 'the old Whig corps' would oppose the peace.

George III, anxious to punish Devonshire's insolence by dismissal from his court office, may have held his hand to await the outcome of this approach. He acted on 28 October, after the Duke had returned to London.[51] Newcastle thereupon sought to build out of this Devonshire incident a campaign of selective resignations. 'There exists the most factious combination of *soi disant* great men against the lawful right and liberty of the King that ever happened in this country', Bute told George Townshend on 2 November.[52] George III was scornful of such a tactic, commenting to Bute that on the contrary 'every officer that votes against government at a time like this ought to be made an example of'.[53] On 3 November the King led the way by the rare step of striking out Devonshire's name from the Privy Council.[54] The young Marquess of Rockingham and Newcastle's nephew and heir Lord Lincoln resigned from Bedchamber posts, but apart from the Cavendish family there were few other resignations, only nine of the thirty-three officeholders listed by Newcastle on 3 November for the campaign.[55] Hardwicke, whose own son Charles Yorke had refused to resign as Attorney-General, told the Duke on 15 November that he should not have expected otherwise. 'This cannot possibly be new to your Grace, who have been conversant in Courts and parties above these forty years. Have you not all along seen such motives to be the great hinges, on which the generality of people's conduct has turned?'[56] The fiasco exposed Newcastle's political weakness out of power, and provided some convenient patronage opportunities for Bute.

It was only gradually that the Parliamentary implications of his new role in opposition dawned on Newcastle. In August and September his lists of the House of Lords optimistically showed a rough equality, but by 6 December conceded the ministry an advantage of 109 to 51. And on 18 December, when the Duke was licking his wounds, he reckoned on only 45 supporters there.[57] Likewise, for the House of Commons he at first weeded out only 56 previous supporters, mostly MPs connected with Bute, Bedford and Fox, making no allowance for the magnetic pull of government power.[58] Fox, unscrupulous and energetic, with a taste and aptitude for political management lacking in Bute, excelled in his task of ensuring a Commons majority for the peace. 'No man knows better than he does the *weakness* and *wickedness* of mankind, or how to make the best use of it', Newcastle commented to Charles Yorke on 25 October. 'He has agents working everywhere. He knows whom to employ and how to work upon different dispositions and constitutions. My Lord Bute had done ably for his purposes in the choice he has made.'[59]

There soon proved to be little substance in early government fears either that independents and old Tories would resent being canvassed by such a Court Whig, or that Pitt's charisma and reputation would carry much weight. For the ministry was offering a good peace and the prospect of an end to high taxation. Fox shrewdly estimated that the opposition would not muster sixty Commons votes.[60] But he nevertheless believed that coercion of known opponents would have a salutary effect, beginning with Newcastle himself. 'Strip the Duke of his three lieutenantcies', he urged Bute in November. 'I'll answer for the good effect of it, and then go on to the general rout. But let this beginning be made immediately.'[61] Fox did not get his way, and the retributive action was postponed until after the Parliamentary triumph, Newcastle not being deprived of his county lord-lieutenancies until 23 December.

After Henry Fox and George III had in their different ways done their work, Newcastle accepted the inevitable. The last of the Duke's numerous Commons lists, compiled just before the meeting of Parliament on 25 November, classified 176 MPs as 'for' Newcastle, 34 as absent, 91 as doubtful, and 256 as 'against'.[62] A ministerial majority of 213 votes to 74 on 1 December was ominous for its effect on any waverers.[63] The opposition was in disarray. No strategy was agreed upon, either by a group of younger men on 30 November or by the old heads on 2 December; while Pitt declined open cooperation when sounded by Cumberland on 17 November, stating that he did not wish to overthrow Bute merely to restore Newcastle to power.[64]

This opposition incompetence and disunity contributed to and enhanced a ministerial triumph that was already assured. Henry Fox had thought there would be a Commons majority for any peace made by Bute long before he himself was called upon to provide it, comprised, so he told Devonshire on 31 July, of 'the Tories, the Scotch, and the Loaves and Fishes'.[65] In other words, the independents and the Court Party would outvote the political factions. And so it happened, without need of the bribery of historical legend.[66]

When it came to the point the opposition leadership momentarily doubted whether it would be wise or expedient to oppose the peace after all: but decided to do so on the realisation that supine acceptance would be a poor start to a Parliamentary campaign wherein support might later be expected from peers and MPs who would certainly vote for the peace terms.[67] It was on 9 December that the ministry sought approval. Lord Shelburne moved the Address in the Lords. The twenty-seven-year-old Duke of Grafton, a Pittite, attacked the terms and imputed corruption to Bute, who mocked him as a callow youth and made a fine speech of two hours. Newcastle and Hardwicke also criticised the peace, the latter condemning the restoration of Havana, the key to the West Indies, and of so many French sugar islands. No vote took place.[68]

In the House of Commons that day Pitt made one of the most famous Parliamentary speeches of all time, calculated by several auditors at three hours and twenty-five minutes, reputedly a record length hitherto. Pitt drank cordial and deployed crutches and bandages for dramatic effect, the better to emphasise his physical self-sacrifice in appearing at all, which the House recognised by permission for him to sit down as required during his oration. His main theme was that Britain had given away most of her economically valuable gains. He dwelt at what many felt to be undue length on the fishery concession to France; and regretted the return of so many West India sugar islands and, above all, of Havana, which would have enabled Britain to dominate the trade with Spanish America. France, too, should not have been given back any slave trade ports in West Africa nor her trading bases in India. Pitt concluded by deploring the loss of the Prussian alliance. His speech was a personal statement rather than an attempt to influence the debate. In that respect it was counter-productive, since his disclaimer of any connection with Newcastle encouraged waverers like Charles Townshend to speak and vote with the ministry: a few days earlier Townshend had resigned as Secretary at War, and had therefore been expected to oppose the peace. After Pitt left during the debate others did the same, including some thirty of Newcastle's followers when the Duke sent word not to force a vote. Horace Walpole noted that 'the secession of Pitt struck such a damp on opposition, that Fox had little to do but to chant *Te Deum* for victory'.[69] Before the debate opposition estimates of the minority vote ranged from an optimistic 170 to a pessimistic 110.[70] The actual total of 65, as against 319 for the ministry, was therefore a morale-destroying disaster.

The length of Pitt's speech prevented many MPs from voicing their opinions, and thirty-six did so next day on the report: among those who criticised the peace were Henry Legge and Attorney-General Charles Yorke, and two of Newcastle's young supporters, Thomas Townshend and George Onslow, both still in office. An attempt to retrieve the voting debacle failed because the Newcastle abstentions now present were matched by an equal number of new absentees, opposition mustering only 63 votes against 227.[71] Newcastle calculated that altogether 103 MPs had voted against the peace, and he hopefully added to them 49 others still thought to be friends.[72] He recognised his numerical weakness, ruefully reflecting to Hardwicke on 14 December that 'it is but too true, what Mr Fox said … viz, my Lord Bute has got over all the Duke of Newcastle's friends'.[73] Already Newcastle's former Treasury Secretary James West had advised the Duke not to instigate 'an opposition to the measures of the publick, in trifling divisions, which become contemptible, by violence being added to weakness'.[74] The problem of organising a credible opposition was

compounded by the difficulty of finding Commons spokesmen. That
political weathercock Charles Townshend was soon negotiating to
rejoin the ministry, and early in 1763 became President of the Board of
Trade. Attorney-General Charles Yorke was inclined to support government, like Hardwicke's other sons, and had abstained from voting
after speaking against the peace on 10 December. In the absence of
support from these two formidable debaters Henry Legge, never a
close friend of the Duke, declined the role of opposition spokesman.
'He says he is not qualified to be sole Leader in the House of Commons', Newcastle told Devonshire on 12 December.[75]

Political retribution meanwhile followed the Parliamentary rout.
Those peers and MPs who sided against Bute over the peace or otherwise must have expected dismissal from any honour or office they
held, whether Newcastle, Grafton and Rockingham from their county
lieutenancies, or MPs George Onslow and Thomas Townshend from
their court sinecures. Such was normal political practice, albeit not
with the thoroughness displayed against Newcastle's followers.
George III himself insisted on immediate dismissal of Parliamentary
offenders, since it would 'frighten others'.[76] The offices thus made
available were distributed to the supporters of those now in power:
among them Welbore Ellis, a Fox man, succeeded Charles Townshend
as Secretary at War; Bedfordite Richard Rigby at last acquired a lucrative post as a Vice-Treasurer of Ireland; and James Harris, a friend of
Grenville, was appointed to the Board of Admiralty. More unusual
and open to comment was the consideration of Tories for office: Sir
Walter Bagot declined a place at the Board of Trade, while the replacement of Lord North by Sir John Philipps at the Treasury Board was
briefly contemplated.[77]

But that the political change inaugurated by the accession of George
III signified more of a political revolution than a mere change of ministry was demonstrated by what George Onslow in a 1785 memoir
described as 'that general massacre [that] was made of almost every
man in office from high to low who had any connection with far better and higher men than themselves, those who composed the Whig
administration of the late reign, especially with the Duke of Newcastle'.[78] The papers of Bute's secretary Charles Jenkinson contain numerous lists of minor officials in various government departments, such as
the Customs, Excise, Salt and Stamp Offices, countrywide as well as in
London. It was Fox who insisted on local dismissals, to show where the
power now lay, and the changes in county lieutenancies also had consequential effects. The victims were men marked out for dismissal

because they had been appointed by Newcastle during his decades of power. The Duke thought this systematic removal of officials appointed by him throughout the government structure, down to local customs officers, to be a breach of political convention: 'such a stretch of power, as is hardly constitutional', he wrote to Hardwicke on 19 December.[79] But the campaign was undertaken just because the old Whig corps had been in power for so long. Newcastle melodramatically compared the political atmosphere to the climate of fear in the reign of James II.[80] But lives were not at stake, and a more accurate comparison would have been with the proscription of Tories after the Hanoverian Succession. Many of these men facing dismissal constituted an electoral and political organisation for Newcastle, on the government payroll. It was naive of the Duke to believe that they would remain in post, unless they demonstrated their allegiance to be to the King's government, and not to Newcastle himself.[81]

'A kind of new trade to learn at a late hour.'[82] That was Hardwicke's wry comment to Newcastle on the prospect of permanent opposition. It was not these former ministers, but their younger friends, who first began to pick up the pieces of the shattered opposition. The Marquess of Rockingham, Lord Bessborough, Lord Villiers, George Onslow, and Thomas Townshend were among a group anxious in late December to form a political club. Newcastle discouraged the idea, commenting that such conduct would appear factious, still to the former minister a mark of opprobrium, and also expose their numerical weakness. No club was to be formed for another year.[83] In January 1763 the Duke equally disapproved of the idea of 'our young friends', as he denoted them to Hardwicke, that an approach should be made to Pitt.[84] Such ducal put-downs can only have further demoralised the opposition, which in January 1763 Rigby, an MP since 1745, reported to Bedford as being disheartened and leaderless. 'I never saw the Parliament look so tame after the Christmas recess since I have been a Member as the *present* one does. The opposition has not got a grain of spirit to support itself. Numbers and Abilities they are totally devoid of.'[85] For a while the journalism of John Wilkes, who maintained a relentless attack on Bute in the *North Briton*, seemed to be the sole recourse of opposition, which, in the opinion of the Duke of Devonshire, would be 'undone' without Wilkes, who was 'the life and soul of it'.[86] Parliamentary opposition did revive later in the session, as the Bute ministry gave hostages to fortune by devising new measures. Policy-making was made necessary by the financial, imperial and international problems put into sharp focus by the end of the war, and any positive moves were likely to incur criticism.

That was less so with respect to foreign policy. British diplomatic isolation, resulting from the breach with Prussia, was perceived by virtually all politicians in Westminster as a situation to be remedied, and disagreements arose over what ally should be selected, not whether one should be sought. For it was evident that France would be seeking revenge, and she had maintained her alliances both with Britain's former partner Austria and with Spain, now even more hostile since Britain was her supposedly predatory colonial neighbour along the Mississippi as well as in the West Indies. Bute's first move was an attempt to revive the Prussian alliance. Britain had, after all, insisted on French evacuation of Prussian territories in western Germany: but it was optimistic of Bute on 26 May 1762 to seek to mend fences with Frederick II by justifying the cessation of the Prussian subsidy on two grounds: the prospect of peace for Prussia, and the new Spanish war for Britain. Frederick II refused to be reconciled, and Prussia gave support to the anti-Bute propaganda campaign in Britain.[87] Frederick not only disliked and distrusted Bute. He had his eyes fixed on the Russian alliance that he was to secure in 1764.

Russia was also cultivated by the Bute ministry, for Peter III, ruler from January to July 1762, was anti-French as well as pro-Prussian. Apart from the obvious attraction of Russian military might, there was a need to renegotiate a lapsed 1734 trade treaty, and a common interest in countering French intrigues in Sweden and Turkey. Even the deposition of Peter III by his wife Catherine II was not perceived as a setback, since she was reputed to be an Anglophile, and a new ambassador, the Duke of Buckinghamshire, left in August 1762 for St Petersburg with instructions to renew a 1742 military alliance as well as the trade treaty. But Catherine would not commit herself, and merely told Buckinghamshire that the evident goodwill on both sides made her consider 'the treaty as already concluded', and a formal alliance might alarm Europe. Meanwhile she made clear her expectation of British support at the anticipated vacancy for the elective monarchy of Poland, currently a Russian satellite; for French intervention was expected, as at the last election in 1733. This issue remained dormant, for the ailing Polish King Augustus III lived longer than expected, until October 1763.[88]

Prussian enmity pointed to an approach also to Prussia's foe Austria. There were many British politicians who through tradition and sentiment hankered after this partnership, even though unsuccessful overtures to Austria and Holland early in 1762 had confirmed that the 'Old Alliance' was dead. Such men included George III, who detested Frederick II, and most 'old Whigs', among them Northern Secretary Halifax. An Austrian alliance was never a viable possibility, for Chancellor Kaunitz regarded his French alliance as the cornerstone of his foreign policy. All the Bute ministry achieved was the restoration of diplomatic relations, Lord Mansfield's nephew Lord Stormont being appointed as ambassador to Vienna.

Imperial measures were as yet as uncontroversial as foreign policy, when the Bute ministry considered problems, old and new, arising in North America. Other imperial matters, in India and Africa, were rather deemed the concern still of the respective trading companies, apart from a decision to station an army regiment in Senegal. An old colonial issue was the depreciated value of the paper money printed by Virginia, whose planters were wont to borrow in sterling and repay their debts in notes worth only about five-eighths of their nominal value. In 1762 the Board of Trade received complaints from the merchants of Glasgow, Liverpool, and London, and in February 1763 the Board warned the colony to mend its ways. Otherwise the local currency would be made illegal.[89] A more obvious problem, highlighted by wartime events, was that of ensuring an amicable relationship with Indian tribes angered by encroaching settlers and cheating traders. In the summer of 1762 three Cherokee chiefs from Virginia visited London, and Southern Secretary Egremont, the minister responsible for America, in March 1763 sought to organise a meeting of southern Indians at Augusta. But northern Indians were being alienated by the establishment of settlements near the Great Lakes, and Egremont, fearing an Indian war, urged the army commander in America, General Jeffrey Amherst, to prevent this. Such events brought to ministerial attention the need to organise and defend Britain's new American territories. Egremont told Amherst on 27 January 1763 that 'a plan' was under consideration; soon afterwards he asked the Board of Trade for ideas on a colonial tax; and early in March approved a scheme, drafted by former Georgia governor Henry Ellis, for the government of the new possessions, including the idea of a western settlement boundary for the old colonies.[90] The Bute ministry ended before any of these ideas were implemented, but they foreshadowed much of what the Grenville ministry was to enact.

These matters of foreign and imperial policy did not come before Parliament, and so in a sense were outside the political arena. By contrast military and financial decisions always needed Parliamentary approval, and in 1763 independent MPs as well as the chastened Newcastle faction were to voice various concerns about such government business.

The wartime army amounted to some 100,000 men in July 1762, including 18,000 in Germany and 6,000 in Portugal.[91] George III, in true Hanoverian tradition, 'looked upon the army to be his own department', so Bute later told Henry Fox.[92] As early as September the King was drawing up plans for the peacetime army.[93] But exactly how much of 'his majesty's plan', a phrase used by Fox, was incorporated into the ministerial decision to have an army of some 54,000 men cannot be ascertained.[94] The cabinet on 29 December 1762 settled on 20,000 men in Britain, 18,000 in Ireland, 10,000 in North America and the West Indies, 2,600 in both Gibraltar and Minorca, and a regiment of 550 men in the new African base of Senegal.[95] This plan represented a substantial increase on pre-war numbers, up from 4,000 in America, and 12,000 in Ireland, the statutory minimum for that country by an act of 1699. The proposed American army was already in place, and was intended to keep the peace between colonists and Indians, overawe the French inhabitants of Canada, and guard the southern coast against potential French or Spanish attack: any need to control the existing colonies by force did not come to mind, in 1763.[96] The proposal for an army almost double the previous peacetime establishment, when it was announced to Parliament, revived old and absurd 'country party' fears of a large permanent army being a threat to political liberty. Sir John Philipps, an old Tory but now a loyal supporter of George III, wrote to Bute on 18 February warning that many MPs would not support it. The King, conscious of his own rectitude, privately denounced the sinister implication as nonsensical, but Bute could not afford to alienate independent opinion.[97] Rigby told Bedford on 23 February that the army estimates had been delayed because of objections from 'most of the Tories, and some even of the Walpolian Whigs'.[98] The next day Secretary at War Welbore Ellis presented revised estimates to an invited group of MPs. They included the reduction of the British army to 17,500 and that in Ireland to 12,000. These altered estimates were approved by all those present, including Philipps and Charles Townshend, except for Sir Roger Newdigate.[99]

The Newcastle faction nevertheless still saw the presentation of the army estimates for Commons approval on 4 March as an opportunity to attack the ministry, but Pitt was known to favour a large army. Newcastle, Rockingham and Henry Legge therefore decided to raise the matter only if he was absent. Since he attended, the sole direct attack came from William Beckford, currently Lord Mayor of London, who opposed the motion on grounds of cost, corruption, and putative tyranny, country party sentiments not endorsed even by the squires, among whom Philipps now commended ministerial economy. Pitt regretted that the proposal was not for a larger army, since the peace was only 'an armed truce'. Legge did venture to criticise such expense at a time when the national budget could barely be balanced, but the Newcastle party deemed it unwise to force a vote.[100]

Even before that problem had been resolved the ministry had also removed the sting from another move by Sir John Philipps, who was proving almost more troublesome to Bute as a supporter than his avowed political opponents. Newcastle had long been fearful that his fall from power would be followed by a vindictive inquiry into the vast financial expenditure of the Seven Years War, when apparent inefficiency had been unavoidable, however honourable the Duke's own conduct. Far more concerned about such a prospect, and with good reason, was Henry Fox, who as Paymaster-General of the Forces during the war had used that post to make a fortune. For Newcastle the intention of Philipps to move for a Commission of Public Accounts, an antiquated procedure and the very method anticipated by the Duke in trepidation, seemed to confirm his suspicion of a deliberate attempt by Bute to harass him. Philipps had in fact acted on his own initiative and put the ministry in an embarrassing predicament, George III deeming the proposal 'very silly'.[101] A demand for an inquiry into suspected government extravagance and corruption could not be voted down, and so it had to be evaded, after the motion by Philipps passed on 11 February. When the formal appointment of the Commission came under consideration on 22 February, Chancellor of the Exchequer Dashwood persuaded Philipps to accept instead the modern procedure of a Commons Committee of Inquiry. The next day Dashwood successfully proposed, on the ground of efficiency, that it should be a Select Committee, chosen by ballot. This decision achieved the ministerial objective of neutering Sir John's initiative, while accepting the principle of accountability; for the Committee chosen on 1 March corresponded exactly with a Treasury list, and progressed no further than an examination of the finance of the Board of Ordnance.[102]

Such a retrospective inquiry paled into insignificance by comparison with the legacy of the financial burden from the Seven Years War that now confronted the British government. Two quite distinct problems were the cost of administering and defending the greatly enlarged empire, and the increased burden of the national debt. For the British taxpayers already felt squeezed beyond endurance.

That imperial possessions should be as small a financial burden as possible on the home country had long been a precept of British politicians: and estimates of the cost of maintaining an army of 10,000 soldiers in America soon led the Bute ministry into contemplating a tax on the colonies there. That was evident from a note sent by George III to Bute early in February, for his comparison between the army establishments of 1749 and 1763 excluded the American army 'as [it is] proposed that being no expense to Great Britain'.[103] For the Bute ministry decided that after the first year the American colonies should bear the cost of the army in their continent, and Secretary at War Welbore Ellis promised this to the House of Commons on 4 March.[104] But no resolution had been taken as to the method of taxation, and George III was therefore indignant when on 18 March Charles Townshend, then President of the Board of Trade, proposed in the House of Commons the conversion of an old molasses duty, designed in 1733 by Sir Robert Walpole to prohibit the import of foreign molasses into British North America, into a revenue to pay for the American army.[105] The King reminded Bute that 'this subject is new to none, having been thought of this whole winter'. He was angry that the silence of the Treasury Board, Fox and Grenville had allowed Townshend to claim the whole credit for the idea. 'All ought to have declared that next session some tax will be laid before the House, but that it requires much information before a proper one can be stated, and thus have thrown out this insidious proposal'.[106] Townshend's idea was so popular that an American Tax Bill was at once brought in; but it was killed in Committee on 30 March, ironically by George Grenville, the minister who was to tax America.[107]

The National Debt, so Chancellor of the Exchequer Dashwood told the Commons on 18 March, amounted to £141 million, with an interest burden of £4,700,000.[108] During the army debate of 4 March former Chancellor Henry Legge had cited this situation as an argument against the proposed increase of the army. His concern was that the debt would never be paid off, still the professed long-term aim of the Treasury: for he conjectured the total taxation revenue at £10 million, the debt interest at £4,500,000, and the cost of the Civil List, army and navy at £3,900,000, which together with sundry other expenses, would leave only £1 million a year to redeem the debt, a 'tedious' process.[109]

Three days later Dashwood presented his budget. Needing to raise a further loan of £3,500,000 to meet remaining wartime expenses, he proposed new taxes to cover the interest thereon, one of which was a duty of ten shillings on each hogshead of cider sold, to bring in £75,000. The proposal was postponed for further consideration at the request of MPs from the cider counties, in the West of England. This minor tax was to provoke a major political crisis. Pitt, to win favour with the squirearchy, then threw out the irresponsible suggestion that the main direct tax, the land tax, should be halved from its wartime level of 20 per cent, four shillings in the pound. Grenville challenged him to state what extra taxes he would raise to meet the consequent shortfall of £1 million a year, only to be mocked by Pitt, who quoted or hummed, a popular ditty, 'Gentle Shepherd, tell me where' and then walked out. Many MPs deemed Pitt's conduct silly and rude, but the nickname 'Gentle Shepherd' long stuck to Grenville.[110] Within a few days the proposed cider duty was changed from ten shillings a hogshead on cider sold to four shillings on all cider, whether sold or consumed privately. This attempt at fairness did not remove the sense of grievance in the West Country, even though the rest of England had long endured a beer duty on their favourite drink. Cider county squires were roused to make maiden speeches in the House, with Worcester-shire MP William Dowdeswell rising to prominence as the chief oppo-nent of the duty. When the tax was confirmed on 13 March by a vote of 138 to 81, diarist James Harris noted, 'the division was such as no object but cider could produce. Against the measure all the members of the cider counties of Devon, Somerset, Worcestershire, Gloucester-shire, and Herefordshire; part of the Tories; part of the Newcastle men, such as Mr Legge'.[111] Attendance at the cider debates was poor, and the burden of argument fell on the squires. The West Country was not Pelhamite territory, and the Newcastle party gave support to the protest only by votes. They raised the minority to 112 as against 181 after a long debate on 21 March, but the political inexperience of the cider MPs led them to force too many divisions, a tactic counter-productive as an annoyance factor.[112]

Opposition was even made to the cider duty in the House of Lords, contrary to the constitutional convention that taxation was a matter for the Commons only. A long debate took place over the second reading on 28 March, when Lord Bute argued that since beer was taxed so should cider be; but he agreed that the method of taxation by excise duty was objectionable; and offered to repeal the tax in the future if it was not equitable. Hardwicke somewhat unfairly por-trayed the cider tax as a second land tax on the western counties. The Lords divided 72 to 40 in favour of the tax, a majority raised by prox-ies to 83 to 41. Another vote was forced after a debate on the third reading two days later, when the tax was voted by 73 to 39.[113] The City of London sheriffs at once presented a petition to the King, who made no reply to what he described to Bute as 'a parcel of low shop-keepers'.[114] Bute's behaviour in the cider controversy belied the image of a timid and spineless politician. He had risen to the occasion both as Prime Minister and as Parliamentarian, persisting with the tax despite the misgivings of Fox, Grenville and even George III, and excelling personally in both Lords debates.[115]

Simultaneously with these attacks at Westminster the reviving opposition also sought to embarrass the Bute ministry at India House, where the dominant Laurence Sulivan was an ally of Bute and Shelburne. Robert Clive had returned to Britain in 1760 with an intention to play a part in Parliamentary rather than Company politics. He created his own small group in the Commons, and obtained an Irish peerage from Newcastle in 1762. But a potential threat to his *jagir* then led him to join a challenge to Sulivan's control, and this dispute within the East India Company became part of the battle between administration and opposition. During the peace negotiations of 1762 the Bute ministry coerced the Company into acceptance of less favourable terms than it sought. This treatment alienated Company Chairman Thomas Rous, Lord Clive, and, so Newcastle thought, 'the Company in general'.[116] Early in 1763 the Company polarised into supporters of Sulivan and Clive, who on 15 March carried in the General Court of the Company, by 359 votes to 298, a motion approving the conduct of Rous.

The Bute ministry, threatened with the prospect of a hostile Company after the next election of Directors in April, threw its full political and financial weight behind Sulivan. Commons Leader Henry Fox and Lord Shelburne took out voting qualifications, and government supporters hastened to follow suit. The Newcastle party backed Clive, with grandees like the Duke of Portland and Lord Rockingham qualifying to vote. This contest of 1763 was distinguished from that of 1758 not only by the intervention of Parliamentary politicians but also by the tactic of stock-splitting. Direct ministerial intervention produced 100 of the 160 votes created for Sulivan, the Pay Office under Fox purchasing £19,000 of stock, equivalent to 38 votes. Clive alone was rumoured to have spent £100,000, and altogether 220 votes were made for his party. Such stock-splitting attracted much censorious comment, but did not decide the contest, for over 1,200 proprietors voted, the great majority of them genuine shareholders. Ministerial canvassing of such proprietors was more successful than the campaign of the Newcastle party, for Sulivan carried all ten places contested, fourteen candidates having been double-listed.[117] Both Clive and the Parliamentary opposition were humbled, even though the Company election on 13 April took place just after the end of the Bute ministry.

The irony of the cider tax episode was that the Newcastle party had exploited the issue in order to force Bute out of office; whereas by then he had already finally decided to resign. After the Lords debate of 28 March Fox reported to Bute that one opposition peer had said that the aim was 'only to get rid of you, which shows that they don't smoke the secret yet'.[118] Even after Bute's resignation Newcastle, to whom such a voluntary retirement was inexplicable, remained convinced that he had been forced out of office by 'the noble stand made in the House of Lords, and the spirit shewed in the House of Commons, the end of the session, with the general sense of the nation'.[119]

That Bute did resign within a week or so of the cider tax controversy was coincidence, not cause and effect. Only constant royal encouragement had persuaded him to persevere thus long in face of incessant personal attacks in press and Parliament. On 3 February he told his son-in-law Sir James Lowther that 'if I had but £50 per annum, I would retire on bread and water, and I think it luxury, compared with what I suffer'.[120] Political resentment of him as an unconstitutional royal favourite was transmuted into personal antipathy. Especially did the prejudice against Bute as a Scot span the whole range of society, from the mob to the aristocracy: it was Lord Rockingham who referred to 'the Thistle Administration'.[121] By early March Bute was resolved to retire, but for long only Henry Fox and George III knew of his intention.[122] It was kept so close a secret that Secretaries of State Egremont and Halifax were not told until 1 April.

Bute's first idea was to recommend Fox as his successor, but he was as reluctant to accept as George III was to agree to this proposal, and urged Bute to reconstruct his ministry and carry on. A detailed proposal written by Fox at Bute's request and submitted to him on 11 March suggested that Lord Gower should replace Egremont as Southern Secretary: not merely because Egremont was 'an useless, lumpish, sour friend', or even because Gower was a man of honour and good humour, who would not quarrel with Charles Townshend at the Board of Trade; but also to 'fix that capricious being the Duke of Bedford, who intends to resign, and would be a fifth Duke at Devonshire House within a year'. Fox also recommended for high office young Lord Shelburne, who 'has uncommon abilities, great activity, and loves you sincerely'. Those to be dismissed along with Egremont were Grenville, 'a tiresome incumbrance', and Halifax, 'vain and presumptuous, aiming at the highest degree of power ... insincere, regardless of his word to a supreme degree'.[123] George III dismissed Fox's suggestions out of hand, commenting to Bute, 'I never saw anything less calculated to cement, and make a firm administration'.[124]

In the same letter Fox commented on the House of Commons that 'there never was one so well disposed to be governed', and it would have been at this time that he gave the King advice Shelburne recalled in 1768. 'Not to be diffident about his first Minister, for let him chuse whom he pleased, such Minister would govern the House of Commons'.[125] The restriction on George III's choice was of his own making, for he was known to be angry at the behaviour of the opposition leaders, 'who not only pretended to tell him who should quit his *service*, but who also should succeed them, that ... *nothing but the greatest extremity* would ever induce him to take them in, particularly the Dukes of Newcastle, Devonshire, and Pitt'.[126] The immature young King might hold such opinions early in 1763, but within months his animosities proved not to be immutable.

By mid-March Fox, as adamant in his refusal to be Premier as Bute was determined to resign, was reluctantly suggesting Grenville as Prime Minister. Halifax could still be Northern Secretary, but Bute's young protégé Lord Shelburne should replace Egremont. Bute accepted this plan, but George III thought Shelburne too young and inexperienced for such high office, suggesting that Charles Townshend should succeed Grenville at the Admiralty and then Shelburne could go to the Board of Trade.[127] Grenville's reluctance to replace his brother-in-law with the raw Shelburne, whose appointment as Secretary of State would arouse widespread resentment among more senior and experienced peers, made this seem the obvious arrangement after Grenville on 25 March accepted both the Treasury and the Exchequer, for Bute was determined to secure some office for Shelburne.[128] The Lord Presidency of the Council, vacant since Lord Granville's death in January, was offered to Bedford, who declined, saying he would be 'a madman' to join men who had treated him so badly during his Paris embassy, being especially angry with Egremont. He resigned as Lord Privy Seal, but his resentment was personal, and there was a strong Bedfordite presence in the new ministry.[129] His own son-in-law the Duke of Marlborough succeeded him as Lord Privy Seal, Lord Gower became Lord Chamberlain of the Household, and Richard Rigby continued as an Irish Vice-Treasurer, while Lord Sandwich re-entered

the cabinet on his return to the Admiralty after twelve years, when
Charles Townshend changed an acceptance of that post into a refusal
after his stipulation that a friend be appointed to that Board was
rejected. Dashwood gladly took a peerage and a court office in lieu of
the Exchequer, but Fox, while claiming a promised peerage as Baron
Holland, refused to give up the Pay Office, as had been expected. In
personnel the new ministry was a continuation of the old one, friends
of Bute, Fox and Bedford being appointed and promoted. Grenville
had few recommendations to make, but among them James Harris
joined him at the Treasury Board, and Thomas Pitt and Lord Howe
went to the Admiralty Board.

Halifax continued as Northern Secretary, but now at last resigned
as Lord-Lieutenant of Ireland, since that post would soon require residence in Dublin. Rumours about his replacement had circulated since
the end of 1762. Among those named were the Marquess of Granby,
heir to the Duke of Rutland and on military duty in Germany as commander of the British cavalry; Lord Hertford, a courtier and elder
brother of General Conway, thought to be keen on the appointment;
and Lord Waldegrave, who died suddenly of smallpox in April.[130]
Lord Granby was offered the post, so Hardwicke ascertained from
Halifax and Egremont, informing Newcastle that 'his Lordship was
apprehensive of the difficulties attending it and the Duke of Rutland
was averse to it for fear it should lead his son into too much claret'.[131]
Granby preferred a post more connected with the army, Master-
General of the Ordnance. George III told Bute on 10 April that 'Lord
Granby's refusal I own hurts me': but he agreed with Bute that 'the
next best' was the Earl of Northumberland, whose son was to marry
a daughter of Bute in 1764. The King suggested that Lord Hertford
be simultaneously made ambassador to France 'to prevent jealousies',
and both appointments were announced on 11 April.[132]

Bute's intention to retire from politics was genuine, motivated by
ill-health and a dislike of 'the fatigue of business'. Grenville therefore
assumed he was being appointed Prime Minister 'in the manner as Mr
Pelham was', so he confided to James Harris on 5 April.[133] Henry Pelham had been the last MP to hold that post. But what Bute and George
III envisaged was rather a power-sharing arrangement. Bute commented to Attorney-General Charles Yorke that 'he should leave the
King's affairs in much abler hands than his own. Lord Halifax, Lord
Egremont, Mr Grenville, whom he had known from 12 years of age, a
very worthy and able man, and whose turn lay towards the revenue,
and to that public economy, that was so much wanted'.[134] The King

specifically described his new administration as 'the Triumvirate'.[135] It was publicly given out that 'the Ministry is Mr George Grenville, My Lord Egremont and My Lord Halifax, and that everything *important* was to be determined by their *unanimous* opinion', so Newcastle told the British ambassador at the Hague. But the Duke added this interpretation. 'People generally think, that my Lord Bute will be minister behind the Curtain, though his Lordship absolutely denies it.'[136] The events of the summer of 1763 would determine whether power lay with Bute, Grenville alone, or 'the Triumvirate'.

Notes

1 *Devonshire Diary*, p. 170.
2 *Devonshire Diary*, p. 170.
3 Malmesbury MSS. Photocopies A172–3.
4 BL Add. MSS. 51379, fos 140–1.
5 Malmesbury MSS. Photocopies B682.
6 BL Add. MSS. 51379, fos 204–5.
7 There is an unclear reference to him in their correspondence. *Bute Letters*, p. 108.
8 *Bute Letters*, p. 109. The printed text has 'see' for 'seek'.
9 Thomas, *John Wilkes*, p. 18. For the search for a Chancellor of the Exchequer see Nicholas, Thesis, pp. 57–62.
10 *Bute Letters*, pp. 104–5.
11 *Grenville Papers*, I, 447, 450. Nicholas, Thesis, pp. 61–3.
12 Walpole, *Memoirs*, I, 334.
13 For a list of the 210 present at the levee of 2 June, compiled for Newcastle, see BL Add. MSS. 32939, fos 309–11.
14 Malmesbury MSS. Photocopies A171.
15 BL Add. MSS. 35421, fos 259–60. Namier, *Age*, p. 328.
16 *Devonshire Diary*, p. 173. *Bute Letters*, p. 129. Malmesbury MSS. Photocopies A172. Namier, *Age*, pp. 326–40.
17 *Devonshire Diary*, pp. 168–9. *Grenville Papers*, I, 450.
18 Nicholas, Thesis, pp. 95–108. Rashed, *Peace of Paris*, pp. 118–42.
19 Rashed, *Peace of Paris*, p. 150.
20 BL Add. MSS. 57834, fos 8–12.
21 *Bute Letters*, pp. 118–21.
22 Walpole, *Letters*, V, 217.
23 BL Add. MSS. 57834, fos 62–3.
24 *Bute Letters*, pp. 126–8.
25 *Devonshire Diary*, pp. 173–4. *Bute Letters*, pp. 128–9.

26 BL Add. MSS. 57834, fo. 63. For accounts of this stage of the negotiation see Nicholas, Thesis, pp. 111–33, and Rashed, *Peace of Paris*, pp. 142–58.

27 *Bute Letters*, pp. 178, 187.

28 BL Add. MSS. 32941, fos 126–7.

29 *Bedford Papers*, III, 96–9. Rashed, *Peace of Paris*, pp. 165–6.

30 *Grenville Papers*, I, 474–6.

31 *Bedford Papers*, III, 128.

32 Malmesbury MSS. Photocopies B77.

33 *Bute Letters*, p. 130.

34 *Devonshire Diary*, p. 184.

35 *Bedford Papers*, III, 130. *Bute Letters*, p. 142.

36 Nicholas, Thesis, pp. 180–1.

37 Bute MSS (Cardiff), no. 188. *Grenville Papers*, I, 483.

38 *Bedford Papers*, III, 133–4.

39 BL Add. MSS. 33000, fos 96–8.

40 Lawson, *George Grenville*, p. 142. Grenville's drop in salary was from about £8,000 to around £2,000. In 1763 Grenville said that he had changed posts over the cession of Guadeloupe, and in 1767 that he had resigned over Havana. Malmesbury MSS. Photocopies B77, 854.

41 *Grenville Papers*, I, 451–2.

42 PRO 30/47/21 (cabinet minute). *Bute Letters*, pp. 142, 149–50, 153.

43 Rashed, *Peace of Paris*, pp. 178–87.

44 On this see Nicholas, Thesis, pp. 77–92, and Rea, *The English Press in Politics*, pp. 28–41.

45 Peters, *Pitt and Popularity*, pp. 241–7. Thomas, *John Wilkes*, pp. 19–23.

46 Namier, *Age*, pp. 339–41.

47 *Devonshire Diary*, p. 173.

48 *Bute Letters*, p. 143.

49 BL Add. MSS. 32943, fo. 266.

50 BL Add. MSS. 32943, fo. 369.

51 *Bute Letters*, p. 152.

52 BL Add. MSS. 38200, fos 89–90.

53 *Bute Letters*, p. 155.

54 The only recent example of such disgrace was Lord George Sackville. Of the other four examples earlier in the century two were for corruption. *Jenkinson Papers*, pp. 77–9.

55 Namier, *Age*, pp. 385–6.

56 BL Add. MSS. 32945, fo. 18.

57 Namier, *Age*, pp. 361–3.

58 Namier, *Age*, pp. 363–4.

59 Yorke, *Hardwicke*, III, 426.

60 *Bedford Papers*, III, 161.
61 Fitzmaurice, *Shelburne*, I, 137.
62 Namier, *Age*, pp. 386–7, 422–4.
63 Walpole, *Memoirs*, I, 175.
64 Namier, *Age*, pp. 387–94.
65 BL Add. MSS. 33000, fo. 96.
66 That story was repeated as late as 1951 by Rashed, *Peace of Paris*, pp. 188–9. Journalist John Almon was a main source for it, pointing out that from Oct. 1761 to Apr. 1763 a credit on the Civil List balance of £130,000 became a deficit of £90,000. *Chatham Anecdotes*, I, 306. That was however an expensive time for the Crown for many reasons, notably those arising out of the royal marriage. Reitan, *BIHR*, 47 (1974), 186–201.
67 Hoffman, *Edmund Burke*, p. 301.
68 Simmons and Thomas, *Proceedings and Debates*, I, 412–15. Walpole, *Memoirs*, I, 175–6. Hoffman, *Edmund Burke*, pp. 302–3. Namier, *Age*, pp. 394–5.
69 Simmons and Thomas, *Proceedings and Debates*, I, 415–24.
70 Hoffman, *Edmund Burke*, p. 301.
71 Simmons and Thomas, *Proceedings and Debates*, I, 424–8.
72 Namier, *Age*, p. 399.
73 BL Add. MSS. 32945, fo. 289.
74 BL Add. MSS. 32945, fo. 278.
75 BL Add. MSS. 32945, fos 280–1.
76 *Bute Letters*, pp. 173–4.
77 Nicholas, Thesis, pp. 262–4.
78 *HMC Onslow*, p. 521. Onslow himself was by then a holder of court office and a peer. Sir Lewis Namier dramatically denoted the episode 'the massacre of the Pelhamite innocents'. Namier, *Age*, p. 403.
79 BL Add. MSS. 32945, fo. 316.
80 BL Add. MSS. 32946, fo. 11.
81 For accounts of the 'massacre' see Nicholas, Thesis, pp. 259–71, and Namier, *Age*, pp. 403–15.
82 BL Add. MSS. 32948, fos 1–2.
83 Watson, *BIHR*, 44 (1971), pp. 56–9.
84 Namier, *Age*, pp. 416–17.
85 Quoted by McCahill, 'The House of Lords in the 1760s', in Jones, ed., *Pillar of the Constitution*, p. 169.
86 Thomas, *John Wilkes*, pp. 12, 24–5.
87 Nicholas, Thesis, pp. 363–9.
88 Nicholas, Thesis, pp. 369–75.

89 Nicholas, Thesis, pp. 326–8. Thomas, *British Politics and the Stamp Act Crisis*, pp. 62–3.
90 Nicholas, Thesis, pp. 315, 322–30. Thomas, *British Politics and the Stamp Act Crisis*, pp. 41–2.
91 Whitworth, *Ligonier*, pp. 373–4.
92 BL Add. MSS. 51379, fo. 141.
93 *Bute Letters*, p. 135.
94 Bullion, 'Securing the peace … ', in Schweizer, ed., *Lord Bute*, pp. 17–18, 36.
95 PRO 30/47/21 (cabinet minute). Nicholas, Thesis, pp. 295–6.
96 Shy, *Towards Lexington*, pp. 45–83.
97 Thomas, *Politics in Eighteenth-Century Wales*, pp. 196–7.
98 *Bedford Papers*, III, 210–11.
99 *Bute Letters*, p. 191.
100 Malmesbury MSS. Harris Diary, 4 Mar. 1763. Nicholas, Thesis, pp. 300–2. Thomas, *British Politics and the Stamp Act Crisis*, pp. 38–9.
101 *Bute Letters*, p. 190.
102 Thomas, *Politics in Eighteenth-Century Wales*, pp. 195–6.
103 Bute MSS (Cardiff), no. 414.
104 Simmons and Thomas, *Proceedings and Debates*, I, 440.
105 Bute MSS (Cardiff), no. 46: printed in Simmons and Thomas, *Proceedings and Debates*, II, 562–3.
106 *Bute Letters*, pp. 201–2.
107 Thomas, *British Politics and the Stamp Act Crisis*, pp. 39–40.
108 Malmesbury MSS. Harris Diary, 18 Mar. 1763.
109 Malmesbury MSS. Harris Diary, 4 Mar. 1763.
110 Malmesbury MSS. Harris Diary, 7 Mar. 1763. Walpole, *Memoirs*, I, 198.
111 Malmesbury MSS. Harris Diary, 7–13 Mar. 1763.
112 Woodland, *PH*, 8 (1989), pp. 68–71.
113 Malmesbury MSS. Harris Diary, 28 and 30 Mar. 1763.
114 *Bute Letters*, p. 208.
115 Bute MSS (Cardiff), no. 143. Nicholas, Thesis, p. 451.
116 BL Add. MSS. 32944, fo. 30.
117 BL Add. MSS. 32948, fo. 130. For accounts of this episode see Nicholas, Thesis, pp. 345–6; and Sutherland, *East India Company*, pp. 100–9.
118 Bute MSS (Cardiff), no. 155.
119 BL Add. MSS. 32948, fos 120–2.
120 *HMC Lonsdale*, p. 132; quoted Nicholas, Thesis, p. 308.
121 Nicholas, Thesis, pp. 381–99.
122 *Bute Letters*, pp. 195–6.
123 BL Add. MSS. 51379, fos 148–52.

124 *Bute Letters*, p. 199.
125 Malmesbury MSS. Photocopies, B912.
126 Malmesbury MSS. Photocopies, B680.
127 Thomas, *British Politics and the Stamp Act Crisis*, pp. 7–9.
128 *Grenville Papers*, II, 33–40.
129 Malmesbury MSS. Photocopies, B684–5, 691.
130 Hoffman, *Edmund Burke*, p. 305. *Waldegrave Memoirs*, pp. 96–8.
131 BL Add. MSS. 32948, fo. 55.
132 *Bute Letters*, p. 216.
133 Malmesbury MSS. Photocopies B677.
134 BL Add. MSS. 32948, fos 92–8.
135 *Bute Letters*, p. 228.
136 BL Add. MSS. 32948, fos 120–2.

5

The Grenville ministry (1763–1765): Wilkes and America

It was a widespread assumption in 1763 that Bute had resigned as Prime Minister with the intention of becoming George III's secret background adviser, enjoying power without responsibility. Active politicians could not envisage any other explanation: Lord Bristol commented to Pitt that Grenville would be 'the phantom of a prime minister';[1] and Newcastle summarised opinion at Westminster for the British ambassador at The Hague. 'People generally think, that my Lord Bute will be minister behind the Curtain, though his Lordship absolutely denies it.'[2] Bute had no intention of playing any such role, as he had assured Secretaries of State Egremont and Halifax on his resignation.[3] But his sovereign would not allow him to withdraw from the political scene. George III insisted on informing and consulting him on political matters during April, at the rate of a letter a day.[4] This correspondence was curtailed when the favourite went to the York-shire spa of Harrogate for the month of May, but after Bute's return to London on 1 June the King began to use him again as his political go-between. Bute was deputed to sound opposition leaders about joining the ministry, ostensibly to fill the office of Lord President of the Council, vacant since the death of Lord Granville in January.[5] Matters came to a head after George III, contrary to 'the positive and repeated advice' of the Triumvirate, formally instructed Egremont in mid-July to offer the post to Hardwicke, with the prospect of some office also for Newcastle. Hardwicke promptly rejected the offer, declaring 'they would never come into office, but as a party and upon a plan concerted with Mr Pitt and the great Whig Lords, as had been practised in the late King's time'.[6]

The behaviour of George III had made the early months of the Grenville ministry a political stalemate, as Lord Chesterfield noted.

'The Triumvirate did nothing, because they had not the power; and Lord Bute did nothing, though he had the power, because he would not have it thought that he had'.[7] George III's approach to the opposition provoked the ministry into confrontation with the King. He was visited by Grenville on 2 August, and the two Secretaries of State the next day, with the demand that he must choose either 'to stand by and support his administration' or 'to form another by taking in the opposition'. He was given only two days to consider this ultimatum, but Grenville agreed on 'ten days or a fortnight' as 'more decent'.[8] George III, aware now that the Newcastle party would insist on a coalition with Pitt, opted for an approach to the Duke of Bedford, made by Bute through Shelburne. The Duke agreed to take the Treasury if Pitt would join his ministry: but this scheme was aborted when Pitt refused to serve with anyone concerned in the Peace of Paris.[9] George III therefore had no choice but to assure Grenville that he would retain and support his ministry. Hardly had he done so on 21 August than Lord Egremont suddenly died the same day, through apoplexy.

What happened next reflected muddle and deception by George III. Having told both Grenville and Bedford that he would not send for Pitt, he informed Grenville on 26 August that he intended to call in Pitt 'to the management of his affairs, declaring that he meant to do it as cheap as he could, and to make as few changes as was possible'. Grenville expressed astonishment at this volte-face, and refused to be party to any such arrangement. George III nevertheless saw Pitt the next day, and offered him the post of Southern Secretary in an apparently otherwise unaltered ministry. Pitt countered with a demand for a complete change of administration. Lord Temple must be at the Treasury, and Charles Townshend the Northern Secretary and Commons Leader, Newcastle was to become Lord Privy Seal, and Hardwicke Lord President of the Council. This would be another Pitt-Newcastle coalition. Pitt bluntly told the King that he intended 'to break this government, which was not founded on true Revolution principles, that it was a Tory Administration'.[10]

George III, deeming Pitt's demands unreasonable, now had to eat humble pie. Admitting to Grenville on 28 August that 'he had no right after what had passed to expect a compliance', he said he now realised 'that it was necessary the direction should be in one man's hands only, and he meant it should be in his'. When Grenville raised the question of 'secret influence', the King assured him that 'Lord Bute desired to retire absolutely from all business whatsoever, that he would absent himself from the King for a while'. The next day George III told Pitt his proposals were unacceptable, and assured Grenville of his full support.[11] To bind his sovereign into fulfilment of his promises Grenville drafted a circular letter to his leading supporters, which he read out to the King on 3 September. This stated that George III had in the recent negotiations merely sought to fill up the vacant posts of Lord President and Southern Secretary; that he had promised full support to Grenville; and that Lord Bute was retiring from politics and would absent himself from the King's presence 'until the suspicion of his influence on public business shall be entirely removed'.[12] No prior royal approval was obtained, and some copies of the letter had been sent out before Grenville obtained the King's consent. The astonished Sir John Philipps sent a copy to Bute, who was angry at this public use of a private promise.[13] He duly passed the winter at his Bedfordshire home of Luton Hoo, and on his return to London in April 1764 did not discuss political issues with either the King or Grenville, merely some matters of patronage. When in May 1765 Grenville stipulated that the King should not consult Bute on politics, George III replied in amazement that he had not done so since August 1763.[14]

Grenville had neatly trapped the King and removed Bute from influence. There remained the reconstruction of the ministry. Bute's adherent Lord Shelburne, embarrassingly involved in the August negotiations, resigned as President of the Board of Trade, and by the end of the year had been attracted to Pitt's orbit. He was replaced by Lord Hillsborough, a friend of both Grenville and Halifax. The most significant aspect of the reshuffle was the complete integration of the Bedford group within the ministry. The Duke now knew of Pitt's proscription of him, while Egremont's death and Bute's loss of influence removed his personal objections to taking office. He became Lord President of the Council, while his ally Sandwich moved from the Admiralty to become Northern Secretary, Halifax choosing to transfer to the Southern Department 'upon account of the colonies'.[15] Lord Egmont, formerly a Leicester House man, was appointed to the Admiralty.

The political crisis of August 1763 resulted in the emergence of Grenville as sole Minister, as the real Prime Minister he had expected to be in April, for the King promised not only to give up Bute but also full support against his Bedfordite colleagues. The episode also witnessed the increasing polarisation of active politicians into factions. In that sense the opposition comprised two, the band of Pitt admirers and the Newcastle group designating itself the Whigs as the heir to the dominant party of George II's reign, but now reduced to the status of a faction. Within the ministry were the Bedford group and that now forming around Grenville. Bute's followers, though often listed as such by contemporaries for some years and revived as a group by his brief return to politics in 1766, were already gradually merging into the general body of the Court Party.

Grenville's establishment in power came only a few weeks before the next Parliamentary session. Political analyses suggested that the Prime Minister would have little difficulty in the House of Commons. On 4 November Thomas Hunter produced a calculation for his Treasury Board colleagues of 349 ministerial supporters there, with 200 MPs as opposition or doubtful.[16] But Grenville knew well enough the contrast between paper majorities and political reality. They could melt away in the face of sustained attacks by opposition spokesmen, and it was the widespread contemporary opinion that the opposition had the best Commons speakers, notably William Pitt, Charles Townshend, and Henry Legge. Henry Fox had gone to the House of Lords, and Grenville himself was not thought to be up to the task of Commons Leader, after his poor showing in the session of 1761–62. Lord Chesterfield observed on 30 September that 'there is not a man of the Court side, in the House of Commons, who has either abilities or words enough to call a coach'.[17] How well Grenville rose to the occasion is implicit in the comment of another man with a low opinion of him, Lord Holland, the former Henry Fox, who wrote in December 1765, when Grenville was in opposition. 'Mr Grenville, who never was thought to speak well, till he was Chancellor of the Exchequer, is now again the most wretched speaker in the House'.[18]

What gave point to this concern about Parliament was the expectation of a major controversy there. For in the opinion of both George III and the Grenville cabinet John Wilkes had at last exposed himself to prosecution for his weekly *North Briton*, when in the forty-fifth issue on 23 April he had attacked the King's Speech at the end of the previous Parliamentary session in terms that the Crown's law officers, Attorney-General Charles Yorke and Solicitor-General Sir Fletcher Norton, deemed 'a scandalous and seditious libel', adding that 'all libels, being breaches of the peace' were outside the Parliamentary privilege of immunity from arrest.[19] Official action was prompted by George III himself, and on 26 April Secretary of State Halifax issued a general warrant, not naming those to be arrested, for the apprehension of 'the authors, printers and publishers' of the anonymous paper. Verbal and written evidence was soon obtained that Wilkes was the author, and he was arrested under the same warrant, on 30 April. Secretaries of State Egremont and Halifax favoured the issue of a new warrant naming Wilkes, but their law clerk Lovell Stanhope and the Treasury solicitor Philip Webb deemed that step to be unnecessary.[20] The whole storm over general warrants arose from their advice. Six days later Wilkes was released on the ground of Parliamentary privilege, a controversial decision by Chief Justice Pratt, amid shouts of 'Wilkes and Liberty' by a mob ignorant of legal niceties. That aspect of the case was irrelevant to the key issue of general warrants, a device often used to arrest spies and other anonymous enemies of the state. But even before 1763 doubts had been raised as to its legality, and the arrest of some fifty persons in the *North Briton* case aroused widespread alarm about the potential threat to individual liberty. Wilkes denounced it as 'a ridiculous warrant against the whole English nation'. Although condemnation of what Wilkes had written was almost universal, the Parliamentary opposition would undoubtedly seek to harass the administration over general warrants.

During the summer recess of Parliament a whole series of lawsuits arose from the episode, Lord Temple playing a crucial role by financing Wilkes. His prosecution for libel was countered by actions for trespass, damage and unlawful arrest, forty-six writs being issued on 26 May alone. Many of these cases came to court, fourteen printers being awarded damages in July. There was also a lively press campaign on both sides. Caught up in the general excitement, Wilkes made the fateful decisions of reprinting *North Briton Number Forty-Five* and privately printing a few copies of an obscene poem *Essay on Woman* that he had written in 1754. Both would expose him to legal retribution.[21]

Before Parliament met the ministry lost its Attorney-General. Charles Yorke, son of Lord Hardwicke, resigned on 2 November, finding himself on the wrong side of the political fence when a clear alignment between administration and opposition developed after the August negotiations. Yorke's behaviour highlighted the adjustments of individual politicians to the new situation. In February 1764 James Harris of the Treasury Board calculated that there had been fifty-six desertions from the ministry in the House of Commons. They included ten in the Yorke family grouping; six in that headed by Lord George Sackville; and four followers of Shelburne, who had joined Pitt.[22]

The ministry duly formulated its Parliamentary resolutions, that the offending issue of the *North Briton* was a seditious libel and that Parliamentary privilege did not cover this crime, thereby exposing Wilkes to legal retribution. He would then be expelled from the Commons, not as a punishment but as an unworthy member. Grenville made it clear to his colleagues and supporters that the successful enactment of this strategy would be deemed a vote of confidence in his ministry, but that was not much of a hostage to fortune, in view of what most MPs thought of Wilkes and his libel. To reinforce that hostile opinion, the ministry attempted a character assassination of Wilkes when Parliament met on 15 November. For Lord Sandwich then read out parts of the *Essay on Woman* to the House of Lords, on a specious pretext that the obscene and impious poem was a breach of privilege.[23]

In the House of Commons that day the ministerial motion, put by Lord North of the Treasury Board, that the forty-fifth issue of the *North Briton* was 'a false, scandalous and seditious libel' was carried by 273 votes to 111 after long debates totalling 82 speeches, 15 of them by Pitt. Many thought he demeaned himself by his vigorous defence of Wilkes. During the debate Buteite MP Samuel Martin denounced the anonymous author as 'a cowardly rascal', and next day Wilkes fought a pistol duel with him, being so badly wounded that he would be unable to attend Parliament again that year. Proceedings against him nevertheless continued. On 24 November North moved the resolution that Parliamentary privilege did not cover seditious libel. He argued that although only treason, felony and breach of the peace were specifically named as exceptions to the immunity from arrest enjoyed by MPs, the distinction was between criminal offences and civil ones. Pitt, though denouncing his former supporter Wilkes as 'an impious criminal', spoke for two hours against the motion, which was carried by 258 votes to 133. Next day the House of Lords endorsed the Commons resolutions by 114 votes to 35: six of the King's detested Dukes were in the minority, Bolton, Cumberland, Devonshire, Grafton, Newcastle, and Portland.[24]

Intense popular interest was generated by the whole sequence of events, and a series of riots in London resulted, notably after a first legal condemnation of general warrants by Judge Pratt on 6 December, for their use to search unspecified houses. The press celebrated that 'every Englishman' could now claim that 'his house is his castle'.[25] During the court proceedings Solicitor-General Norton failed to prove the authorship of the *North Briton* by Wilkes, and henceforth the legal charge against him was merely that of republishing the libel. Wilkes now fled any trials, evading surveillance to escape in late December to France, where he was to spend four years in exile.[26]

Parliamentary and legal proceedings against Wilkes continued in his absence, but Norton, now Attorney-General, advised the ministry to avoid any direct Parliamentary vote on the popular topic of general warrants. On 19 January 1764 North put two motions to the

Commons, that Wilkes was guilty of writing and publishing the relevant *North Briton*, and that he be expelled. Only one MP voiced dissent, for the Parliamentary opposition shunned Wilkes, William Pitt and Newcastle's chief Commons spokesman Henry Legge being deliberately absent. But the ministry could not expect such an easy time over general warrants, where the sacred cause of 'liberty' was under threat. What followed was one of the great Parliamentary battles of the century. A series of long debates, punctuated by the examination of witnesses, culminated on 17 February in a motion by opposition MP Sir William Meredith condemning as illegal the use of general warrants in cases of seditious libel. Norton moved to postpone the resolution for four months, ostensibly lest it prejudice pending legal cases, but tactically to avoid losing support in a direct vote. The longest Commons debate in memory ended at 7.30 the next morning, with a ministerial majority of just 14: 232 to 218. Sir Lewis Namier long ago pointed out that the administration was saved only by a solid Scottish vote, based on personal hated of Wilkes.[27] But even defeat would not have toppled the Grenville ministry. The Prime Minister had completed the series of measures against Wilkes on which he had staked his reputation, and the King had already assured him that he would pay no heed to any defeat over general warrants. Both men knew that few of the deserters over such a popular question, whether placemen or independents, intended to bring down the ministry, and had already agreed not to dismiss any office-holders. The jubilation of the opposition at the prospect of a change of ministry was baseless delusion.[28] After the debate Treasury Secretary Charles Jenkinson listed 49 MPs in the minority 'who are friends or nearly so'.[29] That that desertion by many independent members was only over general warrants was soon demonstrated by a deliberate gesture. On 21 February numerous squires concerted their attendance at the Prime Minister's levee as evidence of their continuing support.[30]

The Parliamentary excitement had barely subsided before the trial of Wilkes for libel took place, on 21 February. As Wilkes never later failed to point out, the charges merely concerned publication, not authorship. It was his May 1763 reprinting of the *North Briton* that formed the basis for the charge of 'seditious and scandalous libel', and his private printing of the *Essay on Woman* for one of 'obscene and impious libel'. The facts of publication were not in doubt, and Wilkes was found guilty on both counts. When he failed to return from France to receive sentence, he was outlawed in November. Some compensation for his exile came with news of further condemnation of

general warrants in 1764 and 1765, this time by Chief Justice Lord
Mansfield. By ending their use for the arrest of persons, these rulings
complemented the Pratt judgment on trespass.[31]

Simultaneously with that first Wilkes case the Grenville ministry
faced a more direct legacy of the Bute ministry, West Country hostil-
ity to the cider tax. During the 1763 summer recess of Parliament
Cornwall, Devonshire, Gloucestershire, Herefordshire, Somerset and
Worcestershire sent in county petitions calling for repeal of the tax.
So did 17 boroughs within these counties, Leominster submitting
two, together with the Bristol Society of Merchant Venturers and the
City of London, as usual eager to stir up trouble for government.
Devonshire, 9 of whose 13 constituencies submitted petitions, formed
the heart of the campaign, for it was masterminded by bookseller Benjamin Heath, town clerk of Exeter. That borough paid for a widely
circulated pamphlet in which Heath urged these six counties, which
returned altogether 113 MPs to Westminster, to follow the example
of Scotland, whose MPs supported national interests even in preference to their notorious compliance with ministerial demands. Heath
urged the cider MPs to lobby the Prime Minister at the opening of the
next Parliamentary session and make their support conditional on
repeal. This phenomenon of local political movements that owed little to the initiative of MPs was a new mid-century development, and
one revived in the West Country at the end of the decade, when the
area submitted a disproportionately large number of petitions on a
second Wilkes case.[32]

The cider tax agitation was a political complication that Grenville
could have done without, faced as he was with a major crisis over the
North Briton case. With characteristic preparation he thought out
what tactic to adopt, as he told Treasury Lord James Harris on 29
October. Repeal was not an option, and he would oppose it in Parliament. Nor would he regard defeat as a vote of no confidence, since
the tax was not his measure. But he was willing to accept alterations
in the method of collecting the tax.[33] After the customary pre-session
meeting of ministerial MPs on 14 November, when Harris noted that
among the 250 MPs present were 'most of the Tories, those even of
the cider counties', Grenville met fifteen 'principal gentlemen' from
the West Country.[34] On 18 November Grenville had further discussions with the three leaders of the movement, Worcestershire MP
William Dowdeswell, Devonshire MP Sir Richard Bampfylde, and
Herefordshire MP Velters Cornewall.[35] At a gathering of cider MPs
on 21 November the majority were inclined to accept Grenville's

compromise, and this became clear when Dowdeswell opened the Parliamentary campaign on 24 January 1764 by moving for a Committee on the Cider Act.

Grenville, to prevent any discussion there of repeal, moved an amendment that the Committee should discuss only alteration. He pointed out that the tax revenue was already pledged to cover interest on the National Debt, and that repeal would make necessary another tax instead. Moreover, such a precedent would lead to demands for repeal of the beer and similar taxes. Grenville announced the firm stance he had long devised, stating that he would offer no concession if repeal was put on the agenda, and this tactic worked, even though some Newcastle men, Lord George Cavendish and Thomas Townshend among them, sought to exploit the situation and drive a wedge between the cider members and the ministry by advocating complete repeal. Disgusted Pittite MP James Grenville reported to Lady Chatham how, with the honourable exception of Dowdeswell, the cider members expressed 'a zeal for the support of the present ministers, even to adulation … In short, the Tory party showed itself in its true colour of devoted attachment to the court'.[36] Even so, Grenville only carried his amendment by 167 votes to 125.[37]

When the Cider Committee met on 31 January Dowdeswell, prevented from proposing repeal, moved to transfer the tax from the makers to the retailers. That would remove most of the tax burden from the cider counties, and Grenville opposed it for that reason. He intended to retain a tax that had yielded £30,000 in the first year. Dowdeswell's motion failed by only twenty votes, 172 to 152.[38] On 7 February the Cider Committee agreed, without voting, on a compromise whereby individuals could compound for the tax at two shillings each, children under eight being exempt. But on 10 February Sir Richard Bampfylde, under constituency pressure and contrary to his own opinion as professed on 24 January, moved to repeal the cider tax altogether. Dowdeswell was among those who spoke in support, but the motion was defeated by 204 votes to 115, with many squires from outside the cider counties swelling the majority. The stand by Grenville did not cost him support over general warrants, diarist Harris noting that 'most of the cider members' were in a majority of 217 to 122 on 6 February.[39]

The political temperature fell after the excitement over the cider tax and general warrants, and Grenville had an easy time in the House of Commons for the American measures he now introduced. The opposition was disheartened after the failure to defeat him on general

warrants, and for a variety of reasons their leading spokesmen were
absent: illness kept William Pitt and Henry Legge away, parental
deaths and other factors Charles Yorke and Charles Townshend.
Grenville and his colleagues had meanwhile not allowed the Wilkes
furore to distract them from devising colonial measures, and even
before Parliament met the ministry had enacted a land settlement for
North America. Egremont and Grenville, in their first territorial plan,
had proposed to include in a new colony of Quebec the area south of
the Great Lakes, between the Ohio and Mississippi rivers, known then
as 'the old North-West'. That was agreed by the cabinet on 8 July. But
the Board of Trade, after news of an Indian rising under Chief Pontiac,
deemed it wiser to leave it as an Indian reservation. After Egremont's
death Grenville found himself alone in objecting to this policy and
gave way, though uneasy about the lack of any form of government for
that wilderness.[40] Halifax and Hillsborough, now Southern Secretary
and President of the Board of Trade respectively, drafted the Proclamation of 7 October 1763, creating three new colonies of Quebec,
East Florida, and West Florida, which was a coastal strip to the Mississippi. Settlement was otherwise prohibited between the Mississippi
and the Atlantic mountain watershed, where local officials were to
map out the so-called Proclamation Line to that end. The royal prerogative was deemed sufficient authority for that measure, but others
were being devised to come before Parliament early in 1764.[41]

For decades British politicians and colonial officials had been concerned about evasion of the customs laws in North America, especially
the breach of the 1733 Molasses Act imposing what was intended as a
prohibitory import duty of 6*d* a gallon on foreign molasses, used to
make rum. By 1763 it was obvious that the British West Indies could
not supply British North America, and the conversion of this duty to a
revenue one of 3*d* was deemed likely to satisfy both colonial rum distillers and also the British Treasury, as the first step in providing finance
for the American army: such a scheme had been killed by Grenville
when prematurely proposed by Charles Townshend in March 1763,
but he now adopted the idea. It was preferred to another potential
source of revenue contemplated by the Treasury Board, 'a sort of
capitation tax' as Treasury Lord James Harris described it.[42] A poll tax
would have been even more unpopular in America than the revenue
duties actually imposed!

Many other provisions to curb smuggling and alter duties were
included in a comprehensive American Duties Bill for 1764. When
Grenville opened his budget on 9 March he also announced his

intention to raise additional colonial revenue by stamp duties, to be levied on legal documents, newspapers and other items, as they had been in Britain since the seventeenth century. This Stamp Bill had been under preparation since September 1763. In his speech Grenville threw out a challenge, which was not taken up, that he would force a vote over Parliament's right to tax America if any MP doubted it. The budget debate focused on this new idea of colonial taxation. Sir William Baker, deputed to speak for the Newcastle group, approved the idea of stamp duties, but when it was attacked as unfair Grenville at once accepted a suggestion that the colonies should first be informed, and the measure was postponed for a year. He later met the colonial agents, on 17 May, and explained that he was open to suggestions for alternative Parliamentary taxation, but that was the extent of his concession.[43] In 1770 Grenville, when talking of the Stamp Act, recalled that 'the King was particularly desirous to have it, and frequently called on him (Mr. G.) to bring it on. That he had told his M. it should be done, and wished it might be done, as it was, deliberately'.[44] It is unclear whether this royal pressure was exerted when Grenville postponed the measure in 1764 or at its introduction in 1765; but the story adds a new, royal, dimension to the usual version of the taxation of America.

When the American Duties Bill came before Parliament there was no challenge to the molasses revenue duty on principle, but in Committee on 22 March an amendment was put to lower it to 2*d* a gallon, the rate sought by the colonial agents. Grenville estimated the revenue from a 3*d* duty at £50,000, and it was confirmed on a division by 147 votes to 55, the minority being composed of the Newcastle group and some American merchants. Charles Yorke absented himself, and Charles Townshend did not speak, being dismayed by the lack of cooperation from the absent Pitt, who, so he told Newcastle, 'is against *all* taxation'.[45] Townshend held the opposite view, and intended to attack Grenville for producing only a derisory American revenue. Both Newcastle and Rockingham supported this idea, so contrary to their own later policy, but Townshend let them down. The Parliamentary debates of 1764 reflected an assumption of the right to tax America, and a unanimity of opinion that the colonies ought to contribute to the cost of the American army.[46]

Grenville had postponed the America Stamp Act for a year, but another colonial measure his ministry had also intended to defer was suddenly enacted at the end of the session. The problem of depreciated colonial paper money being used to repay to British merchants debts borrowed in sterling had been considered by the Bute ministry early in 1763, when Virginia, the chief offender, was told to mend its ways. When that colony did nothing, Hillsborough's Board of Trade took the matter into consideration during the winter of 1763–64, and its report on 9 February 1764 denounced the colonial practice of issuing legal-tender paper money as 'founded on fraud and injustice'. The ministry, however, thought it too late in the session to act, but on 4 April MP Anthony Bacon, an American merchant who had suffered from the practice, proposed a Bill to prohibit colonial currency altogether. The Board of Trade, aware of the shock to the colonial economy, thereupon hastily negotiated with colonial agents a compromise whereby only the issue of new legal-tender currency would be prevented, permitting existing notes, which were dated, to continue until their expiry. This concession took the immediate sting out of the measure, and the American Currency Act passed rapidly without opposition.[47]

Grenville had to concern himself with India as well as America, from motives of political advantage and national interest. In the East India Company Sulivan, after his victory at the Company election of 13 April 1763, exacted immediate revenge on Clive by a Directory decision on 27 April to stop payment of his *jagir*. The indignant Clive preferred political to legal action, but his former Newcastle allies were in impotent opposition, and Pitt warned Clive that he would have no chance in Parliament. By the autumn Clive therefore cast aside his old political connections by negotiating with the new ministry of George Grenville, offering the support of his Parliamentary group in return for help over his *jagir*.[48] Early in December Horace Walpole reported the deal as made. 'The ministry have bought off Lord Clive with a bribe that would frighten the King of France himself: they have given him back his £25,000 a year.'[49] But Grenville could not deliver his side of the bargain, for Sulivan saw no need to conciliate Clive. News from India, that the Nawab of Bengal was at war with the Company, then fortuitously put Sulivan at Clive's mercy. A special General Court on 12 March 1764 greeted with acclamation the nomination of Clive as Governor and Commander-in-Chief for Bengal, but he refused to accept without confirmation of his *jagir* and the election of a supportive Court of Directors. It was now that Clive's compact with Grenville paid dividends. He enjoyed ministerial assistance in the Company election, with Treasury Secretary Charles Jenkinson pressuring voters instead of stock-splitting.[50] Lord Holland, the former Henry Fox, and Lord Sandwich were both as active against Sulivan as they had been for him the previous year. The new Court of Directors, elected on 12 April, had a narrow majority for Clive, and a General Court confirmed his *jagir* for ten years, by 583 votes to 396.[51] Clive then sailed for India in June, and for the next two years Company matters passed from the forefront of the political stage. The Clive party was assisted by the Grenville ministry to another victory over Sulivan at the 1765 election of Directors, and then kept a low profile during the Rockingham ministry, when no Indian issues came to political notice.

Contrary to many expectations Grenville had been in every respect a success as Prime Minister. Charles Townshend acknowledged his triumph in this candid appraisal to Newcastle at the end of the 1763–64 session. 'As things now stand, the ministry are strong. The minority not in strength or reputation. Lord Bute forced to keep a neutrality at least, and the public grow familiarised to an administration they see so little opposed.'[52] The Parliamentary opposition, already at a low ebb, was to suffer further blows. William Pitt, who had rarely attended the Commons after the general warrants case, was not to appear there at all in 1765. Deaths and desertions weakened the Newcastle group. His chief prop and confidant Hardwicke had died on 6 March, and on 2 October the more unexpected demise through epilepsy of the Duke of Devonshire at the age of forty-four deprived the party of a respected figure and Newcastle's probable successor as leader.[53] The death of Henry Legge on 23 August cost the Duke his financial expert, and the group's leadership in the House of Commons was to be further weakened by the gradual desertions of Charles Yorke and Charles Townshend. Both were negotiating with Grenville, and both gave debating support to his ministry in the next session.

Yet all was not doom and gloom for the opposition. This evident loss of experience and ability was partly offset by the zeal of Newcastle's younger supporters. The opposition club that they had sought to create at the end of 1762 came into existence by January 1764. Its membership included the Newcastle peers and their Commons followers, together with Lord Temple, but not Pitt. It was organised by a Thomas Wildman in Albemarle Street, and according to John Almon, who became its official stationer and bookseller, was called 'the Coterie', a designation used also by diarist James Harris in his debate report of 22 March.[54] Newcastle listed 106 members on 9 February.[55] Even during the political doldrums of the 1764 summer recess the club met every week. Newcastle was never enthusiastic about this new development, jealously commenting to Portland on 1 July that 'the boys of Wildmans shall not be the Whig party'.[56] But the gap between the 'zealous young men' and the aristocratic grandees was bridged by the thirty-four-year-old Marquess of Rockingham, who, unlike the Duke, regularly dined at Wildman's. This situation paved the way for his accession to the party leadership early in 1765, when Newcastle tacitly and reluctantly began to step down: and Wildman's Club seems to have ended when he became Prime Minister.[57]

This opposition could still hope to find political mileage in such controversies of the previous session as the cider tax and general warrants. In the autumn of 1764 the cider members sought an alliance with the Newcastle party, which considered the prospect of exploiting the West Country discontent, but rejected the idea for several reasons. Pitt, piqued that the first approach had not been made to him, declined all cooperation. 'I have no disposition to quit the free condition of a man standing *single*', he informed Newcastle in October.[58] Newcastle, too, feared that 'a coalition with the Tories' would give offence to many of his friends, and in any case he rightly deemed the prospect of success uncertain: the cider issue was never to be debated in 1765.[59]

The opposition, by contrast, wasted no time in mounting a challenge on general warrants. On 29 January 1765 Sir William Meredith again moved, as on 17 February 1764, that they were illegal in libel cases. This time the ministerial counter-tactic, immediately deployed by lawyer George Hay, was a destructive amendment to render the motion unacceptable: this was a procedural device hitherto rarely used, and denounced as unfair by the opposition. Hay agreed that general warrants were illegal under common law, but with the caveat that state necessity might justify their use. Pointing out that the matter was pending in the law courts, he put an amendment to that effect, contending that courts decided the law, not Parliamentary resolutions. This tactic was denounced by Henry Conway, an army general now turning politician, who in 1764 had been dismissed from two posts, Groom of the Bedchamber and a colonelcy of dragoons, for speaking and voting against general warrants. His political career was thereby boosted by martyr status, and his personal connections with Cumberland and Grafton took him into the Newcastle party. Two prominent MPs unconnected with the Duke who also criticised the amendment were William Dowdeswell and Lord George Sackville. In a tortuous speech Charles Townshend spoke for administration while at the same time denouncing general warrants as an 'odious, skulking' device of officials. Charles Yorke, for the only time that session, spoke in opposition, again condemning general warrants as illegal. Attorney-General

Norton pointed out that Yorke had argued otherwise in court. This premeditated attack found its mark, for Yorke's weak reply was to distinguish between his legal and political roles, presumably what was and what ought to be the law. A second political martyr who spoke was Colonel Isaac Barré, whose political allegiance Shelburne had now transferred from Bute to Pitt. He complained that of eighteen army officers in the House who had opposed general warrants he alone had been dismissed. That was misleading. His removal from military posts worth £1,500 a year had occurred by December 1763, for opposing ministerial policy on Wilkes before general warrants became the issue. Later Barré poked fun at Grenville. He was glad to see him surrounded by friends, for he remembered when he could have taken them home 'in his chariot'. The House sat until five o'clock the next morning, when the ministerial amendment was carried by 224 votes to 185.[60]

That debate was to contemporaries the highlight of the Parliamentary session, with several new men, Barré, Conway and Dowdeswell, to the fore: but the size of the ministerial majority, compared with that in 1764, was a dousing shock to opposition ardour, and the subsequent American legislation, for which Grenville is so remembered, attracted little controversy. The ministry, however, came to regard the Stamp Act as of great significance, because of the American response to Grenville's announcement. Far from taking up his offer to suggest alternative modes of Parliamentary taxation, the colonies protested against that whole concept.[61] The Grenville ministry perceived the challenge to Parliamentary sovereignty. After a Treasury Board meeting in December 1764 James Harris made this note: 'colonies would reject all taxes of ours, both *internal* and *external* – would be represented'.[62] By early 1765 the assertion of Parliamentary sovereignty over America had become for the ministry more important than the prospective revenue. That, in the final draft of the Stamp Bill, would be derived from stamp duties on newspapers, most legal documents, cargo lists for ships, and numerous other less recurrent items like liquor licenses, calendars, cards and dice. The chief burden would fall on printers, lawyers, merchants, and publicans. It was expected to yield £100,000, and, even with £50,000 from the molasses duty, American taxes would bring in less than half the £350,000 now estimated as the cost of the American army.[63]

Parliamentary discussion of the subject began on 6 February, when Grenville introduced the appropriate resolutions after a carefully constructed speech. The colonial claim to be taxed only by their own representative bodies would apply equally to all other legislation, he said. The colonies were subject to the mother country, and none had been given exemption, by charter or otherwise, from Parliamentary taxation. All taxes were unpopular, like the one on cider, and fairness demanded that everybody should contribute, including the colonists, who were defended by Britain's army and navy. The stamp duties would be efficient and equitably spread, and the colonists had not responded to the invitation to make alternative suggestions. The main criticism came from two Pittites, William Beckford and Isaac Barré, but neither of them or any other speaker challenged Parliament's right of taxation, a point later rubbed in by Charles Townshend, who said that the colonists were well able to pay. Although twelve of the eighteen speakers opposed the taxation, on grounds of inexpediency and impolicy, a blocking motion by Beckford was defeated by 245 votes to 49.[64] 'Many of our people with them', explained George Onslow to Newcastle.[65]

Discussion of the Stamp Bill resumed on 15 February, over the rejection of several colonial petitions, on the procedural ground that Parliament did not accept protests against future taxation. A notable speech came from Charles Yorke, who defended Parliamentary taxation of America by the argument that the two alternatives would be undesirable or unfair: either a federal Congress of the colonies, or an arbitrary quota system. Subsequent Commons discussions concerned only details, and there was no Lords debate on the measure. No MP or peer had challenged Parliament's right to tax the colonies.[66]

Meanwhile there had arrived from America on 1 March a report from the army commander-in-chief, now General Thomas Gage, complaining about colonial obstruction over billeting soldiers. Secretary at War Welbore Ellis promptly drafted a Bill, approved by Southern Secretary Halifax, authorising where necessary the quartering of soldiers on private houses. It was the alert King who expressed concern about the Parliamentary reception of such a proposal, and at his behest Grenville altered it to a vague phrase stipulating previous practice if not enough barracks or taverns were available.[67] MPs like William Beckford were not fooled when Ellis presented the American Mutiny Bill to the Commons on 1 April, and there was much talk of liberty and Magna Carta. Afraid of an unexpected Parliamentary storm, with Pitt being roused to support the Newcastle party, the ministry postponed the Bill until 19 April, to provide the opportunity of changing the alternative choice to one of uninhabited buildings. That met all Parliamentary objections, but a consequent additional stipulation that the colonists should provide at their own expense non-food items such as fuel and bedding was to become a grievance in America.[68]

The concept of 'a Grenville programme' for America has little validity. Many of the measures exacted by his ministry arose from decisions taken by the Bute ministry, such as those for colonial taxation and the general nature of the land settlement; while the American Mutiny Act was a belated postscript. But Grenville was a Prime Minister who got things done, a capable and conscientious man, one especially concerned about financial viability and legal authority, who was shocked by the colonial situation. Therein lies the truth of a retrospective comment by an unidentified official. 'Mr Grenville lost America because he read the American dispatches, which his predecessors had never done.'[69]

The same motivation of tighter imperial control led the Grenville ministry into an important policy decision concerning Ireland. The matter had not been given priority. The ministry, with many other problems calling for attention, sent its new Lord-Lieutenant Northumberland to Ireland with instructions to cooperate with the Undertakers, 'to temporize with the evil', as Halifax phrased it on 26 November 1763.[70] Even so the Parliamentary session of 1763–64 proved a stormy one for Dublin Castle. There was much indignant debate about the granting of Irish posts and pensions to British politicians, even though Northumberland was authorised to announce a government decision not to award any more such pensions.[71] So delicate was the situation that Northumberland advised that it would be unwise to seek approval of the Peace of Paris, pointing out the sensitive position of Speaker Ponsonby, who was closely connected with the Cavendish family, opponents of the peace terms at Westminster. Ministerial pressure caused the Lord-Lieutenant to alter his stance.[72] The Viceroy was also confronted with Irish repercussions of the *North Briton* case. Support for John Wilkes was voiced in a Dublin newspaper *The Freeman's Journal*, launched on 10 September 1763 by Charles Lucas, a radical MP elected for Dublin City in 1761 and sometimes dubbed 'the Irish Wilkes'. Northumberland contrived to secure on 20 December 1763 the passage, by 130 votes to 42, of an Address that both commended the Peace and condemned Wilkes. That was a notable triumph for the Viceroy, who had retained the support of the Ponsonby faction, but the price of this success was surrender to the Undertakers.

When Northumberland returned to England, Stone, Shannon and Ponsonby were left as Lords Justices: and in July 1764 they forced the resignation of Chief Secretary Hamilton, whose attempt to create an embryonic 'Castle Party' was a potential threat to their power. He was replaced by Lord Drogheda, an ally of Stone and, contrary to recent practice, both an Irishman and a peer: Dublin Castle would not have an official spokesman in the Commons.[73] The Grenville ministry was then fortuitously presented with an opportunity to redress this situation, when Stone died on 19 December and Shannon the next day. The power vacuum was more apparent than real. The new Lord Shannon was the son-in-law of John Ponsonby, and inherited his father's electoral and Parliamentary influence. His close alliance with the Speaker continued a powerful Undertaker interest, but the demise of Archbishop Stone was an opportunity too good to miss. George III later recalled that 'on the death of the Primate of Ireland it was deemed expedient to re-examine the state of Ireland'.[74] The cabinet that met on 1 February 1765 to consider Ireland included Northumberland and his two immediate predecessors, Bedford and Halifax. After Northumberland expressed doubts as to whether his health would permit him to return to Ireland, the cabinet came to this resolution. 'That whenever a new Lord Lieutenant should be appointed by His Majesty he should be directed to reside constantly.'[75]

Such a tightening of control over Ireland would chime in with Grenville's American policy, and form a stronger pattern of imperial government. Contemporaries noted the parallel, for early in 1765 there were rumours in Ireland that the British Parliament intended to tax that country as well as America.[76] Subsequent events were to demonstrate that the logical implication of the decision, the creation of a Castle Party in the Dublin Parliament, had not been fully grasped; but, in any case, the Grenville ministry did not have the opportunity to implement its Irish policy. Their intention to replace Northumberland, with his Bute connection, by the Bedfordite Weymouth met with stiff resistance from the King, who deemed the choice unsuitable on grounds of character and competence. Weymouth was not appointed until 5 June, and the dismissal of the Grenville ministry the next month meant that he never went to Ireland.

During the Grenville ministry, as later, political and imperial matters took precedence over foreign policy.[77] That was initially left to Sandwich, Northern Secretary from September 1763. Southern Secretary Halifax was more concerned with his responsibility for the colonies, while the priority for Grenville was the ramifications of the *North Briton* case. Although there seemed after the Peace of Paris to be a prospect of European tranquility for the first time in several decades, Sandwich acted on the assumption of French hostility universal among British politicians, and continued the quest for a Russian alliance that would last, intermittently, for a decade. He soon found that Russia was not content to renew the 1742 and 1755 treaties by which she had simply agreed to hire soldiers to Britain. Catherine II now insisted on equality, specifying particularly what came to be known as 'the Turkish clause', British assistance if the Ottoman Empire attacked Russia. That stipulation was made in a draft alliance proposal presented to British ambassador Lord Buckinghamshire in August 1763; and a secret clause also requested British financial support in the anticipated forthcoming election of a Polish King. These terms were unanimously rejected by the Grenville cabinet on 16 September.[78] The idea that Britain should have to pay a peacetime subsidy to obtain an ally was deemed insulting, while the financially prudent Grenville jibbed at the expense. Fear of a threat to Britain's trade in the Mediterranean from Turkish hostility was a further consideration.

The death of King Augustus III of Poland on 5 October then caused Russia to offer more favourable terms. Russian minister Nikita Panin dropped the Turkish stipulation, and asked only for a £100,000 subsidy for use in Poland. This was a window of opportunity for a cheap Russian alliance, but the British government still balked at a peacetime subsidy, and the chance was lost. Frederick II of Prussia signed a treaty with Russia in April 1764, and his assistance enabled Catherine II to secure the election of her candidate Stanislaus Poniatowski in September 1764. Panin, aware of the benefits of British financial and naval strength, always favoured a 'Northern System' in which Britain would be an ally as well as Prussia, but Frederick II's enmity and the Turkish clause were henceforth invariably to be obstacles. In 1764 the inept Lord Buckinghamshire was replaced by the able and energetic Sir George Macartney, just when Britain and Russia were finding common ground against France in Sweden. That country had been the scene of party strife since a 1720 constitution restricted royal power. Britain and Russia supported the Caps party against the hitherto dominant Hats, backed by Choiseul. A key figure in Stockholm was the British envoy Sir John Goodricke, as both Britain and Russia spent money in the 1765 elections to the Swedish Diet that led to a Caps victory.

Such a success, in which Russia allowed Britain to take the leading role, cannot disguise a British inability to read the European scene correctly. The most serious misunderstanding was the outmoded belief that, as Sandwich commented to Grenville on 6 June 1764,

Britain and France were still 'the two great Powers of Europe'.[79] This lack of perception was underlined by an abortive approach to Austria, as Sandwich's strong desire to revive 'the old System' clouded his judgement. Even Austrian Chancellor Kaunitz's categorical statement in January 1764 to the British ambassador that Austria would adhere to her French alliance was not seen as a final rebuff, merely as a postponement of hopes cherished by many in Britain.

Unrealistic as the main thrust of British foreign policy may have been, under Grenville it was nevertheless a success. Quite apart from the 1765 coup in Sweden, which was to prove short-lived in the face of French countermeasures, the Premier himself, continuing his hard-line attitude already evident during the Bute ministry, resorted to what in the next century came to be known as 'gunboat diplomacy'. Still resentful about the leniency of the Peace of Paris, Grenville took a firmer line than his colleagues, the pacifist and Francophile Bedford, the lethargic Halifax, and a Sandwich mistakenly anxious about the navy, when in 1764 and 1765 confrontations occurred with the Bourbon Powers. The status of the British settlements in Honduras to cut logwood, which yielded a dye for wool, had been confirmed in 1763, but the Spanish harassment of them in 1764 was not unjustified, for they were both illegally cutting mahogany for furniture and engaging in contraband trade. News of this situation was overshadowed when a local French governor expelled British subjects from Turk's Island, south of the Bahamas, on 1 June 1764. At Grenville's instigation Britain put together a naval task force, including four ships of the line, designed to overcome any local opposition and to deter any prospect of a major conflict. Spain and France promptly conceded the points in dispute, respectively promising not to molest the Honduras settlements and disavowing the Turk's Island action, with the French government professing ignorance of its location! Likewise, early in 1765 the threat of a naval attack on a new French settlement on the Gambia River in West Africa, an area not mentioned in the peace settlement but assumed in London to be a British preserve, caused its immediate evacuation. This naval coercion by Britain of her Bourbon foes set the tone for the decade, since Choiseul was all too aware of Britain's superiority at sea.[80]

By the Easter of 1765 the Grenville administration appeared to be a success in every respect. Ministers could congratulate themselves on a quiet and productive Parliamentary session, and Grenville seemed to be settling in for a long spell as Premier. 'Mr Grenville establishes himself upon very solid foundations every day, and gains credit both by his

Parliamentary abilities, and by the improvements he is gradually making in the revenue', courtier Hans Stanley wrote on 24 February.[81] A 1763 prophecy that Grenville would be Prime Minister as long as Sir Robert Walpole did not now seem foolish.[82] He was dominant in the cabinet as well as the House of Commons. His colleagues, after some early disputes over patronage and policy, had soon displayed an unexpected harmony, with Grenville their acknowledged head.[83] But the third centre of power, the Crown, had not been secured, despite George III's initial assurances to Grenville. Both men later dated the deterioration of their relationship to the autumn of 1764, although earlier the King had already looked askance at the growing cabinet solidarity, for two reasons: it weakened his own bond with Grenville; and he held a low opinion of most of his ministers. Halifax he thought lazy and incompetent, while the Bedfords were self-seeking, apart from the Duke himself, who was merely idle.[84] The heart of the matter was George III's growing personal dislike of the boringly verbose Grenville. 'When he has wearied me for two hours', the King complained to Bute, 'he looks at his watch to see if he may not tire me for an hour more.'[85] Patronage was the issue, not policy. George III, in political memoranda he compiled at the end of 1765, made frequent references to the 'insolence' of Grenville in his demands. 'No office fell vacant in any department that Mr G. did not declare he would not serve if the man he recommended did not succeed.'[86]

It was the Bute phenomenon again. During the winter of 1763 to 1764 Bute had absented himself from London, and as late as June 1764 Grenville confided to James Harris that 'he was perfectly well with Lord Bute', at whose request he had accepted the Admiralty and the Treasury, whereas he could never ally with 'the Newcastle Party', because they wanted 'a sole possession of all power'.[87] But thereafter Bute's personal contact with the King led to Grenville's belief that his patronage recommendations were constantly being refused in favour of Bute nominations. It was an opinion widely held. Lord Chesterfield wrote on 14 September that Bute 'names absolutely to every employment, civil, military, and ecclesiastical'.[88] Especially was there an ongoing dispute over Scottish patronage between Grenville and Bute's brother Stuart Mackenzie, Lord Privy Seal of Scotland. Grenville's attitude to Bute soon changed from trust to hostility. Whereas earlier he had attempted to curb Bedfordite animosity to Bute, he now shared their hostility. This antipathy became mutual, with Bute men uncooperative, absent from meetings, and conspicuously silent in the Parliamentary debates of 1765.[89] On 18 April 1765

Horace Walpole could write that 'the enmity between Lord Bute and Mr Grenville is not denied on either side.'[90]

Suspicion of Bute naturally coloured Grenville's reaction when on 3 April George III, intermittently ill since January, informed him that he wanted a Regency Bill to cover the contingency of his death. For when the King reserved to himself the nomination of regent, Grenville's mind immediately flew to the Princess Dowager of Wales, and the fear that Bute would thereby become regent by proxy. But George III always had the Queen in mind, and kept this decision secret only to preserve harmony in the royal family. Ill health precluded his uncle, the Duke of Cumberland, and he had no intention of choosing his frivolous brother Edward, Duke of York, but wished to avoid a public snub to him as long as possible. Grenville and his colleagues were barking up the wrong tree when they pressed George III to reveal his choice. When the possibility of the King's mother being considered for this role was raised in the House of Lords by opposition peer Richmond, Halifax was instructed to move on 3 May a relevant definition of the royal family as the Queen and descendants of George II. No one thought it a point of consequence until the Princess Dowager was now persuaded she had been insulted. Grenville declined to move a Commons resolution that would contradict his colleague, but supported one by a minor government lawyer John Morton on 9 May to insert her name. Grenville himself, reflecting on the incident three years later, did not believe the episode contributed to his subsequent dismissal from office, but many thought so then and afterwards.[91]

George III had indeed already decided to change his ministry, but postponed any move until the Regency Bill had passed through Parliament on 13 May: though Grenville thought the 'decisive' event was a riot of Spitalfields silk weavers after Bedford contrived the rejection of a protective Silk Bill in the House of Lords that same day.[92] Bute was not this time the King's negotiator, for George III had ceased having private discussions with his former favourite in March: Holland was incredulous when Bute told him so on 7 November. 'I thought with the whole world, that you saw the King in private, at Leicester House, and at Kew 3 or 4 times in a week'.[93] But long afterwards it remained a Grenvillite belief that Bute caused the downfall of the ministry.[94] The King was now on good terms again with the Duke of Cumberland, and in April sounded his uncle on acting as an intermediary to replace the ministry with the opposition, a request with which the Duke willingly complied.[95] Since 1762 his political associations had been with the Newcastle Whigs, and he had always resented

Bute having supplanted him in the natural role of his nephew's adviser. On 13 May the King authorised Cumberland to form a ministry out of 'Mr Pitt and Lord Temple, with the other great Whig families'.[96] But Pitt declined to discuss any ministerial plans, and the Newcastle group refused to take office without him.

This fiasco played into Grenville's hands, for the attempt was soon public knowledge, as the Premier told the King on 21 May. Next day the cabinet now set out its terms for continuing in office.[97] The first were Bute's complete withdrawal from politics, and his brother's dismissal from his Scottish post. Nor must Cumberland have anything more to do with the government. Weymouth was to become Lord-Lieutenant of Ireland, in succession to Lord Northumberland, and Charles Townshend would replace Lord Holland at the Pay Office: both changes were deemed further blows at Bute, since Northumberland's son had just married one of his daughters, and Holland was thought now a Bute man. The King resisted only the dismissal of Mackenzie, having promised him the post for life, but yielded on 23 May. His colleagues pushed Grenville into this demand, which he perceived in retrospect as the last straw for the King: 'the consequences are known', he observed to James Harris when recalling the incident in 1768.[98] The public rebuff to Bute made the ministry widely popular in the political world, notably at the Cocoa Tree, and Grenville's levee on 23 May was crowded.[99]

The Grenville cabinet thought this episode of May 1765 a repetition of the events of August 1763, and that another royal failure to remove the ministry left it in a stronger position than before. This confidence was strengthened by the sudden reconciliation, political as well as personal, of Lord Temple with his brother, Premier George Grenville, by 22 May.[100] Since Pitt always made it a condition of his return to office that Temple should accompany him, and the Newcastle group seemed unwilling to act without Pitt, this event may have explained Pitt's refusal, and now appeared to rule out any immediate prospect of a change of administration.[101]

That was an illusion. Whereas in 1763 George III had given genuine support to Grenville, in 1765 the King was alienated from his ministry, which indeed made little attempt to conciliate him. At the end of May George III complained to Bute that 'every day I meet with some insult from these people'.[102] James Harris observed with concern the coldness Grenville met with at a royal levee on 4 June. 'These and many other little events show that the *present* system of power, however strong in its constituent parts, is founded on *compulsion*.'[103]

Matters came to a head when Bedford, without consulting Grenville, sought to clear the air by confronting the King on 12 June, reporting to the Duke of Marlborough what he had said. 'I proceeded to beseech him to permit his authority and his favours and countenance to go together; and if the last can't be given to his present ministers, to transfer to others that authority.'[104] This interview strengthened the indignant King's intention, already mentioned to Cumberland, to change the ministry, and he promptly gave the Duke appropriate instructions. If Pitt again refused, an approach should be made to 'those worthy men, Lord Rockingham, the Dukes of Grafton, Newcastle and others; for they are men who have principles and therefore cannot approve of seeing the Crown dictated to by low men'.[105] For George III, as later in his reign, paid no heed to a Parliamentary majority if he wished to overturn an administration, and, contrary to ministerial opinion, he did have somewhere else to turn. 'The Duke of Cumberland has certainly removed all the prejudices to the Whigs', reflected Newcastle to Rockingham on 1 June.[106] The King was appealing to the very same Whig aristocracy whose removal from power he had intended at his accession.

The next few weeks were recalled by the second Lord Hardwicke as the time when 'the Duke of Cumberland was settling a ministry for the King'.[107] The approach to Pitt foundered on Temple's unwillingness to replace his brother at the Treasury.[108] Cumberland then opened negotiations with the Newcastle connection, to the incredulity of men like Lord Chancellor Northington, the former Lord Henley, who on 26 June 'talked with contempt of a ministry to be formed by that old fellow ... and a parcel of boys'.[109] Newcastle, now seventy-two, was devoid of ambition for high office, but favoured the attempt to form a ministry without Pitt, from a sense of duty to his sovereign, and also to redress the treatment of his supporters in 1762. On 30 June Newcastle, Rockingham and General Henry Conway visited Cumberland at Windsor, and there agreed that Rockingham, aged thirty-five and Cumberland's choice, should take the Treasury, while the two Secretaries of State would be the Duke of Grafton, not thirty until September, and either Conway or Charles Townshend. Construction of the ministry was hampered by Pitt's refusal to promise support, and bedevilled by suspicion of Bute. Rumour had it that when Pitt was consulted about policy he talked of general warrants, repeal of the cider tax, and a Prussian alliance, but would give no assurances.[110] Attempts to secure his goodwill included a peerage for Judge Pratt as Lord Camden, given, said Temple when he later claimed credit for the creation, for Pratt's behaviour towards Wilkes in 1763;[111] an unsuccessful offer of the Board of Trade to Lord Shelburne; and acceptance of Grafton's insistence that he would become Northern Secretary only if Pitt could take over the post, and presumably head the ministry, whenever he chose.[112]

If the prospective neutrality of Pitt seemed to jeopardise the ministry's survival, fear of Bute's influence was exaggerated. It was reflected in an early stipulation, suggested by the Duke of Portland, that Bute's brother Stuart Mackenzie should not be restored to his Scottish post, and in a demand for the dismissal from office of some men deemed Buteites. George III was astonished by these demands, for Cumberland's role ought to have made it apparent that Bute no longer had the King's ear: but he authorised his uncle to give assurances that Bute would not be allowed to interfere in political matters and that any of Bute's followers who did not support the proposed administration would face immediate dismissal. That the incoming ministry had grounds for such unease was demonstrated by an approach to Grenville on 3 July by three men associated with Bute, Lords Denbigh, Egmont and Talbot. They suggested that he should seek a reconciliation with the King, but the Prime Minister replied that such a move would be 'impossible and absurd' while negotiations to replace him were in progress.[113] This omen that the Rockingham administration would not enjoy the full support of the Court Party was to be borne out by the future course of events.

Another courtier, Lord Townshend, the former General George Townshend who had succeeded his father in 1764, was unwilling, so he told George III, to act against 'men whose principles he had always approved', the outgoing Grenville ministry; he persuaded his younger brother Charles to decline the Secretaryship of State, and was rumoured to have himself refused the Lord Lieutenancy of Ireland and a Marquessate.[114] Even when pressed by George III Charles Townshend refused to become either Secretary of State or Chancellor of the Exchequer, and remained at the Pay Office recently given him by Grenville. If the attitude of the Townshends was ambivalent, that of the Yorkes, another family long a part of the old Whig corps, was merely cautious. Charles Yorke delayed acceptance of his old post of Attorney-General, which he eventually took only after a personal promise from George III that the next year he would be made Lord Chancellor.[115] His brother, the second Earl of Hardwicke, refused to head the Board of Trade. Lack of confidence in the prospects of the new ministry rendered recruitment to it difficult, but the key posts

were soon filled. Conway became Southern Secretary, the Board of
Trade went to Lord Dartmouth, a nephew of Henry Legge, and the
Exchequer to William Dowdeswell, a surprise choice, since the only
link that old Tory had with the old Whigs was resistance to the cider
tax. Continued from the former ministry were Lord Chancellor Northington and First Lord of the Admiralty Egmont, both men loyal to
the King rather than to their new colleagues. Newcastle became Lord
Privy Seal, and Rockingham's uncle, old Lord Winchelsea, Lord President of the Council. Contemporary opinion identified two key weaknesses in the new ministry, lack of both administrative experience and
Parliamentary debating strength. Neither Secretary of State had held
executive office, nor any members of the Treasury Board, where
Rockingham and Dowdeswell were joined by three young MPs hitherto with an aptitude only for opposition speeches, George Onslow,
Thomas Townshend, and Lord John Cavendish. In the House of
Lords the Bedford group alone might prove more than a match for
ministers, and it was not expected that Conway and Dowdeswell
would fare well against Grenville in the Commons.[116]

The formal change of ministry took place on 10 July, when
Grenville and his chief colleagues were summoned by George III.
'The King's reception of him and the two disgraced Secretarys was
cold and short', so James Harris was told. When Grenville, conscious
no doubt of having been a successful Premier, asked why they were
being dismissed, 'the King admitted his business had been well done,
but that they had formed a plan to give him law'.[117]

When Grenville dined his former Treasury Board on 17 July, he
stated that he would cooperate with the new ministry if his measures
were adopted, and oppose if contrary ones were put forward.[118] That
was political correctness at a time when good reasons had to be
adduced for opposition to the King's government not to be
denounced as factious. But Grenville's opposition was already the
probable outcome. For Dowdeswell was expected to repeal the cider
tax, and by the end of July it was being rumoured that the ministry
would 'affect popularity by concessions to the Americans'.[119]

Notes

1 *Chatham Papers*, II, 217–18.
2 BL Add. MSS. 32948, fos 120–2.
3 BL Add. MSS. 32948, fos 54–7.
4 *Bute Letters*, pp. 212–34.

5 Thomas, *British Politics and the Stamp Act Crisis*, pp. 10–12. Lawson, *George Grenville*, p. 158.

6 *Grenville Papers*, II, 191. Mrs Grenville's Diary.

7 *Chesterfield Letters*, VI, 2,531.

8 *Grenville Papers*, II, 83–5.

9 Malmesbury MSS. Photocopies B975. Fitzmaurice, *Shelburne*, I, 199–204.

10 *Grenville Papers*, II, 193–9. Mrs Grenville's Diary.

11 *Grenville Papers*, II, 200–1. Mrs Grenville's Diary.

12 *Grenville Papers*, II, 104–7, 203.

13 *Jenkinson Papers*, p. 394. Tomlinson, Thesis, pp. 61–3.

14 BL Add. MSS. 38335, fos 120–34; 38338, fos 274–81.

15 *Chesterfield Letters*, VI, 2,543.

16 Tomlinson, Thesis, p. 110.

17 *Chesterfield Letters*, VI, 2,543.

18 BL Add. MSS. 51406, fos 120–1.

19 Malmesbury MSS. Photocopies B89.

20 Malmesbury MSS. Photocopies B97–9.

21 Thomas, *John Wilkes*, pp. 27–36.

22 Malmesbury MSS. Harris Diary, 17 Feb. 1764.

23 Thomas, *John Wilkes*, pp. 37–9, 42.

24 Thomas, *John Wilkes*, pp. 41–5.

25 *St James's Chronicle*, 8 Dec. 1763.

26 Thomas, *John Wilkes*, pp. 45–7.

27 Namier, *Structure of Politics*, p. 153.

28 Thomas, *John Wilkes*, pp. 47–54.

29 BL Add. MSS. 38337, fo. 193.

30 Tomlinson, Thesis, p. 101.

31 Thomas, *John Wilkes*, pp. 54–5.

32 Woodland, *PH*, 4 (1985), 115–36.

33 Malmesbury MSS. Photocopies B108.

34 Malmesbury MSS. Harris Diary, 14 Nov. 1763. *Corr. of George III*, I, 63.

35 Tomlinson, Thesis, p. 83.

36 *Chatham Papers*, II, 282.

37 Malmesbury MSS. Harris Diary, 24 Jan. 1764. Walpole, *Memoirs*, I, 281.

38 Malmesbury MSS. Harris Diary, 31 Jan. 1764.

39 Malmesbury MSS. Harris Diary, 6, 7, 10 Feb. 1764. Walpole, *Memoirs*, I, 285.

40 *Additional Grenville Papers*, pp. 317–18.

41 Thomas, *British Politics and the Stamp Act Crisis*, pp. 40–3.

42 Malmesbury MSS. Photocopies B708.

43 Thomas, *British Politics and the Stamp Act Crisis*, pp. 69–77.
44 Malmesbury MSS. Photocopies B996.
45 BL Add. MSS. 32957, fos 239–40.
46 Thomas, *British Politics and the Stamp Act Crisis*, pp. 56–61.
47 Thomas, *British Politics and the Stamp Act Crisis*, pp. 62–6.
48 *Grenville Papers*, II, 160–1.
49 Walpole, *Letters*, V, 403.
50 *Jenkinson Papers*, pp. 270–2.
51 Sutherland, *East India Company*, pp. 117–32. For the *jagir* issue see Lenman and Lawson, *HJ*, 26 (1983), 801–29. The *jagir* was extended in 1767 to 1784, but Clive died in 1774.
52 *Lyttelton Memoirs*, II, 659.
53 *Chesterfield Letters*, VI, 2,613.
54 Almon, *Memoirs*, p. 16. Malmesbury MSS. Harris Diary, 22 Mar. 1764.
55 BL Add. MSS. 32955, fos 409–14.
56 BL Add. MSS. 32967, fo. 187.
57 Watson, *BIHR*, 44 (1971), 59–77.
58 *Chatham Papers*, II, 293–7. Walpole, *Memoirs*, II, 28–9.
59 Woodland, *PH*, 8 (1989), 78–9.
60 Malmesbury MSS. Harris Diary, 29 Jan. 1765. For the debate see also *Ryder Diary*, pp. 239–53, and Walpole, *Memoirs*, II, 37–45.
61 Morgan and Morgan, *Stamp Act Crisis*, pp. 51–8.
62 Malmesbury MSS. Photocopies A56.
63 Malmesbury MSS. Photocopies A57. For more detail see Thomas, *British Politics and the Stamp Act Crisis*, pp. 77–88.
64 Thomas, *British Politics and the Stamp Act Crisis*, pp. 89–94.
65 BL Add. MSS. 32965, fo. 346.
66 Thomas, *British Politics and the Stamp Act Crisis*, pp. 96–9.
67 *Grenville Papers*, III, 11–14.
68 Thomas, *British Politics and the Stamp Act Crisis*, pp. 102–8.
69 *Rockingham Memoirs*, I, 249.
70 *CHOP*, I, 330.
71 *Grenville Papers*, II, 147. *Additional Grenville Papers*, pp. 56–7, 65–6.
72 *CHOP*, I, 314, 317, 337–8. *Additional Grenville Papers*, p. 66.
73 Powell, Thesis, pp. 95–100. *HMC Charlemont*, I, 22.
74 *Corr. of George III*, I, 168.
75 *Additional Grenville Papers*, pp. 335–6.
76 Powell, Thesis, pp. 106–7.
77 On this see Scott, *British Foreign Policy*, pp. 53–89.
78 *Additional Grenville Papers*, pp. 317–18.
79 *Grenville Papers*, II, 344.

80 Tracy, *Navies*, pp. 42–53.
81 BL Add. MSS. 22359, fo. 44, quoted Langford, *First Rockingham Administration*, p. 7.
82 Tomlinson, Thesis, pp. 124–5.
83 Walpole, *Memoirs*, I, 234.
84 Tomlinson, Thesis, pp. 151–6.
85 Walpole, *Memoirs*, II, 115.
86 *Corr. of George III*, I, 162–75.
87 Malmesbury MSS. Photocopies A51.
88 *Chesterfield Letters*,VI, 2,613–4.
89 Tomlinson, Thesis, pp. 156–64.
90 Walpole, *Letters*, VI, 215.
91 Malmesbury MSS. Photocopies B608–12, 685. For accounts of this episode see Tomlinson, Thesis, pp. 165–90; Jarrett, *EHR*, 85 (1970), 282–315; and Brooke, *King George III*, pp. 110–13.
92 Malmesbury MSS. Photocopies B618–9.
93 BL Add. MSS. 51379, fos 175–6.
94 Malmesbury MSS. Photocopies A70.
95 BL Add. MSS. 51406, fo. 114.
97 *Rockingham Memoirs*, I, 191. Cumberland's narrative.
97 *Grenville Papers*, III, 41.
98 Malmesbury MSS. Photocopies B882.
99 Malmesbury MSS. Photocopies B615, 886–7. *Grenville Papers*, III, 177–88. Tomlinson, Thesis, pp. 180–6.
100 *Grenville Papers*, III, 183.
101 Thomas, *British Politics and the Stamp Act Crisis*, pp. 118–19.
102 *Bute Letters*, p. 241.
103 Malmesbury MSS. Photocopies B630–1.
104 *Bedford Papers*, III, 286–90.
105 *Corr. of George III*, I, 116–19. These letters are printed in the wrong sequence.
106 BL Add. MSS. 32967, fos 3–5.
107 BL Add. MSS. 35428, fo. 22.
108 One rumour was that the plan was undermined by Grenville's refusal to be merely Chancellor of the Exchequer, as the key to the whole arrangement. Malmesbury MSS. Photocopies B640–4.
109 Malmesbury MSS. Photocopies B646.
110 Malmesbury MSS. Photocopies B650.
111 Malmesbury MSS. Photocopies B913.
112 BL Add. MSS. 32973, fos 68–71.
113 Malmesbury MSS. Photocopies B652.

114 Malmesbury MSS. Photocopies B661, 670.
115 BL Add. MSS. 35428, fo. 22.
116 For the construction of the new ministry see Hardy, Thesis, pp. 307–64;
     Langford, *First Rockingham Administration*, pp. 4–39; and Thomas,
     British Politics and the Stamp Act Crisis, pp. 119–26.
117 Malmesbury MSS. Photocopies B662–8, 887–8.
118 Malmesbury MSS. Photocopies B669.
119 Malmesbury MSS. Photocopies B671.

6

The first Rockingham ministry (1765–1766): the Stamp Act Crisis

Lord Rockingham, who is at the head of the Treasury, is so infirm in his health, that it hardly seems possible for him to stand an active session of Parliament. One of the Secretaries of State [Grafton] is a very young man, and the other [Conway] new in the business. In general they want authority, and seem to have no head except the Duke of Cumberland, whose health and life are thought to be very precarious.[1]

This appraisal was by an opponent, Grenvillite Lord Lyttelton, but it helps to explain the widespread contemporary opinion that the new ministry would be short-lived. Inexperience and a perceived lack of ability; Pitt's indifference; Bute's reputed influence; the indignant hostility of the displaced Grenville and Bedford factions: none of this boded well for the new administration. Prime Minister Rockingham, devoid of administrative experience, had seemingly been promoted above the level of his ability. But his charm and integrity made him a good team leader, and he was to remain head of his party until his death in 1782. That was despite his nervous inability to speak in the House of Lords, where he only spoke twice during the session he was Prime Minister. Not until 1770 did the Marquess become a regular speaker in debate.[2] One undoubted asset was his new private secretary Edmund Burke, who contributed industry as well as Commons oratory. Of the two Secretaries of State Grafton was able but lazy, and Conway notoriously weak and indecisive for a man named Commons Leader by the end of the year. How the ministry would manage the House of Commons was a puzzle to contemporaries, with Pitt neutral, Grenville hostile, and Charles Townshend unwilling to commit himself by accepting high office: but Charles Yorke did his duty as Attorney-General, and an unexpected bonus was the blossoming performance of William Dowdeswell, both as Chancellor of the

Exchequer and as a Commons spokesman. And the ministry was strong there in terms of numbers: a Parliamentary list compiled in September named 294 MPs as 'Pro', only 113 as 'Con', with 127 as 'Doubtful'. Pitt's followers were put in this last group, but he himself was unclassified.[3] Such a majority was usual for almost every new ministry during the century, with the intangible factor of loyalty to the Crown being reinforced by the practical pull of patronage. But there would be vigorous opposition from the factions of Bedford and Grenville. That there was a Grenville party owed much to the Rockinghamite purge of office-holders, but more to Grenville's skill in winning support as man and minister. A score of MPs were dismissed from office or resigned in protest at Grenville's removal. There was also a group of Grenville admirers, notably Lord Clive with his own small band of MPs. And Grenville's policy of financial retrenchment – contemporary cartoons mocked him as saving candle ends – had won him the support of numerous independents. Grenville's potential support in the new session comprised some 70 MPs, and his debating performance cemented his followers into a firm voting bloc.[4]

George III's support was assured, if only because Pitt's recalcitrance and his own dislike of Grenville left him with no choice. To strengthen this royal link the ministers invited the King's uncle to attend cabinet, and Cumberland did so, until his death on 31 October. Grenvillite unease at this development was voiced by Augustus Hervey, who spoke of 'the danger of the precedent in making a Prince of the Blood, like ye Duke of Cumberland, a Minister. The Duke of York has parts and spirit, and might one time or other think that he had a right to the same power.'[5]

In a sense Cumberland was playing the role Newcastle had marked out for himself. Although Newcastle had taken the non-departmental post of Lord Privy Seal, he had expected, as the party's elder statesman, to be involved in policy consultations. Rockingham was wary of his pressure, and rejected Newcastle's suggestion of reappointing the Duke's confidant James West as Secretary to the Treasury.[6] Finding himself cold-shouldered, Newcastle by October intended to lay before Cumberland his grievance about 'the total want of confidence and communication in the two young lords, and particularly, the Marquess of Rockingham, from whom I think, I had a right to expect a very different conduct'. His concern rose above personal resentment, for on 30 October he commented to Lord Albemarle. '*These young men* do not know the world, and *what Ministers* must do, and ought to do, to be able to serve the Public, and support *themselves*'.[7]

Parliament did not meet until December, and during the first three months of the recess the administration was so dominated by Cumberland that the period was recalled in 1768 as 'the late Duke of Cumberland's ministry'.[8] The Duke had been its creator, and was its chief link with the royal court. Despite his poor health he routinely attended cabinet, which more often than not met at his own house. He was heavily involved in patronage and other decisions. It was Cumberland who killed the idea of a tactical general election. He concerned himself with matters of policy, and strongly favoured the foreign policy initiative of the new ministry.[9]

A deliberate alteration of foreign policy had always been the intention of the men who comprised the new cabinet. Criticism of the loss of the Prussian alliance and of the soft line towards the Bourbon Powers had been voiced over the last few years by Pitt, Newcastle, and their followers, and the change of administration in 1765 was perceived as the opportunity to remedy the situation. The ministry adopted 'Mr Pitt's plan' as put forward to the King in his abortive negotiations of May and June, one for a triple alliance of Britain, Russia, and Prussia.[10] George III feared that this would involve 'Austria deeper with France' and risk 'a new war by unnecessary alliances'.[11] But the King had to allow his cabinet to pursue that objective, which aimed to balance the alliances France enjoyed with both Austria and Spain. The decision was taken at a cabinet of 22 July to form a 'general system … to unite all the powers of the North together with Prussia'.[12] This policy was doomed by the refusal of Frederick II, made known in November, to make any such treaty.[13] But it would in any case have been rendered difficult by Russia's constant insistence on the Turkish clause, and by the demands of Denmark and Sweden for subsidy payments. The only success the ministry could claim was Macartney's negotiation of a 1766 trade treaty with Russia, regaining 'most favoured nation status' for Britain: but the instructions had come from Sandwich during Grenville's ministry, and the Rockingham cabinet played little part in the final outcome.[14]

Grenville's 'gunboat diplomacy' obviated earlier criticism of weakness towards the Bourbon Powers, but there was one matter over which his ministry could be attacked, failure to press the so-called Manila Ransom issue with Spain. There was a strong British case to claim payment of the sum agreed upon at the capture of the Philippines capital to prevent looting of that city. But a belligerent stance in Madrid of the British ambassador Lord Rochford was undermined by the feebleness of Southern Secretary Conway, who betrayed Rochford's bluffing and reduced British claims. Conway was then nonplussed by the Spanish suggestion of mediation by Frederick II of Prussia. This episode was part of the reason why conduct of foreign policy contributed to the Rockingham ministry's reputation for weakness.[15]

So too did the ministry's policy concerning Ireland, for it dropped the aim of permanent residence for the Viceroy. John Ponsonby was closely related to the influential Cavendish family, a chief prop of the new administration, and correctly anticipated little interference from the new regime. 'What matters it to us who are ministers in England? Let us stick to our own circle and manage our own little game as well as we can.'[16] The new Lord-Lieutenant was the Earl of Hertford sent as ambassador to Paris as consolation for not obtaining the same post in 1763. Now he was pushed for it by the Duke of Cumberland and his own younger brother Henry Conway, Commons Leader and as Southern Secretary his immediate link with government.[17] That the new Chief Secretary was not an experienced politician chosen to lead the Dublin Parliament, but merely Hertford's eldest son, the twenty-two-year-old Lord Beauchamp, confirmed the assumption that there would be no Castle challenge to Undertaker rule, and this was evident before America engrossed ministerial attention. Ponsonby was laden with spoils, and Shannon was made Master-General of the Irish Ordnance. But the Undertakers failed to deliver a quiet Parliamentary session, for the Commons opposition was led by a formidable trio, orator Henry Flood, radical Charles Lucas, and adept Parliamentarian Edmond Pery. When a Septennial Bill passed, Hertford sent it to London for rejection, on news of which there were stormy debates and two Castle defeats.

This concurrent weakness over foreign policy and Ireland strengthened the impression of a similar pusillanimity towards the colonies when, unexpectedly, the ministry faced a serious American problem. News of the Virginia Resolves of May, denying the Parliamentary right of taxation, arrived during August: but the cabinet, misled by the colony's lieutenant-governor, believed them to be the work of an unrepresentative minority. Even after news of other colonial protests the ministry did not anticipate undue difficulty in enforcing the Stamp Act, and leisurely referred the problem to the consideration of Parliament. Reports in October of violence in Boston, Massachusetts, and Newport, Rhode Island, were a rude awakening, especially when it became known that such behaviour, or the mere threat of it, was causing the resignation of Stamp-Distributors in several colonies: for they were the officials appointed to enforce the new taxes.[18]

The ministry responded by ordering colonial governors to preserve the peace and to apply, if necessary, to General Gage for military assistance. That decision was taken at a cabinet meeting on 13 October, and formally confirmed on 23 October in the Privy Council, the institution nominally responsible for the colonies. Southern Secretary Conway sent a circular letter next day, but this was so hedged about with qualifications that no governor asked for soldiers. It is difficult to avoid the impression that all this was a face-saving exercise, to anticipate any future criticism and perhaps to mollify Cumberland. For the ministry knew full well that the long delay before the orders arrived, and the current dispersion of the American army in Quebec, Florida, and the Indian reservations, would render impossible any military enforcement of the Stamp Act, which was due to come into operation on 1 November.[19] It must remain conjecture what administration policy would have been devised for America if Cumberland had not died, on 31 October. Some contemporaries assumed the Duke would have favoured the deployment of military force, and that was certainly the reaction of Lord Chancellor Northington. Even those reluctant to adopt that course of action did not necessarily wish to concede political ground. But one immediate consequence of the Duke's death was a decision to take more time for information and contemplation before any policy was devised for America.[20]

More pressing matters needed attention. Cumberland's death seemed to many contemporaries to doom the ministry. The cabinet therefore decided on 7 November to approach Pitt, but George III himself killed that idea.[21] The King assured Rockingham that there would be no change in royal support, but their lack of credibility rendered vain the efforts of ministers to recruit additional strength. Charles Townshend declined to enter the cabinet and become Commons Leader, a role then reluctantly undertaken by Conway. Lord North and Hans Stanley were among those who refused to return to office, and a rather desperate appeal to another former 'old corps' member Lord Halifax also failed. The only man to accept an important post was Lord George Sackville, glad of political rehabilitation after his military disgrace of 1759, who became an Irish Vice-Treasurer in December. But his appointment gave Pitt one more reason to disapprove of the administration.[22]

The delusive hope that the American crisis would solve itself was one reason for delaying any decision. For long the official view was that the more responsible and respectable colonists were not involved in the resistance to British authority. General Gage, in a letter of 12 October that arrived on 15 November, fuelled such expectations by

the opinion that 'it is impossible to say whether the execution of the
Stamp Act will meet with further opposition; but from present appearances, there is reason to judge, that it may be introduced without much
difficulty, in several of the colonies, and if it is begun in some, that it
will soon spread over the rest'. That was an extraordinary conclusion
to his report of defiant resolutions from various colonial assemblies,
and of the current meeting of delegates at the Stamp Act Congress in
New York, that had ended with this comment. 'It is to be feared in general, that the spirit of democracy is strong amongst them. The question
is not of the inexpediency of the Stamp Act, or of the inability of the
colonies to pay the tax, but that it is unconstitutional, and contrary to
their rights.'[23]

During the last two months of 1765 the ministry came under
pressure to suspend or repeal the Stamp Act, from colonial agents and
British merchants. The threat to British trade became an important
factor in the equation, emphasised in interviews Rockingham gave to
leading American merchant Barlow Trecothick and hyperactive Pennsylvania agent Benjamin Franklin. It so happened that, quite unconnected with the political situation, there already was a recession in
Anglo-American trade, part of a wider economic depression affecting
most of Europe.[24] Bristol merchants had sent in a petition on 29 October. There was alarm that threatened American trade boycotts would
convert this slump into a national disaster when they took effect in
1766. A new American Merchants Committee, elected by a general
meeting on 4 December with Trecothick as Chairman, two days later
sent a circular letter to thirty trading and manufacturing towns in
Britain, urging action by petitions to Parliament. Rockingham's approval
of this missive was an early sign that he intended a policy of conciliation,
for a barrage of petitions to Parliament would assist such an aim.[25]

By the end of 1765 the news from America had brought the crisis
to a head. Nowhere had the Stamp Act come into operation on the due
date of 1 November, and that day was marked by a riot in New York.
The choice between military enforcement and concession was discussed in the press, and since complete repeal would be an overt
surrender to mob violence, the most popular form of concession being
mooted was the face-saving device of suspension.[26] Although the ministry had come to no decision on policy, Parliament had to meet before
Christmas to permit the issue of by-election writs for new office-
holders. That would be inconvenient, for the Grenville and Bedford
groups would launch an immediate attack. The administration, so
Massachusetts agent Dennys De Berdt reported on 14 December,

'expect a warm opposition from the old ministry and what they call the Country Party'.[27] But the main Commons debate, on 17 December, was an anticlimax. Grenville overplayed his hand by describing the American situation as a rebellion, comparable to the Jacobite Rising of 1745, and did not force a vote after most speakers, including Charles Townshend and Buteite Gilbert Elliot, declared that more information was needed before any decisions were made. In the Lords, where the opposition was formidable in personnel and numbers, the ministry won the vote by 80 to 24, for the Bute group sided with the administration.[28]

The first skirmishes had gone in favour of the ministers, but the real test would come over their policy. And there was the rub. By now it was apparent to the administration that conciliation was the only possible short-term solution. General Gage had pointed out that the military situation in America precluded any attempt to enforce the Stamp Act.[29] But no ministry could simply present Parliament with that unpalatable fact. How to devise a strategy that would make concession acceptable to peers and MPs exercised the minds of ministers during the next few weeks. During December Rockingham preferred unofficial meetings to cabinets. One motive may have been to avoid pressure from Newcastle, who complained on 3 December to his old friend John White that 'these gentlemen ... are afraid of being thought to be influenced, or advised, by *any* of their predecessors'. Since matters were being settled beforehand, cabinet consultations with Newcastle, Northington and Egmont had become a formality.[30] Rockingham's confidants were Southern Secretary Conway, and two non-cabinet men, Dowdeswell and Charles Yorke. The Attorney-General made the key suggestion of a Declaratory Act asserting the legislative power of Parliament over the colonies. 'It was principally owing to my brother', so Hardwicke later wrote, 'that the dignity and authority of the Legislature were kept up ... I must do Lord Rockingham the justice to say that as far as theory went he declared for asserting the sovereignty of the Mother Country, though he was averse to the exercise of it in point of taxation.'[31] Yorke's tactical suggestion, too, formed the basis of ministerial strategy: that this declaration should precede any conciliation, and that any concession should ostensibly be for economic reasons. There was no agreement as to what form that should take. Lawyers Yorke and Northington were for minimal relief, others like Rockingham and Newcastle for complete repeal. Any policy, moreover, had to be acceptable to King, Lords and Commons. George III seemed to present no problem, voicing no

opinions of his own and simply pressing his ministers for some decision. But it soon became apparent that the Court Party would be split,
with Bute men siding against conciliation along with the Bedford and
Grenville groups. In a letter of 10 January 1766 to Bute, before the
ministry's American policy was known, George III, mindful of his
promise to Rockingham, stated that office-holders should not vote 'to
overturn those I employ': but he followed this injunction by saying
that 'my friends' could vote against ministers when 'their honour and
conscience requires it'.[32] Bute's friends, in and out of office, were to
do so with impunity during the Stamp Act Crisis.

Already what threatened to be an ominous Parliamentary situation
had caused the ministry to sound out the opinion held on America by
the absent Pitt, whose adherents in Parliament, notably Shelburne and
Beckford, had spoken for conciliation. Informal soundings in December had been hopeful, with Beckford assuring George Onslow that Pitt
did '*not* doubt' on America and was 'thoroughly and unalterably
averse to the late people'.[33] Pitt was unhelpful when approached
directly by Thomas Townshend, stating, with constitutional punctil-
iousness, that he would give his opinion in Parliament. That feeler was
sanctioned by the King, but not the simultaneous offer to join the ministry. Pitt replied that he was willing to serve with Rockingham,
Grafton and Conway, but not with Newcastle, since 'there could not
be two ministers'. Rockingham was annoyed by the implication that
Newcastle headed the ministry, and angered by a stipulation that
Temple, now Grenville's ally, should be offered his own post at the
Treasury. Conway and Grafton, at first eager for Pitt on any terms,
agreed that his conditions were unacceptable.[34]

The ministry, awaiting Pitt's opinion, met Parliament on 14 January 1766 before any final policy decision on America. The King's
Speech was therefore a masterpiece of vagueness, referring to both
Parliamentary authority and economic prosperity, two potentially
conflicting criteria in the American context. The ensuing debate was
dominated by a verbal duel between Pitt and Grenville, during which,
so diarist James Harris thought, 'the ministry stood by, like the rabble
at a boxing match'. Pitt, after keeping MPs in suspense, denounced
the attempt to tax the colonists. Adopting what was widely believed
in Britain to be the American constitutional stance, he declared that
Parliament had no right to lay an 'internal tax' on America, since
it was not represented there. Grenville denied that argument, but
Conway warmly welcomed Pitt's speech and was generally understood to have promised repeal on behalf of the ministry.[35]

The contemporary opinion, echoed by some historians, that Pitt had made up the ministry's mind for it, was not the whole truth. The administration had already been moving towards repeal, and the significance of Pitt's pronouncement was that Rockingham could now argue that such a policy was, with Pitt's support, a practical one in Parliamentary terms. But the ministry had got more than they had bargained for. Pitt's denial of complete Parliamentary sovereignty threatened to be counter-productive. Independent MPs might accept repeal on grounds of expediency, but not for the reason Pitt had given. 'The doctrine has not been very pleasing to the country gentlemen in the House', noted South Carolina agent Charles Garth.[36]

American policy was finally settled on 19 January, at an unofficial meeting of Rockingham, Conway, Grafton, Dowdeswell and Charles Townshend, after Rockingham had consulted Charles Yorke earlier that day. The Declaratory Act would merely use the phrase 'in all cases whatsoever' concerning the right of legislation, and not specifically assert Parliament's right of taxation over the colonies, to minimise the disagreement with Pitt. The Stamp Act would be repealed because of inherent defects and more especially the detrimental effect on the British economy. Newcastle, still deliberately excluded from all discussions, was concerned about the strong wording of the proposed resolutions that would form the background to the Declaratory Act. These condemned the colonial disorders, proposed punishment of the rioters, demanded compensation for victims, and asserted the full sovereignty of Parliament. Charles Yorke, on the other hand, wanted the Declaratory Act strengthened by the deliberate mention of taxation. Rockingham, anxious not to offend Pitt, refused to make that change, informing Yorke that most ministerial supporters already thought the resolutions too strong. All this concern reflected ministerial awareness that Parliamentary acceptance of this American policy might founder on a reluctance to accept a surrender to colonial defiance, whatever the verbal packaging.[37]

Grenville hoped to prevent repeal, and was openly scornful of the ministerial hypocrisy of simultaneously asserting Parliamentary right and giving it up. He deemed Pitt's denial of the right of taxation to be a more honest approach. The administration faced an attack on two fronts in Parliament, but they were safe at Court, where George III declined as yet to make public his personal policy preference for modification rather than complete repeal, and refused to respond to suggestions about changing the ministry. On 30 January he rebuffed an approach from Lord Harcourt by saying that 'he would never influence people in their Parliamentary opinions, and that he had promised to support his ministers'.[38] The administration acted with similar propriety by keeping Parliament fully and promptly informed of American news, perhaps with the ulterior motive of making clear the full gravity of the colonial situation. This negative point of the difficulty of enforcing the Stamp Act was reinforced by the positive one of the advantages of its repeal, as hinted by the 24 petitions from British ports and industrial towns, all asking for relief, that were presented to the Commons in January 1766.[39]

The ministry opened its Parliamentary campaign on 28 January, several days being passed in the reading of papers and hearing of witnesses about colonial defiance and violence, in order to provide ostensible justification for the Declaratory Act.[40] That was preaching to the converted, and the presumed ulterior motive of showing that the alternative to concession was the dispatch of a large army from Britain carried the risk of so alienating Parliamentary opinion as to render conciliation impossible. It was a difficult path to tread.

On 3 February the resolution asserting Parliament's right to legislate for America was moved in the Lords by Grafton and in the Commons by Conway. In the Lords Pittite peers like Shelburne and Camden forced a division and lost by 125 votes to 5.[41] In the Commons Pittite speakers also denied the right of taxation, and Barré moved to omit the words 'in all cases whatsoever', but his amendment was negatived without a vote. Charles Garth reckoned that only ten MPs would have supported it.[42] The full discussion can have left no doubt that the phrase did include taxation. Every lawyer in the debate condemned the Pittite and American link between taxation and representation, and also the supposed colonial distinction between internal and external taxation. When Edmund Burke suggested that taxation of the colonies was a dormant part of the constitution, like the royal veto, opposition sought to out-Whig the ministry by contending that Parliamentary taxation of the colonies was preferable to the old method of requisitions by the Crown, for that was a relic of the royal prerogative.[43]

Next day there came a ministerial defeat in the Lords, when Lord Suffolk, a Grenvillite, carried by 63 votes to 60 an amendment to substitute the stronger word 'require' for 'recommend' in the instructions to assemblies concerning compensation. Two days afterwards, on 6 February, the ministry was again defeated there, by 59 votes to 54. Bute spoke and voted against the administration, and the majority on both occasions included not only the Bute, Bedford, and Grenville factions, but also Lord Chancellor Northington and the King's brother the Duke of York, and another royal brother the Duke of Gloucester the second time.[44] Meanwhile in the House of Commons on 5 February an amendment implying that repeal would be a surrender to colonial violence was withdrawn after Grenville expressed a desire for unanimity; but he then carried two other resolutions, concerning protection for loyal subjects and a merely conditional indemnity for those who had failed to pay stamp duties. Grenville had captured the initiative, and announced a motion for 7 February which was expected to be for the enforcement of the Stamp Act.[45]

The beleaguered ministry had already decided to make repeal a matter of confidence, its defeat the ground for resignation. After these Parliamentary setbacks Rockingham therefore had a crucial meeting with George III on 7 February. The King stated that in a choice between repeal and enforcement of the Stamp Act he was for repeal, and gave Rockingham permission to make his opinion public. The Prime Minister did so before the important Commons debate that day.[46] Grenville, encouraged by recent events, overplayed his hand and moved to enforce the Stamp Act. Charles Townshend, in his only important speech of the session, opposed this as premature and prejudging the main issue of policy. Pitt, in a much-celebrated speech, declared that passage of Grenville's motion, and the consequent dispatch of military orders to America, would lead to bloodshed, futilely so if repeal followed. Grenville's blunder, the King's declaration, and the course of the debate, resulted in a ministerial majority of 140, 274 votes to 134, double the most optimistic government forecast.[47] Indeed, so Horace Walpole later heard, the opposition had expected a probable majority vote of 220, with 90 Bute men and 120 from the Grenville and Bedford factions.[48] Analysis of the minority by Sir William Meredith identified 37 each for Bute and Grenville, 34 for Bedford and 27 'Tories'.[49] A list of 131 MPs among Rockingham's papers classifies only five differently, a correlation testimony to the hardening of party groups.[50]

This debacle caused the opposition to abandon its attempt to defend the Stamp Act, and to adopt instead the policy of amendment now soon known to be the King's own personal preference, though George III's pledge to his ministers of support for repeal remained unwavering. The tactic of Grenville and his allies was simply to resist complete repeal, even though they never produced any specific amendment as an alternative, and rumours circulated that they intended only a token duty on playing cards and dice.[51] But there was much error and deception in the ministerial strategy that afforded opportunities for attack. One mistake that escaped detection was the belief that the already existing economic recession in Britain was caused by the colonial boycott of British goods. That could not yet have had any direct impact, and the British economy did not in fact recover for some years after the boycott ended. A clear sham was the pretence that America could not both pay Grenville's taxes and buy British goods, for the taxes had never been paid, and the colonial boycott arose from political will not economic necessity. Also part of the deception was the misrepresentation of the American resistance as spontaneous riots rather than deliberate violence, and as being a challenge to merely 'internal taxation' and not all Parliamentary revenue.

The parade of ministerial witnesses before the Commons from 11 to 13 February was intended to convince MPs that only repeal of the Stamp Act could end the economic depression, and that it would do so.[52] The first and most important witness was Barlow Trecothick, who stressed the importance to Britain of American trade, worth nearly £3 million a year. American orders had now either been cancelled or made conditional on repeal. Trecothick also said that much of the £4,450,000 of colonial debts owed to British merchants was at risk. Opposition cross-questioning failed to shake the unanimous opinion of successive witnesses that only repeal would do; and the accounts by merchants and manufacturers of economic distress in England and Scotland had its effect. Henry Cruger, an American currently a Bristol merchant, wrote back to his father that 'the country members are somewhat alarmed at so many people losing employ: if anything repeals the Act, it must be this'.[53] This tale of economic woe was followed on 13 February by a four-hour examination of Benjamin Franklin. His claim that by 'taxes' Americans meant only 'internal taxes' carried weight, and he cleverly pointed out that since no one could be compelled to buy stamps there could be no question of military enforcement of the tax. Opposition witnesses were heard on 17 and 18 February. Grenville was unable to produce any testimony to counter the weight of evidence about the economic depression and the importance of American trade. The opposition tactic therefore was simply to arouse prejudice against America by highlighting illicit trade there, colonial prosperity, and the scanty tax burden on Americans.[54]

The stage was now set for the great Commons debate on repeal, scheduled for 21 February. Conway put forward the ministerial argument, that Parliament had the right to tax the colonies but should not exercise it. The estimated tax revenue of £60,000 was not worth the sacrifice of Britain's American trade, and still less so would be a token duty. Nor should colonial resistance be used as an excuse for retaining the tax. Britain was not yielding to force, and could subdue the colonies if necessary; but he warned that the Bourbon Powers might exploit a civil war. Charles Yorke admitted his previous support for the Stamp Act, but now declared that repeal was political wisdom. The high point of the debate was a first major speech by Edmund Burke, arguing that historically Britain had never sought to tax the colonies. Pitt's line was that it was unfair both to tax America and to control her economy. He would support coercion if America was not now quiet, words that came back to haunt him. No speaker, not even Grenville, argued for retention of the Stamp Act. The debate ended long after midnight in a vote of 275 to 167 to retain the word 'repeal' instead of the opposition alternative of 'amend'.[55]

The Bedford and Grenville factions were again joined by Bute's followers, and the minority therefore contained many office-holders. One list named 52.[56] An analysis of Scottish MPs put 17 for the ministry, 8 absent, and 20 against.[57] These desertions from the Court Party derived immunity from George III's unguarded remark to Bute in the previous month. Fortunately for the ministry the campaign to win over independent opinion to the economic and political case for repeal had succeeded beyond expectation. It was of the country squires that the Speaker's Chaplain was thinking when he commented that 'as many voted for the repeal who are in the Opposition as who are with the ministry'. The fear of such MPs was over the social repercussions of widespread unemployment coinciding with an existing food shortage: the Spitalfields riots of silk-weavers in May 1765 were fresh in the memory. There had already been hunger riots in 1765 and early 1766, over the high price of bread, and Parliament, in February 1766, passed legislation prohibiting for six months the export of grain and permitting the import of American corn duty-free. MP Horace Walpole captured the mood when he wrote that 'a general insurrection was apprehended as the immediate consequence of upholding the bill'.[58]

Nationwide rejoicing was reported as the news of this vote spread, with its implication of a consequent economic upturn. The Declaratory Bill and Repeal Bill passed through the Commons with little discussion until the third reading stage of both on 4 March. Pitt rose to oppose the former measure, and when Bedfordite Rigby said that it would be of no value if repeal passed there suddenly appeared the prospect of, in ministerial eyes, an unholy alliance against the Declaratory Bill of Pitt's friends with the Bedford and Grenville parties. That possibility was deliberately killed by Pitt when he moved to omit the words 'in all cases whatsoever'. Grenville at once said that he could not support this, and Dowdeswell consolidated Bedfordite-Grenvillite support for the Declaratory Bill by saying that it was essential to show the colonists that Parliament had not surrendered the right of taxation. Pitt's amendment was rejected without a vote. He made a second long speech that day on the Repeal Bill, extravagantly declaring that he was more proud of his part in securing that measure than in obtaining victory in the Seven Years War. Grenville defied a noisy House to justify the Stamp Act, but the Repeal Bill was passed before midnight by 250 votes to 122.[59]

The House of Lords, always more hardline on America than the Commons, had long been seen by the ministry as an obstacle to surmount, and the King's recent behaviour had made the situation there worse. His known personal preference for modification and his declaration to Bute that Parliamentarians, even office-holders, could vote as they thought fit had been damaging factors in the Commons. They might well spell defeat in the Lords. Here the ministry adopted different tactics. Rockingham overruled Newcastle in deciding not to summon witnesses, for there were few independent votes to win over. The economic argument was used, but more significant was the case for avoiding a clash between the two Houses of Parliament, with the additional point that defeat of repeal would effectively mean the Lords were usurping the right of taxation from the Commons. Rockingham persuaded George III to put pressure on Lord Northington, hitherto an opponent of repeal, and that proved decisive: the ministry was to carry repeal in the Lords by the conversion of a small group of peers headed by the Lord Chancellor.[60]

The main Lords debate on repeal took place on 11 March. Newcastle and Grafton rehearsed the economic case, while opposition sought to counter the argument that the Lords should avoid a clash with the Commons. Sandwich declared that repeal had 'forced its way through another House by means of that Democratic Interest which this House was constituted to restrain'. Suffolk declared that the Lords constituted 'the hereditary Council of this kingdom, not subject to the caprice of interested electors'. This blatant appeal to the *esprit de corps* of peers was checked by the key speech of Northington. That he was known to hold hardline opinions, and he voiced them again first, deeming the colonial opposition as equivalent to rebellion, only strengthened his constitutional argument that the Lords should give way to the Commons on finance. The ministry secured a narrow majority of twelve for repeal, 73 to 61, albeit raised to one of 105 to 71 by the addition of proxies. As in the Commons the minority included many of the Court Party, among them the Duke of York, Lord Bute, Lord Talbot, Lord Townshend, and seven Lords of the Bedchamber.[61] On 18 March George III was cheered in the streets of London, a rare experience for him, as he went to give the royal assent to both Bills.[62]

Grenville, on leaving office in July 1765, forecast to George III that the new ministry would seek to overturn his colonial policy.[63] He can hardly then have anticipated repeal of the Stamp Act, but must have been aware that other measures had aroused discontent in Britain and America. The Rockingham party especially prided itself on support of trade, a legacy from Newcastle, and cultivated mercantile connections. During the Stamp Act Crisis the ministry cast a benign eye on requests for the removal and alteration of trade restrictions, even giving West Indian and North American merchants a free hand in devising proposals, the most important of which was the reduction to $1d$ of the $3d$ a gallon duty on foreign molasses imported into North America that had been imposed by Grenville in 1764. Merchant witnesses justified this to the House of Commons, claiming that the British islands could not supply 5 per cent of the molasses needed by the rum distillers of North America, nor consume more than 25 per cent of the fish sent to the West Indies. Unless molasses from foreign islands were purchased, the New England rum industry and fishery would both suffer: that such molasses were currently being smuggled in to solve this problem was passed over in silence. The economic interdependence of the British Empire was demonstrated by evidence that most British exports to North America either were bought with profits from this trade, or directly formed part of it as re-exports.[64]

At the same time there were demands from within Britain for the creation of a free port at Dominica, for the duty-free import of foreign produce. This pressure came especially from Bristol, anxious for more sugar to re-export when refined, and from merchants and manufacturers involved in the nascent cotton industry of Lancashire, for at this time cotton was grown only in the West Indies. Chancellor of the Exchequer Dowdeswell thought the advantage of duty-free cotton imports self-evident, and on 7 April witnesses told the House of Commons that Dominica as a free port could replace the Dutch island of St Eustatius as an international entrepôt for West Indies trade. But just when all seemed to be plain sailing, British West Indies merchants objected to this threat to their trade monopoly; and what rendered

this obstacle formidable was that behind their leader William Beckford loomed William Pitt, by now out of humour with a ministry
increasingly disregardful of him.[65]

Pitt had remained on amicable terms with the Rockingham administration even after his opposition to the Declaratory Bill on 4 March,
finding common ground in the cider tax issue. Three days later
Dowdeswell produced his long-expected Cider Bill, transferring the
tax burden to dealers, while growers and home consumers would pay
nothing. The existing Cider Act, he said, had subjected over 100,000
families to the tax. Pitt, at his own request, seconded him. Eager to
take up a popular cause, Pitt argued that private houses should be safe
from excisemen. Grenville vainly applied the cold water of realism by
pointing out that taxes had to be raised somehow, and said that lenity
to the cider counties was unfair to the beer counties, which paid
£2,900,000 in similar duties. There was no vote then, nor at the short
subsequent debates until the motion to pass the Bill on 18 March,
when it was carried by 145 votes to 48.[66]

It was the hostility of the West India interest that alerted the ministry to the realisation that Pitt was now an enemy. He had been
offended by the increasing independence of the cabinet ministers,
who had long since ceased to press him to join them in office and were
now presuming to formulate policies without consulting him in the
way they had done during the Stamp Act Crisis. Grenvillite James
Harris noted in his diary for 14 April that 'happily for us, Pitt had
quarrelled with his creatures the ministry, and the West Indians with
the North Americans'.[67] Pitt saw the West Indies cause as the first
opportunity to vent his displeasure on the ministry. A cabinet meeting
on 12 April was so dismayed that Rockingham thought that only the
reduction of the molasses duty could now be proposed. It was
Dowdeswell, who, so he told the Commons in 1771, pushed the idea
of a free port in defiance of Pittites and 'King's Friends' alike.[68]

Other business meanwhile intervened. On 18 April Dowdeswell as
Chancellor of the Exchequer produced his budget, which included a
controversial proposal for an extension of the window tax to smaller
houses. Grenville criticised 'making the poor pay for the light of
heaven', when the repeal of the Stamp Act had cost £110,000 in revenue, and the opposition took the unusual step of voting against a tax,
losing then by 162 votes to 112, and again on 21 April by 179 to 114.
Pitt absented himself from this attack on the administration.[69] But he
was to join forces with Grenville when the Rockingham ministry sought
to demonstrate political consistency by a Parliamentary resolution on

general warrants. It was a superfluous gesture, for in 1765 the use of
such warrants had been condemned in the law courts, and in any case a
Commons resolution had no legal validity. On 22 April a motion virtually identical to those defeated in 1764 and 1765 was once again put
forward by Sir William Meredith. George Grenville explained that he
had opposed the motion earlier as improper before any legal decision.
Now he criticised it as too narrow, since condemning the use of the warrants for libel implied their validity in other respects. Pitt agreed with
Grenville on this point, sarcastically welcoming him as 'a good recruit
to liberty'. Since he said Meredith's motion was not now necessary, Pitt
may have been in the minority of 71 voting for a previous question
moved by Grenville, as against a ministerial majority of 173.[70] On 25
April Pitt followed up Grenville's suggestion by a general resolution to
correspond with the legal condemnation of general warrants, and during the debate Grenville was described as co-sponsor. Attorney-General
Charles Yorke weakly concurred, and the resolution was carried without a vote.[71] Grenville also sought to win credit for himself, by proposing on 29 April a Bill to condemn seizing papers by general warrants.
Supported by Pitt, it passed the Commons but was defeated in the
Lords.[72] Edmund Burke suspected an ulterior motive behind this opposition activity: there were also militia debates on 14 and 22 April, and
further opposition to the window tax on 28 and 29 April.[73] All this
Burke thought to be a deliberate tactic by Grenville and Pitt to delay and
thereby prevent further trade regulations.[74]

Although this alliance of Pitt and Grenville might have seemed to
pose the threat of defeat for that ministerial policy in the House of
Commons, Dowdeswell judged the political temperature there better
than his colleagues and his opponents. On 30 April he moved a series
of resolutions, drafted in concert with Charles Townshend, notably
one to reduce the duty on foreign molasses to 1d a gallon, and
another for a free port in the West Indies. Beckford denounced both
ideas as prejudicial to the British islands, and was supported by
Grenville. Pitt favoured the lower molasses duty but not the idea of a
free port, and MPs accepted his compromise proposal that witnesses
called by Beckford should be heard before any decisions were made.[75]
Pitt had shot his bolt. Aware of the mood of the House, he left
London for Bath that same day, on the pretext of ill health, abandoning the West India interest to its fate. Beckford therefore decided to
negotiate the best possible terms, while his witnesses paraded before
the House of Commons as filibuster became farce. The ministry was
resolved to enact the free port plan for Dominica, and obtained the

further concession that molasses from the British islands should also pay the 1*d* duty, in return for the cancellation of an unpopular duty on inter-island sugar trade. This change would add only an estimated £4,000 to the revenue, but would eliminate the fraud of foreign molasses being deemed British at American ports. It finally converted the molasses duty from a trade regulation to a tax, the only productive American tax devised. Concessions to the West Indies interest included stronger protection of the closed British sugar market, for sugar from Dominica and North America were to be deemed foreign. Another was the establishment of Jamaica as a second free port, to legalise the flourishing but hitherto illicit exchange of Spanish bullion for British manufactures, a trade harassed by the Grenville ministry. All these provisions formed part of a wide-ranging agreement signed on 8 May, when the procession of witnesses before the Commons was halted. Appropriate resolutions were voted the same day, for what became the American Duties Act and the Free Ports Act of 1766.[76]

The new-found hostility of Pitt to the Rockingham ministry had not prevented the enactment of its legislative programme, but it was now the key to the political situation. By providing the King with an alternative it would enable George III to dismiss an administration that he increasingly came to regard as incompetent. Pitt's speech of 14 April on the Militia Bill was widely perceived as an attack on the ministry.[77] More significant was one ten days later when he sent a coded message to the King that he would be willing to form a ministry on his own terms. 'Wishes for such a ministry as the King himself should choose', diarist Harris noted him as saying. 'That the people grow weary of our divisions'.[78] This was a hint that Pitt would form a ministry of the most able men in disregard of their political connections, exactly what had been George III's idealistic aim at his accession: Pitt was cleverly pressing the right buttons. The King took due notice, but decided to allow the Rockingham ministry to complete its Parliamentary business and 'hobble out the session'.[79] He also needed time to discover whether Pitt was genuinely willing to form a ministry.[80] Meanwhile the Duke of Grafton responded four days later by intimating to his sovereign and colleagues his decision to resign as Northern Secretary. The Duke had only entered the ministry in the expectation that Pitt would soon take over, and saw no reason to continue in an onerous post that also obliged him, in default of the silent Rockingham, to take the government lead in the Lords.[81] He now told that House that he was resigning because the ministry needed strengthening by Pitt, not because he had quarrelled with his colleagues or objected to measures. Since Pitt would not join the administration, Grafton was sounding its death knell. This was demonstrated by the difficulty found in replacing him. Those who now refused the Northern Secretaryship included Charles Townshend, Lord Egmont, Charles Yorke, and his brother Lord Hardwicke. The vacancy was filled by yet another political novice, the Duke of Richmond, currently ambassador in Paris, who became Southern Secretary on 23 May, for Conway opted to move to the Northern Department and shed his colonial responsibility.[82]

There was one way by which Rockingham might have saved his ministry, recourse to an alliance with the Bute faction; this would not only provide a secure Parliamentary foundation but also have the advantage of pleasing the King. The Marquess always refused to entertain the idea, even after Bute had opened the way by announcing in a Lords speech of 17 March that he would never take office again himself, and urging the ministry to enlarge its base. Grafton's resignation announcement did cause Rockingham to shift his ground slightly and inform his ministerial colleagues that he would be willing to buy an alliance by giving a lucrative post to Bute's brother Stuart Mackenzie. During discussion before and at a cabinet meeting of 1 May Egmont said that such a meagre offer would not suffice. Rockingham replied that anything more would alienate his own friends.[83] It was Rockingham and Newcastle who vetoed any alliance with the Bute party, memories of the early years of the reign having created a psychological barrier in that respect. Richmond noted how 'Lord Rockingham bounced off his seat and the Duke of Newcastle put on his hat to go away' when he revived the idea at a June cabinet, but consciousness of ministerial weakness led Rockingham to hope he might 'buy the Bedfords, that he always reckoned about £8,000 a year would be sufficient to buy most parties'.[84] If such an approach was made, it foundered on a realistic Bedfordite assessment of the poor prospects of the ministry.[85]

During the last few months of his ministry Rockingham behaved towards his sovereign with remarkable insouciance, as if he was either confident that the King had no alternative Premier or entirely indifferent as to his fate. He did nothing to conciliate George III, making demands concerning appointments and dismissals that the King deemed unreasonable; failing to carry out a promise to transfer to his brothers the allowance given to his deceased uncle, Cumberland; and otherwise confirming George III's opinion of his incapacity.[86] Whereas personal antipathy had led the King to dismiss the efficient Grenville, incompetence was the prime motive for the removal of

Rockingham. George III was to tell Bute on 12 July that he had 'suffered greatly from the conduct of my ministers, and my own contempt of their talents'. By May the King had confirmed that Pitt
would be willing to form a ministry: but his earlier promises made
him feel obligated to support the ministry until given 'some handle of
blame to dismiss them'.[87]

The pretext arose from a proposal of the Board of Trade concerning the new colony of Quebec. This recommended the use of English
criminal law, but French civil law in property cases, and altogether
made too many concessions to the French Catholic population for the
taste of ultra-Protestant Lord Chancellor Northington, who sought to
kill the measure by refusing to attend cabinet after 27 June. The ministry nevertheless decided to implement the policy without him, and
Rockingham asked the Lord Chancellor to resign in favour of Charles
Yorke, in accordance with the King's pledge to Yorke a year earlier.[88]
George III saw his opportunity. On 6 July the angry Lord Chancellor,
by pre-arrangement, formally advised the King that the ministry was
too weak to continue. This treachery to his colleagues Grenvillite
James Harris ascribed to Bute's malign influence.[89] Charles Yorke later
simply attributed it to his character, commenting in 1767 on 'the bru-
tality and falsehood of Lord Northington, whom he wondered Ministries had so long endured, who had so often betrayed them'.[90]
George III next day sent to Pitt, and on receipt of his favourable
response informed the Rockingham cabinet on 9 July that they would
be dismissed.[91]

Notes

1 *Lyttelton Memoirs*, II, 683.
2 Langford, *First Rockingham Administration*, pp. 16–20. Hoffman,
   Edmund Burke, p. 466.
3 Thomas, *British Politics and the Stamp Act Crisis*, p. 128.
4 Lawson, *George Grenville*, pp. 220–4.
5 Malmesbury MSS. Photocopies A69.
6 BL Add. MSS. 32967, fos 371–2; 32972, fos 126–33.
7 BL Add. MSS. 32971, fos 177–8, 187–8.
8 Malmesbury MSS. Photocopies B913.
9 Langford, *First Rockingham Administration*, pp. 83–4, 97.
10 BL Add. MSS. 32968, fos 177–8. *Grafton Autobiography*, pp. 83–4.
11 *Corr. of George III*, I, 124–5.
12 BL Add. MSS. 32968, fo. 167.

13 BL Add. MSS. 33078, fo. 75.
14 Roberts, *Macartney in Russia*, pp. 13–33. Scott, *British Foreign Policy*, pp. 95–7.
15 Escott, Thesis, pp. 66–100. Scott, *British Foreign Policy*, pp. 91–5.
16 Powell, Thesis, p. 110.
17 Walpole, *Memoirs*, II, 144–5.
18 Thomas, *British Politics and the Stamp Act Crisis*, pp. 132–6.
19 Thomas, *British Politics and the Stamp Act Crisis*, pp. 137–8. This view is confirmed by Lord Hardwicke's later comment. BL Add. MSS. 35428, fo. 22. For a more literal interpretation, see Langford, *First Rockingham Administration*, pp. 80–2.
20 Thomas, *British Politics and the Stamp Act Crisis*, pp. 138–41.
21 *Bute Letters*, pp. 242–3.
22 Langford, *First Rockingham Administration*, pp. 98–105.
23 *Gage Corr.*, I, 69–70.
24 Langford, *First Rockingham Administration*, pp. 186–8.
25 Thomas, *British Politics and the Stamp Act Crisis*, pp. 142–50.
26 Thomas, *British Politics and the Stamp Act Crisis*, pp. 150–3.
27 *De Berdt Letters*, p. 308.
28 Simmons and Thomas, *Proceedings and Debates*, II, 55–60.
29 *Gage Corr.*, II, 30.
30 BL Add. MSS. 32972, fos 126–33.
31 BL Add. MSS. 35428, fo. 26.
32 *Bute Letters*, p. 242. Langford, *First Rockingham Administration*, pp. 126–32. Thomas, *British Politics and the Stamp Act Crisis*, pp. 160–6.
33 BL Add. MSS. 32972, fo. 251.
34 BL Add. MSS. 32973, fos 55–7, 90–1. Langford, *First Rockingham Administration*, pp. 136–9.
35 Simmons and Thomas, *Proceedings and Debates*, II, 80–92.
36 Quoted, Thomas, *British Politics and the Stamp Act Crisis*, p. 174.
37 Thomas, *British Politics and the Stamp Act Crisis*, pp. 181–4.
38 *Grenville Papers*, III, 353.
39 Thomas, *British Politics and the Stamp Act Crisis*, pp. 185–9.
40 Simmons and Thomas, *Proceedings and Debates*, II, 113–23.
41 Simmons and Thomas, *Proceedings and Debates*, II, 123–33.
42 Quoted, Thomas, *British Politics and the Stamp Act Crisis*, p. 199.
43 Simmons and Thomas, *Proceedings and Debates*, II, 135–51.
44 Simmons and Thomas, *Proceedings and Debates*, II, 151–6, 163–6.
45 Simmons and Thomas, *Proceedings and Debates*, II, 156–63.
46 Thomas, *British Politics and the Stamp Act Crisis*, pp. 205–6.
47 Simmons and Thomas, *Proceedings and Debates*, II, 166–76.

48 Walpole, *Memoirs*, II, 204.
49 BL Add. MSS. 32974, fos 167–8.
50 Simmons and Thomas, *Proceedings and Debates*, II, 177.
51 Thomas, *British Politics and the Stamp Act Crisis*, pp. 209–13.
52 For this evidence see Simmons and Thomas, *Proceedings and Debates*, II, 183–251.
53 Quoted in Thomas, *British Politics and the Stamp Act Crisis*, p. 221.
54 Simmons and Thomas, *Proceedings and Debates*, II, 264–77.
55 Simmons and Thomas, *Proceedings and Debates*, II, 264–77.
56 BL Add. MSS. 33001, fos 200–1.
57 BL Add. MSS. 32974, fo. 245.
58 Walpole, *Memoirs*, II, 212. Shelton, *English Hunger and Industrial Disorders*, pp. 24–9. Williams, Thesis, *passim*. Thomas, *British Politics and the Stamp Act Crisis*, pp. 248–9.
59 Simmons and Thomas, *Proceedings and Debates*, II, 311–16. Thomas, *British Politics and the Stamp Act Crisis*, pp. 239–41.
60 Langford, *First Rockingham Administration*, pp. 193–4.
61 Simmons and Thomas, *Proceedings and Debates*, II, 335–46.
62 *London Evening Post*, 18 Mar. 1766.
63 *Grenville Papers*, III, 215–16.
64 Simmons and Thomas, *Proceedings and Debates*, II, 359–65, 571–4.
65 Simmons and Thomas, *Proceedings and Debates*, II, 575–9. Thomas, *British Politics and the Stamp Act Crisis*, pp. 259–60.
66 Malmesbury MSS. Harris Diary, 7, 11, 17, 18 Mar. 1766.
67 Malmesbury MSS. Harris Diary, 14 Apr. 1766.
68 *Burke Corr.*, I, 251–2. BL Add. MSS. 32974, fos 348–9, 370–1. Walpole, *Memoirs*, IV, 209–10.
69 Malmesbury MSS. Harris Diary, 18, 21 Apr. 1766.
70 Malmesbury MSS. Harris Diary, 22 Apr. 1766.
71 Malmesbury MSS. Harris Diary, *sub* 26 Apr. 1766.
72 BL Add. MSS. 32975, fo. 49. Malmesbury MSS. Harris Diary, 29 Apr., 2, 5, 9, 12, 13, 14 May 1766.
73 BL Add. MSS. 32975, fos 35, 52–3. Malmesbury MSS. Harris Diary, 14, 22, 28, 29 Apr. 1766.
74 *Burke Corr.*, I, 252.
75 Simmons and Thomas, *Proceedings and Debates*, II, 376–8.
76 Thomas, *British Politics and the Stamp Act Crisis*, pp. 254–6, 267–73.
77 BL Add. MSS. 47584, fos 42–3.
78 Malmesbury MSS. Harris Diary, *sub* 23 Apr. 1766.
79 *Bute Letters*, p. 247. *Corr. of George III*, I, 301.
80 *Bute Letters*, pp. 250–1.

81 *Bute Letters*, p. 246. *Grafton Autobiography*, p. 73. *Rockingham Memoirs*, I, 333.
82 *Chesterfield Letters*, VI, 2,742. Langford, *First Rockingham Administration*, pp. 221–4.
83 *Corr. of George III*, I, 297–301.
84 Olson, *EHR*, 75 (1960), pp. 477–8.
85 Walpole, *Memoirs*, II, 222–3.
86 Langford, *First Rockingham Administration*, pp. 236–52.
86 *Bute Letters*, pp. 250–1.
87 BL Add. MSS. 47584, fos 52–3.
89 Malmesbury MSS. Photocopies B828.
90 Malmesbury MSS. Photocopies B883. Northington was in the cabinet from 1761–67, serving in the first five ministries of the reign.
91 Langford, *First Rockingham Administration*, pp. 252–8.

7

The Chatham ministry I. The year of Charles Townshend (1766–1767): India and America

On 7 July 1766 George III summoned William Pitt to form a ministry in accordance with 'the opinion you gave on that subject in Parliament a few days before you set out for Somersetshire'.[1] On that occasion, 24 April, diarist James Harris recorded Pitt as wishing for 'such a ministry at the King himself should choose, the people approve, and who should be eminent above others for their ability and integrity. That the people grow weary of our divisions'.[2] The King had noted this signal, expressing an opinion, so he now told Pitt, 'entirely … consonant' with his own 'ideas concerning the basis on which a new administration should be erected'.[3] And he soon ascertained from Camden, through Northington, that Pitt was 'ready to come if called upon, that he meant to try and form an administration of the best of all party's [sic] and an exclusion to no descriptions'.[4] Pitt's ministry has therefore traditionally been depicted as a famous experiment in non-party government. It was nothing of the kind. No meaningful offer was made to the Bedfordite group, and none at all to Grenville. Pitt at first merely sought to construct a ministry from an alliance of his own small band of followers with some Bute men and a rump of Rockinghamites. That arrangement was one of the two alternative possibilities envisaged by political observers. The other would have been a ministry based on Pitt's brothers-in-law Lord Temple and George Grenville, together with the Bedford party, an arrangement that would in some opinions have led to a more efficient ministry than the one Pitt created. That was not a practical idea, for, quite apart from policy differences, it depended on Grenville's willingness to serve as a mere Chancellor of the Exchequer: he had refused to do so earlier under Bute, and would never now accept such a demotion.[5]

Far from being a successful attack on the 'factions', the new ministry was soon opposed by all three of them, and ironically the only political group that dissolved was the one to which George III would not have affixed such a stigma, that hitherto owing allegiance to Bute. Pitt did what Rockingham had refused to do, pleasing the King by concessions to Bute's friends. He restored Bute's brother Stuart Mackenzie to his post as Lord Privy Seal of Scotland, and obtained a Dukedom for the Earl of Northumberland, father-in-law of one of Bute's daughters. By the end of the year other men associated with Bute had returned to the government fold: Charles Jenkinson was at the Admiralty Board; Robert Nugent President of the Board of Trade; and Hans Stanley both ambassador designate to Russia and Cofferer of the Household. Pitt approached such men directly without consulting Bute, whose quarrel with George III over this issue in August 1766 ended his political career. Those personally associated with him merged into the general body of the Court Party, and 'the King's Friends', though surviving as a myth in the minds of George III's critics, ceased to exist as a political entity.[6]

Arrangements for the new ministry were not completed until the end of July.[7] After Temple, unwilling to be a figurehead, had as expected refused the Treasury, Pitt insisted that the thirty-year-old Grafton should take that post, and then bullied Charles Townshend into being Chancellor of the Exchequer.[8] Camden became Lord Chancellor, with Northington moving to be Lord President. Shelburne was the new Southern Secretary, but Conway remained as Northern Secretary, and also as Commons Leader: for Pitt revealed that he was taking a peerage, as Earl of Chatham, and the non-executive post of Lord Privy Seal. This he did on 30 July, when Grafton, Camden and Townshend formally took office: soon afterwards Lord Granby joined the cabinet as army Commander-in-Chief. Grenvillite Harris cynically noted that 'Pitt, having by this arrangement a cabinet place void of business, interferes in measures just as far as he pleases, while both the responsibility of office, and the drudgery of it fall totally upon others'.[9]

Pitt's decision to take a peerage baffled contemporaries, for he thereby forfeited both popularity and his power base in the House of Commons. Lord Villiers noted in his diary for 30 July. 'Much discontent in general, and particularly in the City, upon Mr Pitt's peerage, and a great deal of abuse in the public papers upon him'.[10] His nickname was the obvious one of 'Lord Cheat-em'. Fellow politicians deemed foolish his retirement from the Commons. Lord North commented to his father, 'I should have thought administration more steady with him in the House of Commons'.[11] That old political hand

Lord Chesterfield was puzzled by Pitt's decision 'to withdraw in the fullness of his power, ... from the House of Commons (which procured him his power, and which alone could insure it to him) and to go into that Hospital of Incurables, the House of Lords'.[12] Historians have generally echoed this contemporary opinion, but a recent biographer has argued that the peerage was not the blunder it seemed, since his power as Prime Minister came from the Crown rather than the Commons.[13] That opinion retains validity only while he was in office. Return to opposition was to show that he was indeed the shorn Samson Choiseul thought on news of the peerage.[14] The shrewd Chesterfield lighted on the most immediate consequence. 'Charles Townshend has now the sole management of the House of Commons; but how long he will be content to be only Lord Chatham's vice-regent there, is a question which I will not pretend to decide.'[15]

Pitt, lacking sufficient followers to form an administration, but also because of the principles he had laid down, was disposed to retain those office-holders who wished to stay. This chimed in with the Rockinghamite attitude, as Lord Villiers noted. 'It seems to be the plan of those in the late Administration who disapproved of this change, to remain in their places unless turned out, but not to accept others nor to give any assurances of support.'[16] Rockingham and Newcastle obviously had to go, and not only because their offices were needed. Their dismissal was an essential public demonstration that the old Whig corps, in power since the days of Sir Robert Walpole and Henry Pelham, was now out of favour. Others left whom Chatham wished to retain. Charles Yorke resigned as Attorney-General on 28 July, incensed by news of Camden's appointment to the post of Lord Chancellor he himself had been promised the previous year. Dartmouth resigned on 30 July, after refusal of his request to have his post as President of the Board of Trade upgraded to cabinet rank as a Secretaryship of State for the Colonies. When Dowdeswell refused it Hillsborough returned to the office he had held under Grenville, albeit briefly.

A more important vacancy occurred on 13 August, when Lord Egmont resigned the Admiralty, being annoyed at Chatham's dictatorial attitude and critical of his proposed foreign policy.[17] Grafton's confidant Lord Villiers noted that on this resignation 'it becomes necessary for the Ministry to call in a new set of men, not as a party, but only to enlarge the foundation. Which this set should be is under consideration'.[18] Grafton suggested the Duke of Bedford should be sounded, and saw his son the Marquess of Tavistock on 15 August, to offer the Admiralty to Lord Gower. Lord Tavistock asked 'whether this was the full extent of the proposal to be made to me', so Bedford reported to Gower, 'or whether my other friends were likewise to be considered. The reply was that this was the only offer to be made at present, but that Lord Chatham's idea was a great and conciliatory plan, but not to turn out those, who should be willing to act with the present administration, but that time was requisite to bring it about.'[19] Bedford left the decision to Gower, who refused the post on 20 August, 'saying he should be quite *isolé* if he was the only man of his Party to take so responsible a post'.[20] This refusal of the Bedfordites to come into office except as a group was an early omen of the failure of Chatham's attack on party. The Admiralty was meanwhile given to one of Chatham's favourite admirals, Rockinghamite Sir Charles Saunders, promoted from within the Board.

The attitude of Rockingham and Newcastle to this ministerial arrangement was ambivalent and unrealistic. It stemmed from the concept of a Whig party in which Chatham was just another leader, whom they would keep under control by surrounding him with their friends. 'We think ourselves perfectly safe in your hands and the Duke of Grafton's', Newcastle wrote to Conway on 29 July.[21] Yet the first allegiance of both these men was to Chatham. Resignations were accordingly discouraged, Newcastle noting on 24 July that 'the remaining of our friends in employment, is the surest way to support the party, and the cause'.[22] Rockingham was irate when Lord John Cavendish resigned from the Treasury Board.[23] This bizarre political strategy survived even a personal quarrel. Pitt totally ignored Rockingham when constructing his ministry, a snub so marked that Conway persuaded him to visit the Marquess on 27 July, only for Rockingham to refuse to see him.[24] The disinclination of Rockingham and Newcastle to oppose Chatham was surrendering to him, not surrounding him. The outcome might well have been the disintegration of their own following into a rump, while Chatham emerged as leader of a Whig and Court Party entrenched in power, if he had not thrown down the gauntlet three months later.

'Measures not men' had always been Chatham's political maxim, and his ministry was not only a supposed experiment in non-party government but also a launching pad for policy initiatives. Moves for closer control by Britain over America, India and Ireland can be construed as a grand imperial design, and in European diplomacy Chatham pursued his own ideas. All of this was to be almost as much a failure as his 'attack on party' within Britain.

As befitting his past career, it was foreign policy to which Chatham gave priority, with an early initiative to achieve his favourite project of a northern alliance. The concept was impractical. Northern Secretary Conway echoed the fear of George III the previous year that news of it would alienate Austria: and Chatham's idea of sending Hans Stanley as a special envoy, first to Berlin and then to St Petersburg, was the wrong way round to go about the negotiation.[25] Chatham's overweening self-confidence brushed aside all doubts and difficulties, whereas his return to office made Frederick II even more wary of being involved in an Anglo-French war by the defensive alliance on offer. In two interviews with the British ambassador to Berlin, Sir Andrew Mitchell, he made his hostility to the idea so clear that by the end of 1766 the British cabinet accepted the futility of any such approach, Mitchell's advice being that only a prior Anglo-Russian treaty might cause Frederick to change his mind. Chatham's health had by then collapsed, and nothing more was heard of that diplomatic initiative.[26] The whole scheme, moreover, was counter-productive in its consequence for the Anglo-Russian relationship. Offence was given to Russia by both the initial approach to Prussia and a subsequent failure to inform Russian minister Panin until April 1767 that Stanley's journey had been cancelled. There was in any case no prospect of an alliance, for Panin had bluntly told British ambassador Macartney that 'we wanted Russia more than Russia could ever want us'.[27]

Confrontation with the Bourbon Powers of France and Spain was the motive behind this search for allies, and Chatham never lost sight of that seemingly perennial circumstance. At this very time another ground for dispute arose from the establishment in 1766 of a British settlement in the Falkland Islands, envisaged by Lord Egmont at the Admiralty as a base for Pacific trade, and named after him. This idea had been approved by the Rockingham ministry, seeking to follow up Grenville's browbeating of the Bourbon Powers. Two years earlier France had established a base in an island group named Les Malouines. Spain promptly protested that the 1713 Treaty of Utrecht gave her a monopoly of settlement in the South Atlantic, and Choiseul agreed to cede to his ally the settlement in what Spain renamed the Malvinas Islands. Realisation gradually dawned in Europe that this was the same group as the Falklands. Britain did not accept the Spanish claim to all uninhabited islands, and Choiseul, afraid that Chatham would seize any pretext for a war, told Spanish Minister Grimaldi that France would not be able to fight for another three years. But Chatham, belying his imperial reputation, was disposed to accept a French proposal to link the two Anglo-Spanish disputes over the Manila Ransom and the Falkland Islands. That policy was agreed at a cabinet meeting of 15 November 1766, Egmont having already resigned over this and other issues. Southern Secretary Shelburne pursued the idea throughout 1767, for payment of the Manila Ransom would bring, he thought, enough diplomatic prestige to outweigh any concession over Port Egmont. But no firm financial offer was made by Spain, and concern with India and America pushed the issue lower down the ministerial agenda. Only the threat of war would cause Spain to pay up, and by October 1767 the Bourbon Powers were convinced that Britain's imperial problems and ministerial weakness precluded any such possibility. In February 1768 Spain finally disclaimed any responsibility, and no compensation was ever to be made for the Manila Ransom.[28] Spain had been playing for time, intending to locate and seize Port Egmont: on 25 February 1768 Governor Bucareli of Buenos Ayres was instructed to expel any British settlement there without further orders. A Falkland Islands crisis was postponed only by Spanish failure to find the British base before this dispute was in 1768 temporarily overshadowed on the international scene by the Corsica question and the outbreak of a Russo-Turkish war.[29]

The failure of British foreign policy during the Chatham ministry can be ascribed to internal factors as well as the unfavourable international scene, the distractions of party politics at home and the need to devise measures for India and America. Yet when the new Parliamentary session began in November, only one of the three political groups out of office intended to oppose the ministry. The ambiguity of the Rockinghamite position, with many supposed adherents still in post, was reflected by their large-scale attendance at the pre-sessional meetings of administration supporters.[30] And in October the Duke of Bedford was deep in negotiations with Chatham. On 24 October, after preliminary soundings by Northington, Chatham visited the Duke 'to express his desire, that I and my friends would take hands with administration', so Bedford noted in his diary. Chatham soft-soaped Bedford over policy, stating his wish for peace in Europe: declaring he was against 'foreign alliances', but with a possible qualification over Russia; and even promising 'that measures for the proper subordination of America must be taken'. Bedford stolidly replied that he would adhere to measures adopted in office and supported in opposition, evidently meaning a tough line on America, but he stated that 'we did not desire opposition'. At a second meeting on 31 October, after Gower, Weymouth and Rigby had approved

Bedford's stance, Chatham clarified his colonial policy by saying he should not be understood 'to intend any violent measures towards the Americans at this time'. When Bedford raised the, to him, key question of posts for his friends, Chatham regretted that there were hardly any vacancies, repeating what he had told the Duke in August: 'the King having determined on a conciliatory plan, those who would continue and act with them should not be removed'. The only offer Chatham made was that Weymouth could be Joint Postmaster, with later prospects of office for Gower and Rigby. The next day the Bedford group unanimously rejected this proposal as inadequate, but 'we parted on good terms', so thought the Duke.[31] In Parliament the Bedfordites adopted a stance of watchful neutrality, having, as Horace Walpole put it, 'openly advertised themselves for sale'.[32]

When Parliament met on 11 November only the Grenville faction was openly in opposition, at a time when there was a strong constitutional case to argue against the ministry, arising out of the government reaction to widespread food riots of 1766. The Rockinghamite legislation of February prohibiting the export of corn had expired on 26 August. The harvest was again poor, some 20 per cent below average, but much worse in Europe, and large-scale exports thence of corn began. News of this led to disturbances at over a hundred places in central and southern England, caused by the hardship of high prices and the fear of starvation.[33] George III was much concerned about both this 'licentiousness' and the distress of his people. He and Chatham favoured an export embargo, and that was agreed unanimously by the Privy Council on 24 September, a Royal Proclamation being issued on 26 September prohibiting corn exports until three days after the meeting of Parliament.[34] This action, taken under the royal prerogative, met with general approval, earning the King some popularity and producing an abatement of the disturbances: even though prices did not fall, there was no longer a sense of public alarm and indignation. But the first provision of the Bill of Rights in 1689 had declared that 'suspending of laws, or the execution of laws, by royal authority, … is illegal'. Lord Chancellor Camden had used the argument of necessity, '*salus populi suprema lex*'; but there remained an obvious question mark over its legality. Some merchants initiated prosecutions of custom officials who prevented corn exports, while Grenville's opinion was that Parliament should have been recalled to take action.[35]

On 11 November the ministry obtained Parliamentary consent to extend the embargo, pending the appropriate legislation, which

passed by 27 November.[36] But its previous legality was debated in
both Houses of Parliament after the King's Speech stated that 'necessity' had caused him 'to exert my royal authority for the preservation
of public safety'. In the Lords Chatham, making his first speech as a
peer, conceded that the Proclamation was 'not strictly speaking legal',
but argued that it would also have been illegal, and a dangerous precedent, to summon Parliament before the date to which it had been pro-
rogued. Such a decision, too, would have greatly inconvenienced
peers and MPs, and also have removed them from their roles of magistrates and Lord-Lieutenants in the suppression of local disorders.[37]
Grenvillites Temple and Suffolk cut through these specious arguments
by asserting that an indemnity was needed for those who had advised
the Proclamation, the legality of which was queried by both Bedford
and Rockinghamite Richmond: but none of these peers forced a vote.
The key speech was made by the most respected lawyer of the age,
Lord Chief Justice Mansfield, whom Grafton dubbed 'neutral' in his
report to the King. Mansfield declined to comment on the legality of
the proclamation, since relevant court cases might come before him
in a judicial capacity. But he did put forward a significant line of argument that would get the ministry off the hook: that the law was
broader than statute law, and the King had a right to act under common law. His suggestion was therefore an Indemnity Bill to cover officials who had acted under the Proclamation, but not the members of
the Privy Council who had advised it.[38] In the Commons Grenville
also suggested an Indemnity Bill, but did not force a vote after Rigby
told him the Bedfordites would be neutral.[39]

   Public opinion accepted that the delay necessary to call Parliament
would have increased the prospect of disorder and starvation, but
there existed a general view that the ministry had broken the law. In
a neat correction of historical legend, such reputed King's Friends as
Sir Gilbert Elliot and Jeremiah Dyson were critical of 'the tyrannical
principles of Lord Chatham and Lord Camden'.[40] On 18 November
Conway moved for the Indemnity Bill suggested by Mansfield, one to
cover all administrative action taken under the Proclamation.
Grenville argued that it should be extended to the advisers in the
Privy Council, the implication being that ministers had been guilty of
breaking the law. An angry Beckford rashly claimed that the King had
a suspending power in times of necessity, but Grenville forced him to
recant by a motion declaring such opinions, contrary to the Bill of
Rights, to be unconstitutional. Temple afterwards congratulated his
brother on his triumph 'not only over the wild alderman, but in him

over the whole crew of new converts to tyranny and despotism'.[41] The
lustre of Chatham and Camden as champions of liberty had been tar-
nished by the episode. Grenville won his argument, for when Conway
introduced the Indemnity Bill on 24 November it covered responsibility for the Privy Council decision, and to Grenville's applause he
disclaimed Camden's doctrine of necessity.[42]

Before this legislation could pass, there was a significant reconfig-
uration of the political map in Parliament. Chatham provoked the
Rockingham party into opposition, and for no very good reason. In
order to fulfil a promise of the post to MP John Shelley, on 17
November he dismissed from the court office of Treasurer of the
Chamber Rockinghamite Lord Edgcumbe, a Cornish borough mag-
nate. According to journalist John Almon, when Edgcumbe told
Chatham that it was 'impolitic to turn out persons of rank, persons of
great Parliamentary interest, Chatham replied, "I despise your Parliamentary interest ... I dare look in the face the proudest connections
in the country".'[43] The Pittite antipathy to aristocracy was marked in
both father and son when Premiers.

The Rockinghamite leadership perceived an intention of Chatham
to remove their friends from office one by one. 'It appeared to everybody', wrote Edmund Burke, 'that Lord Chatham had resolved the
ruin of the party.'[44] A meeting on 19 November decided to pre-empt
this tactic by a campaign of resignations, intended especially to
embarrass Conway into following suit and thereby force Chatham
into meaningful political negotiation. Four peers, headed by the Duke
of Portland, would lead the way, with an anticipated effect on the
Commons. Newcastle, remembering 1762, did not believe the tactic
would work, and he was right. Only three MPs resigned, all at the
Admiralty Board, the First Lord Sir Charles Saunders among them.
The other supposed followers of Rockingham, headed by Conway
himself, retained their posts. The Rockingham party therefore now
lost most of its careerist element, including the Onslow cousins and
others of Newcastle's young friends who had been so active in the
opposition of 1762 to 1765. Newcastle listed as friends staying in
office Lord Ashburnham and 26 MPs.[45] The loss of Conway and
Charles Townshend was a grievous blow, and much of the next year
saw unsuccessful Rockinghamite attempts to win them over: for, as
Burke wrote on 28 March 1767, 'we have no leader but Dowdeswell,
who though by far the best man of business in the Kingdom, and
ready and efficient in debate, is not perhaps quite strenuous and pug-
nacious enough for that purpose'.[46] Nevertheless the die was now cast,

and on 25 November the Rockingham group voted for the first time against the administration, embarking on a period of opposition that was to last until 1782.[47] This development finally destroyed the concept of a Whig party embracing both Newcastle's friends and Pitt that had confused political tactics earlier in the decade. By the end of 1766 the Rockinghamites and Chathamites were as distinctly separate parties from each other as from the Bedford and Grenville factions.

The Rockingham party in opposition differed significantly from that which had taken office in 1765. The second haemorrhage of careerists, those who had remained with Newcastle in the first split of 1762, divided equally the active members of the former Wildman's Club between the Chatham ministry and the Rockinghamite opposition. The basic structure of the Rockingham party was not unlike that of the Bedford group, centred on a small band of influential peers, with their relatives and clients: Rockingham, Portland, Albemarle, Newcastle, together with the Cavendish and Yorke families. But there was an added dimension. Like other Premiers Rockingham had gained friends in office, the Duke of Richmond, George Dempster and Frederick Montagu among them, together with a few of Tory ancestry, notably William Dowdeswell. The shift of membership from office-seekers to independents, and the lack of interest of some leaders in acquiring office, has led some historians to perceive the Rockingham group as purified into a new country party.[48]

Earlier popular expectations of a large-scale Rockinghamite defection had been matched by assumptions that any vacancies would be filled by the Bedford party. Chatham made the expected move on 27 November, but his offer was hardly better than in October, three posts of no political weight, even though the Rockinghamite resignations had now vacated seven places, including the cabinet post of the Admiralty. Bedford demanded better terms, but at a final interview on 2 December Chatham told the Duke 'the King would agree to no more … upon which all further negotiation broke off'.[49] Rumour had it that George III, remembering Bedford's behaviour in the Grenville ministry, had himself opposed any offer to the Duke, and that Chatham, in contrast to his behaviour in October, had deliberately chosen to emphasise their policy differences by condemning the peace terms negotiated by Bedford and announcing his plan for a Prussian alliance.[50] Rebuffed in this manner, the Bedford party followed that of Rockingham into opposition.

The Admiralty was destined for another admiral, Sir Edward Hawke, a long-standing courtier, while the other posts were mostly filled by men, like Charles Jenkinson, associated with Bute, consolidating that erstwhile group into the government fold. On 13 December Secretary at War Lord Barrington reported the whole episode to his friend Francis Bernard, Governor of Massachusetts.

> It seems to me on the whole that there was both passion and faction in the resignations. The Minister (who declares himself the strenuous opposer of faction) would willingly have brought in several of the Duke of Bedford's friends as individuals, but they wanted to come in as a body, which was not permitted. The vacant offices have been given partly to old servants of the Crown displaced by different administrations, and partly to men who take employment by themselves.[51]

The first consequence of the changed political situation in Parliament came on 5 December in Committee on the Indemnity Bill. Members of all three opposition factions, Grenville, Rigby and Burke, sought to harass the ministry by seeking compensation for the losses suffered by those who had obeyed the Proclamation. But that subject was one that embarrassed the Rockinghamites because of their previous support of the decision, as by Newcastle at the Privy Council of 24 September.[52] Dowdeswell therefore only said he would support the motion unless 'some *person* on the Treasury Bench' gave an assurance that compensation would be paid. Conway did so, apparently on cue, for Rockingham thought that 'this was well contrived', and Grenville did not then force a vote.[53] Rigby and Grenvillite lawyer Alexander Wedderburn nevertheless did so on an adjournment motion, when the Rockinghamites either abstained or voted with the ministry, which won by 166 to 48.[54]

At this point Chatham, physically ill and unhappy at his failure to construct a ministry as he wished, quitted the political scene. He left London for Somerset in December 1766, and even when he returned to London in March 1767 remained long confined to his house.[55] There existed the power vacuum of a ministry lacking guidance from its head and afraid of acting without knowing his opinion. The initiative was seized by the most junior member of the cabinet, who only late in 1766 had established his right as Chancellor of the Exchequer to attend. Charles Townshend's hour had come.

In 1767 this weakened ministry faced a formidable opposition, as the three factions of Rockingham, Grenville and Bedford found common ground on India and even America. India was the foremost policy issue. By 1766 the wealth and territory of the East India Company made it a focus of government attention, public concern, and private interest. Lord Clive, dispatched to India on news of a war there, arrived in 1765 to find that the Company had already defeated the combined forces of the disaffected Nawab of Bengal and the Mughal Emperor himself.[56] But it was Clive who negotiated the political settlement of August 1765. This acknowledged the nominal authority of the Emperor, who then granted to the Company the *diwani* of Bengal, Bihar, and Orissa. That was a virtual transfer of sovereignty, for it comprised the right to collect and retain the territorial revenue of those provinces in return for undertaking their military defence, while a new Nawab would supervise the civil administration. The Company, so Clive was to inform the House of Commons in 1769, thereby became effective sovereign of a territory larger than France and Spain combined, with a population of 20 million, an army of 50,000 men, and a gross income of £4 million, that clear of expenses was expected to yield half that amount for remittance to Britain.[57]

News that the Company could now expect a net territorial revenue of £2 million in addition to normal trading profits reached Britain early in 1766, and led to a rush to buy India stock, the price rising from 165 on 19 April to 210 on 10 September.[58] Speculators perceived that a price rise could be maintained by an increase in the dividend, which was raised from 6 per cent to 10 per cent at the September General Court of Proprietors.[59] That was a foolishly provocative move, for the ministry had already informed the Company that Parliament would take India into consideration next session.[60] The cabinet unanimously believed that the state should take a part of the Indian revenue, but was divided as to whether the Company had a right to its territory. Conway and Townshend thought so, as against the opinion of Chatham and Grafton that such a situation was 'preposterous'.[61] Chatham, with his two leading Commons spokesmen hostile to his idea that Parliament should declare that the Indian territory belonged to the Crown, entrusted the management of the Parliamentary campaign to William Beckford, who for the last decade had led an attack on the Company's Asian trade monopoly. On 25 November Beckford moved for a Committee to inquire into the state of the Company. His aggressive posture produced such a hostile reaction that Edmund Burke wrote that 'never ministry made a more shameful figure. They were beat about like footballs'. Burke opened the attack, and Charles Yorke also championed the Company's right. There was a formidable barrage of speakers against the motion: lawyer Edward Thurlow and Richard Rigby from the Bedfords; George Grenville and Alexander Wedderburn, taking their cue from

Lord Clive; and William Dowdeswell and Lord John Cavendish among other Rockinghams. Isaac Barré and, despite their own opinions, Charles Townshend and Henry Conway spoke for an inquiry. Observer Henry Flood, renowned for his eloquence in the Dublin Parliament, paid this tribute to Townshend. 'He is the orator; the rest are speakers.' Although the opposition thought they won the debate, the motion was carried by 129 votes to 76.[62]

The ministry, to avoid internal discord, decided to move only for papers and not witnesses, and Beckford's motion on 9 December was seconded by Grafton's brother Charles Fitzroy to lend it ministerial respectability. Beckford declared that the Company revenues should be used to national advantage, and Barré claimed that they belonged to the Crown. When Townshend, closeted beforehand by Grafton, spoke strongly for the motion Edmund Burke taunted ministers for their subservience to Chatham, but failed to detach Conway even though his former mentors Newcastle and Rockingham were known to be against an inquiry. After the ministry defeated an adjournment motion by 140 votes to 56, the date of 22 January 1767 was fixed for the Committee.[63]

By then Chatham's absence had changed the political climate. Deliberately defying what he knew to be Chatham's wishes, Charles Townshend conducted negotiations with the Company and repeatedly postponed the Commons Committee of Inquiry, until 6 March. Grafton bemoaned the lack of Chatham's leadership, and warned the Company Directorate that landowners were well aware that the Company's estimated territorial revenues were equivalent to the entire burden of the four-shilling land tax, a hint of what the Commons attitude might be. Meanwhile both ministry and Directors anticipated with foreboding the behaviour of the selfish and irresponsible Court of Proprietors, an unpredictable factor in the situation. During early 1767 the disunity of the ministry was becoming public, and Beckford urged Chatham to return to London and take charge.[64] But the great man proved unhelpful, replying from Bath on 9 February to a request to comment on Company proposals that 'Parliament is the only place where I will declare my final judgement upon the whole matter', behaviour perhaps proper in 1766 when he had been consulted by the Rockingham administration on America, but hardly appropriate for the head of a ministry in desperate need of guidance.[65]

The Company Directorate asked for a fifty-year guarantee of its trade monopoly and territory. In return it would pay £500,000 within a year, and, after deductions for civil and military costs and an unspecified dividend, share its future income with the state, merging trade profits and territorial revenue. The cabinet thought this too vague, but a request for clarification produced only a stronger emphasis on the territorial claim.[66] Matters were at an impasse when Chatham finally returned to London on 2 March; but he still declined to give an opinion, or even to attend the cabinet next day. That meeting deemed the Company proposals unacceptable, by a majority of six to two, Conway and Townshend, who thereupon refused to conduct the India business in the Commons on the due date of 6 March.[67] Immediately afterwards, on 4 March, Chatham vainly tried to persuade Lord North to replace Townshend at the Exchequer, a move long anticipated by Lord Chesterfield. 'Charles Townshend has talked of him, and at him, in such a manner that henceforward they must be either much worse or much better together.'[68] This failure, soon public knowledge, served to strengthen Townshend's position: he was to have his way over India, and lead on America.

By this time the administration had suffered a severe battering in Parliament from combined assaults by the three opposition factions, even though Grenville and Rockingham were so inhibited from embarking on deliberate attacks that they had to convince themselves it was the correct course of action. Grenville professed to shun opposition for its own sake, commenting to his confidant James Harris on 30 January that, although George III had been induced to believe the contrary of Bedford and himself, 'he wished not to put himself at the head of a Party, nor to force himself on the King'. But he was concerned about 'the East India affair [and] the state of America'.[69] Rockingham had likewise explained to Newcastle that he would go into opposition 'upon such points only, as were wrong in themselves, and not inconsistent with our former behaviour, in the last opposition'. Specifically he would defend the American policy of his own ministry, and oppose the inquiry into the East India Company.[70] But the Marquess at this time certainly had the intention of regaining office. His aim, however, was to form a ministry by detaching Conway and Townshend from their current affiliation, not to construct a coalition with Grenville and Bedford. Rockingham was aware that in the event of a ministerial change he and Grenville would be rivals for the Treasury. Another barrier to an opposition alliance was America, though Bedford did not harp on that topic in the way Grenville did, and he was not a rival for power. Cooperation between their factions was made easier early in 1767 by the circumstance that India rather than America was the chief subject of Parliamentary attention, for they could unite in defence of the East India Company.

America was nevertheless the first major topic of debate in 1767. It is now evident that Charles Townshend's famous promise of American taxation in the Commons debate of 26 January on the army estimates was not, as was long assumed by historians, an irresponsible whim by the Chancellor of the Exchequer. Rather was it an indiscreet revelation of ministerial thinking. Chatham's conduct during the Stamp Act Crisis had given him a reputation of being the champion of American liberty that was somewhat undeserved. Even then he had declared support for firm measures if conciliation failed to produce quiet in the colonies, and he had given a similar assurance to Bedford in their abortive negotiation of October 1766. Chatham's concept of the British Empire embraced the American colonies in an essential but certainly subordinate role, and Chathamite reaction to the ongoing defiance of the 1765 Mutiny Act by New York and other colonies was to be as stern as Grenville and Bedford could have wished. More pertinent to the current American situation was that Chatham's condemnation of the Stamp Act had concerned only 'internal' taxation. It was therefore no contradiction of this doctrine that his ministry at once began to search for an American revenue. In September 1766 the Chatham administration, with the cost of the American army at about £400,000 a year, initiated two inquiries. One concerned American quit-rents, in the hope of an income from land already or soon to be granted for settlement. The other asked about the official income and expenditure within each colony. Further revenue, as ever, might be derived from an attack on smuggling. In a letter of 11 December to General Gage Southern Secretary Shelburne stated that what the ministry had in mind was 'raising an American Fund to defray American expenses in part or in the whole'.[71]

In the next debate over army costs, on 18 February, Townshend stated that he was thinking of import duties as a source of colonial revenue.[72] Soon afterwards evidence from America showed that existing quit-rents, the alternative idea, yielded a derisorily low income. It was some months before Townshend put his American tax proposals to Parliament, and during that interval he, with cabinet assent, changed the purpose of the tax from meeting army costs to paying civil government expenses in the colonies, intending thereby to free officials there from financial dependence on the assemblies.[73]

Both these Parliamentary declarations of Townshend, on 26 January and 18 February, had been the result of pressure from opposition spokesmen like Grenville. And the opposition now brought off a notable coup to damage the ministry's prestige. That the land tax still remained at the wartime level of four shillings in the pound, or 20 per cent, was a long-standing grievance of the squirearchy, so over-represented in the Commons. It was an issue on which the three opposition groups could launch a united attack, with independent support. The Rockinghamite leadership decided that Dowdeswell should move a reduction of one shilling to forestall Grenville's known intention. This he contrived to do when on 27 February Townshend proposed the usual four shillings, and his amendment was carried by 206 votes to 188. This tactic did not deprive Grenville of credit for the success, his wife's diary recording 'all the country gentlemen coming round Mr Grenville, shaking him by the hand'.[74] The opposition challenge was not a surprise, but earlier 'the calculations were that the Ministry would carry it by about fifty', wrote Lord George Sackville.[75] Grafton and Conway, however, compared with Grenville and Newcastle, were political innocents in the game of organising Parliamentary votes. Grafton explained to Chatham that 'the majority was composed of the gentlemen composing the Cocoa Tree. The Bedfords, Grenvilles, Rockinghams, and Newcastles united with most others, who had county or popular elections'.[76] The last word can be given to Chesterfield, who laconically wrote that 'all the landed gentlemen bribed themselves with this shilling in the pound'.[77]

This triumph stimulated opposition zeal, and Newcastle was back at his old pastime of compiling Parliamentary lists. One of 2 March named altogether 547 MPs: 232 ministerial supporters, 91 Tories, 101 Rockinghamites, 54 adherents of Bedford and Grenville, and 69 MPs noted as doubtful or absent.[78] A Grenvillite calculation, noted by James Harris, assessed the balance of opposition strength rather differently. 'This March 1767 it was supposed the friends of Bedford and Grenville were 90, the Rockinghams 70, the country gentlemen 60', giving a total of 220.[79] The existence of such a calculation implied an intention by Grenville to engage in wholehearted opposition, despite his earlier disclaimer. But the Rockinghamite tactic still centred on detaching Conway and Townshend from the administration, not on a coalition with the other opposition factions; and the India question that now came before Parliament seemed to provide an excellent opportunity to achieve that aim. Not until that hope faded did Rockingham negotiate with Bedford and Grenville for an alliance to defeat the ministry at Westminster.

Chatham, before his two-year withdrawal from public life in March 1767, instructed Shelburne how to conduct the Indian business in Parliament. The land tax defeat showed that it would be risky to raise the question of territorial ownership. Instead there should on 6 March be motions to lay the Directors' proposals before the House of Commons, and to print the Company papers already submitted.[80] That date saw Beckford move these resolutions. Townshend and Conway opposed printing the Company proposals. Hawke and Granby followed this by informing the House that in any case they had been rejected by a cabinet majority, a notable indiscretion even for non-political service ministers. Leading opposition speakers like Grenville and Burke denounced the motions as improper, but no vote was forced.[81] Afterwards Townshend commented that that had been a tactical blunder, since an amendment might have obliged Conway and himself to vote against the ministry. The opposition sought to remedy this mistake by arranging for the Company Directors to submit on 9 March a petition against publication of their papers, since that would reveal information to foreign competitors.[82] Newcastle busied himself in mustering Parliamentary support, in secret, so as 'not to give alarm' to the administration.[83] Although the ministry had only a few hours' warning that something was planned for that day, enough support was mustered to avert another debacle like that on the land tax. Townshend absented himself, avoiding the trap of his own making, but Conway rose to the occasion by proposing a two-day adjournment so that the Directors could specify papers not to be printed. In an able speech he turned on its head the opposition attempt to exploit cabinet disunity by pointing out that such ministerial differences of opinion 'showed that there was no such dictator', obviously Chatham, as had been often claimed in earlier debates. A long debate of nearly thirty speakers, in which Grenville, Rigby, Dowdeswell, and Burke spoke for opposition, and Barré and Lord North for administration, ended in a ministerial victory by 180 votes to 147.[84]

That the ministry could scrape only a narrow win over a conciliatory motion encouraged the opposition to redouble its efforts. 'The House was very full', noted diarist Nathaniel Ryder, when on 11 March the Company officials objected to printing any papers except the charter and treaties already in the public domain. This stand was supported by Townshend and Conway, whose motion to that effect was seconded by Grenville. The administration conceded the point without risking probable defeat, Burke writing afterwards that 'our best numberers thought ... we should beat them'.[85]

It now seemed obvious that no Parliamentary declaration of territorial right in favour of the state would succeed, and that basic tenet of Chatham's policy was abandoned, except by Beckford. The cabinet turned its attention to securing the best financial terms, and the Parliamentary setbacks led to a tactical change of battleground, from Westminster to East India House. Lord Shelburne and his ally Laurence Sulivan moved to centre stage, the aim being to persuade the General Court of Proprietors to offer better terms than the Directorate had done. When on 12 March the Directorate sought General Court approval of their proposals as Company policy, Sulivan warned that uniting trade profits with territorial revenue would effectively hand over control of the Company to the government, and secured permission to put forward his own plan on 16 March. This proposed that the Company should obtain from the territorial revenue payment of all administrative and military costs, together with money sufficient for a 14 per cent dividend. The government would receive the surplus, without any troublesome commitment, together with an immediate cash payment of £800,000. The Company would retain all commercial profits. But on 19 March the scheme was in effect rejected, being referred by 456 votes to 264 to the hostile Directorate.[86] This decision Rockingham welcomed as a 'majority against Shelburne, i.e. Lord Chatham ... This is very good, ... and will be a very unpleasant hearing for the Great Man'.[87] On 2 April the Directorate duly condemned Sulivan's plan, as inviting continuous Parliamentary interference, and then produced an alternative scheme on 6 April. This made no promise of any specific payment to government, merely a share of any surplus revenue, after payment of costs and a dividend that was unspecified but hinted at being 16 per cent. Two days later this scheme was approved by 546 votes to 347 at a General Court, where the Directorate was also re-elected. The ministry had been outbid, as might have been expected, and would have to turn again to Parliament.[88]

Here the Commons Committee of Inquiry read papers for three days and examined witnesses on a further eight days in late March and early April.[89] The trend of the evidence was markedly in favour of the Crown's right to the Indian territory, none more so than that on 27 March of Henry Vansittart, Governor of Bengal during Clive's absence from 1760 to 1764, which 'brought over many persons to that side'.[90] 'All they do is to run a blind muck at the Company's right to their acquisitions', complained Edmund Burke.[91] By 7 April Beckford, when challenged as to his intention, was confident enough to say that he meant to decide that right.[92] The opposition was aware of the need to strike before the Easter recess sent many country gentlemen home for the summer and left government its usual free hand at the

fag end of a session. All the opposition groups were at one on the
India question, and to counter Beckford's tactic they hoped for support from Conway and Townshend, and from independent MPs.
Their decision to move on 14 April for an end to the Committee
threatened the ministry with another Parliamentary humiliation. Such
calculations overlooked the role of the Company as a player in the
game. In their own attempt to anticipate Beckford's motion, the
Directors presented their new proposals to the House. Their
manoeuvre succeeded, for the ministry was being offered revenue
without responsibility, and Beckford announced he would abandon
his motion, thereby taking the wind out of the opposition's sails. 'Mr
Beckford's dropping his motion was an unfavourable circumstance
for us', Newcastle and Bedford agreed.[93] For many MPs believed that
the ministry should now be given time to digest the evidence and consider the Company's proposal. After a long debate on 14 April, during which Conway spoke for the ministry while denying the Crown's
right to Indian territory, the opposition motion to end proceedings
was defeated by 213 votes to 157.[94]

The cabinet decided upon a negotiated settlement with the Company, and on 27 April authorised Grafton, Conway and Townshend
to make the bargain.[95] The Directors, alarmed by the implication of
the Parliamentary evidence, were anxious to conclude an agreement,
but on 6 May the General Court of Proprietors again kicked over the
traces. It voted both a dividend of 12.5 per cent and a resolution
against government interference, having been provoked by a ministerial request the previous day for dividend restraint. There followed
two more declarations: that an extension of the Company's charter
was a prior condition of any agreement, and that if the Crown took
the Company's territories it should refund the cost of their acquisition, over £12 million.[96]

MPs and ministers alike were outraged by this behaviour. When on
8 May Jeremiah Dyson of the Board of Trade moved on behalf of the
administration for a Bill to restrict Company dividends, he was seconded by Dowdeswell and thirded by Grenville, and the motion
passed unanimously. At the first reading on 11 May Dyson announced
a dividend restriction of 10 per cent.[97] The impasse between Company
and ministry was resolved on 18 May when, despite prior objections
by the Directorate, Laurence Sulivan persuaded the General Court of
Proprietors to accept a double proposal: that £400,000 a year be paid
to government, and that the Company be empowered to make a
dividend of 12.5 per cent. This compromise scheme, guaranteeing a

fixed payment to government and promising a higher dividend for stockholders, had been devised between Sulivan and Townshend, who had promised to oppose the Dividend Bill.[98]

He did so, but was unable to fulfil his part of the implicit bargain. In a heated Commons debate of 26 May, in Committee on the Dividend Bill, Townshend and Conway joined with Grenville and Dowdeswell to argue for the 12.5 per cent dividend, but were defeated by 151 votes to 84.[99] Contemporaries noted this event with amusement and amazement. Charles Jenkinson wrote that it had 'convinced the world that the personal influence of these gentlemen who affect to be leaders is in fact nothing'.[100] A chagrined Townshend next day publicly displayed his mortification, and, according to diarist Ryder, 'as he was going out of the House he said "see where the ministry is now", meaning to intimate that it was in Lord Bute's hands'.[101] That myth should be translated into appreciation of the strength of the Court Party, as in this appraisal by Grenvillite James Harris. 'Though two such great officers as Secretary of State and Chancellor of the Exchequer went to an opposite side, *scarce any* followed them, such [is] the fidelity of troops well-disciplined.'[102] Conway's friend Horace Walpole later recorded the same shock reaction that 'so subordinate a placeman as Dyson could lead the House of Commons against the chief Ministers there, when they disagreed with the measures of the Court'.[103] The reality of political power had been starkly revealed.

On 23 May the House of Commons accepted Sulivan's idea of a fixed annual payment of £400,000 for three years, later reduced to two, and allowed the Company to retain the territorial revenue. Despite Grenville's objections, a 1s a lb internal duty would be removed on tea re-exported to America, to enable the Company to undersell smugglers in the colonial market: but the Company would compensate government for the revenue loss. Legislation to enact these proposals, and to curb the impact of stock-splitting by a six-month voting qualification, passed without incident through the Commons.[104]

A temporary, and for many unsatisfactory, solution had been found for what to contemporaries seemed the most important problem of India. That was the issue over which the Rockingham faction had sought to detach Conway and Townshend from the ministry, and thereby precipitate its collapse. It was always a futile hope, as some in the party early perceived. After the Commons debate of 9 March John Yorke commented to his brother Lord Hardwicke that Conway had spoken 'not like one who meant to resign. I am sick of this intrigue between our friends and that division in the ministry. Each aims to dupe the other, and in the mean time it makes any approach to George Grenville impracticable'.[105] Rockingham saw both Conway and Townshend frequently in March, but even his optimism had faded before the end of the month.[106] There followed tentative negotiations among the opposition factions. From the first Rockingham insisted on 'a majority of friends in the cabinet' and the specific exclusion of Temple, as a troublemaker.[107] Grenville and Rockingham never met face to face, communicating through Bedfordite Rigby. Which of them would have the Treasury in a prospective new ministry proved to be an insuperable barrier to any formal alliance.[108] The Rockinghamite view was that 'the Treasury in Mr Grenville's hands was the whole administration'. Bedford contended that Grenville was 'the most able man' for that post, but could be balanced by Rockingham as a Secretary of State and Charles Yorke as Lord Chancellor.[109] These negotiations in the spring of 1767 failed over disputes about office, not policy, for Grenville volunteered assurances that he would not seek to renew the policy of American taxation reversed by the Rockingham ministry.[110]

Opposition parties therefore could combine to harass the Chatham administration on America as well as India, when colonial matters increasingly came to the attention of Parliament. Chatham's last pronouncement on America, before his political retirement, had been that Parliament, not the cabinet, should deal with New York's disobedience of the Mutiny Act.[111] On 12 March the cabinet was presented with three policy proposals, and adopted Townshend's idea of suspending the New York Assembly until it complied with that Act: this was preferred to both Shelburne's direct action plan of billeting soldiers on private houses, and Conway's suggestion of extra customs duties for New York.[112] Two months were to pass before the enactment of this decision.

Meanwhile in Parliament Bedford had taken the initiative on America, without consulting Grenville or Rockingham. On 25 February and 5 March he pressed in the House of Lords for American papers, which were laid before the House on 12 March. But Bedford was then removed from the political scene by a hunting accident on 9 March to his heir, the Marquess of Tavistock, that resulted in his death on 22 March. The Duke was absent from an American debate of 30 March when Grafton anticipated any opposition move by announcing that the cabinet had devised a policy. The Lords debates revealed a hardline ministerial attitude on America, courtier Lord Talbot tartly commenting that 'new converts were always the more zealous'.[113]

Bedford returned to the Parliamentary scene on 10 April, according to Burke being persuaded by his friends 'to plunge into politics as a diversion from the grief occasioned by his late great loss'.[114] Angry at the breakdown of the opposition negotiations, he regarded himself as having a free hand to propose whatever he wished on America.[115] The subject he raised was a Compensation and Indemnity Act passed by the Massachusetts Assembly, which encroached on the royal prerogative by combining pardon of offenders in the 1765 Boston riots with payment of reparations to the victims. British condemnation of this audacity was universal, but the ministry, slow to act, still had the matter under consideration when Bedford proposed its reference to the Privy Council. Fearing a leak through the Cavendishs to Conway, he did so without prior notice to Rockingham.[116] The Marquess took offence, and the result was an opposition debacle. Rockingham and five friends supported administration, two others voted against, and fourteen more led by Newcastle walked out. The ministry won on a previous question by 63 votes to 36, but Newcastle soon calculated that a united opposition would have lost by only one vote, and lamented the lost opportunity. 'It would have shewed my Lord Bute, and my Lord Chatham (and that is my point) that with the Duke of Bedford etc we were masters of the House of Lords'.[117] But the ministerial weakness there had been revealed, and the debate was the prelude to a sustained opposition attack. It began on 6 May over a motion for papers on the same subject, when a combined opposition lost by only nine votes, 52 to 43. A worried Grafton told George III that 'the whole of the opposition had brought their united strength which his Majesty will see is numerous'.[118] Yet another challenge on the same topic failed on 22 May by six votes, 62 to 56.[119] There followed the rare event of whipping for the next Lords debate of 26 May, also on the Massachusetts issue, when the ministry won two divisions each by 65 to 62, having had the votes of two of the King's brothers and of 'some Lords brought down from their very beds', so Grafton told Chatham. Such was the Duke's despair that the King on 30 May asked Chatham to save the situation. 'I have uniformly relied on your firmness to act in defiance to that hydra faction … Though your relations, the Bedfords and the Rockinghams are joined with intention to storm my Closet, yet if I were mean enough to submit, they own they would not join in forming an administration, therefore nothing but confusion could be obtained.' Chatham responded to this appeal by allowing Grafton to visit him on 31 May and 4 June, and sufficiently restored his morale for the Duke to see out the session.[120]

On 2 June Richmond moved a resolution censuring administration for not having produced a plan for Quebec, which the ministry defeated by 73 votes to 61, having, so Newcastle said, 'fetched up Lords who had scarce ever been in the House or had been absent many years'.[121] This reinforcement put the ministry beyond danger of defeat. When opposition forced a vote over the East India Company Dividend Bill on 17 June the administration majority was 73 to 52, raised after proxies to 98 to 57, a margin of victory that disheartened even Newcastle, and one that George III saw as decisive.[122] Opposition tried again on 25 June, in Committee where proxies were not permitted, and lost by 59 votes to 44.[123]

While Grafton felt beleaguered in the Lords, Charles Townshend dominated the Commons, as these weeks saw the full flowering of his talents. He proposed his budget on 15 April, when government expenses totalled £8,894,000. It proved a triumphant occasion, a masterpiece of financial skill and of presentation. 'He contrived to make all his calculations understood', wrote Lord George Sackville, 'and to make that dry subject agreeable and entertaining to those the least conversant in business.'[124] Faced with an unexpected deficit of nearly £500,000 because of the land tax defeat, Townshend had made up this loss by scouring government departments for spare money, especially the Treasury and the Pay Office, where he claimed £90,000 from Lord Chatham and £70,000 from Lord Holland as money still not paid in by them as former Paymasters.[125] He later explained to Newcastle that he had 'collected above £469,000 out of the savings of office, and from cash dormant in the Exchequer, unseen by others and fairly applicable to replace the fourth shilling of the land tax'.[126] A recent surmise that the £400,000 from the East India Company was intended to meet the land tax shortfall therefore has no more validity than the long-exploded belief that Townshend's American taxation had that motive.[127] The budget was balanced before that fixed sum payment was devised.

This impressive exhibition of financial competence was followed by incomparable Parliamentary eloquence in his famous 'champagne speech' of 8 May, a display of verbal pyrotechnics that delighted MPs, and one that may have owed less to alcohol and more to premeditation than most contemporaries thought. 'It lasted an hour', wrote Horace Walpole, 'with torrents of wit, ridicule, variety, lies and beautiful language ... in this speech he beat Lord Chatham in language, Burke in metaphors.' Among Townshend's wide range of targets was the appointment to high office of young peers without ability and experience, and the damaging frequency of recent ministerial changes, palpable hits at Grafton and George III. He said the Prime Minister should be in the Commons, and seemed to hint he could head a ministry of Rockinghamites. But if the speech was a bid for high office, it was counter-productive. 'It showed him capable of being, and unfit to be, First Minister', opined Horace Walpole.[128]

Yet only five days later, on 13 May, Townshend triumphantly carried his New York policy proposal after a speech described this time by Walpole as 'consonant to the character of a man of business, and so unlike the wanton sallies of the man of parts and pleasure', evidently pointing the contrast.[129] Townshend explained to the Commons that only that colony had been completely defiant of the Mutiny Act, and that it would be coerced by a prohibition on all Assembly legislation until it complied with that Act. Beckford was alone in deeming this too harsh a policy. It was criticised as too lenient by Dowdeswell, who put forward an agreed Rockinghamite suggestion for billeting on private houses, Shelburne's proposal in cabinet. Grenville was scathing, recalling the promise by Chatham on 21 February 1766 of military action in the event of further colonial defiance, and criticising Conway for deserting the Southern Department to avoid dealing with America. His suggestion was that the New York colonial treasury should simply be ordered to pay army costs directly. Conway, though Commons Leader, spoke against the agreed ministerial policy, repeating his cabinet proposal of a local tax on New York, and he voted in opposition. Townshend nevertheless won by 180 votes to 98, a victory margin that shocked the united opposition parties. There was no resistance to the subsequent legislation, but it never came into force, since New York meanwhile gave way in June.[130]

On this occasion Townshend took the opportunity of informing MPs about his plans for American customs duties, a method he was adopting to meet the supposed colonial distinction between internal and external taxes. He gave a list of items to be taxed, one that was to be greatly altered in the next few weeks, and estimated the total revenue would be £40,000. Townshend also for the first time announced that the aim was to pay civil government costs, to free officials and judges from financial dependence on the assemblies. The only comment was a denunciation by Grenville of the taxes as inadequate. In retrospect the most conspicuous omission from Townshend's list was tea, because not until 20 May did he negotiate an agreement with the East India Company. Townshend finally presented his proposals to the Commons on 1 June. The import duty of 3*d* a lb on tea would produce £20,000, and the same total would come from duties on china, glass, paper, and paints. This total of £40,000 was the same as that from the markedly different set of duties announced on 13 May, and would seem to have been the target sum, one which almost exactly matched the estimated cost of colonial government. Grenville again attacked the total as paltry, but this fateful American taxation apparently met with no opposition at Westminster.[131]

After the Parliamentary session ended in June the Duke of Grafton drew the conclusion from his buffeting in the House of Lords, and set-backs in the Commons, that he ought to strengthen the ministry by recruiting part of the opposition, and early in July he obtained royal permission to do so. George III, the Duke told Conway and Horace Walpole, 'was not disinclined to take Lord Rockingham, but protested he had almost rather resign his crown than consent to receive George Grenville again'.[132] Grafton's own preference was for the Bedfords, but after an initial rebuff he was persuaded by Conway to approach Rockingham on 7 July, when he offered his own post of the Treasury. The Marquess assumed that he was being invited to form a new administration;[133] and he conducted prolonged negotiations during the next fortnight under that misapprehension. Rockingham was not now prepared, as he had been in 1765, to base a ministry only on his own following. He wanted a comprehensive administration, to include the Bedford group, and at their request some Grenvillites, together with some selected Chathamites: but he would not have potential rivals like Chatham, Grenville or Temple in his cabinet. His plan for a coalition ministry differed completely in principle from Chatham's 1766 attack on the factions. Rockingham was seeking to coerce the Crown by an alliance of factions too strong to be resisted, or removed. He had learnt his lesson. The Bedfords initially agreed to take part, and consulted Grenville, who, aware that he had no chance of office himself, raised with them the issue of America, infuriating the Marquess by deeming Rockinghamite and Chathamite views to be identical. Rockingham and Bedford contrived a verbal compromise formula, an agreement that British sovereignty there would be asserted 'with firmness and temper': this implicit contradiction the signatories were never called upon to resolve. These opposition nego-tiations broke down not on policy but over Rockingham's adamant insistence on having Conway as his Commons Leader. Bedford vainly suggested Dowdeswell, in view of Conway's proven incompetence during the last two sessions.[134] On 22 July Rockingham reported to the King his failure to form a ministry, only to be informed that he had not been asked to do so. The Marquess was astonished, and also angry, thinking he had been deceived by Grafton.[135] Grenville had already perceived that the ministry would gain from the failure of the negotiation, as well as its success; for discord would be sowed among the opposition factions. Whether or not that was Grafton's deliberate aim, as Grenville suspected, the prognosis was correct, and Grenville himself the greatest loser. His alliance with the Bedfords had been born out of past events, and nurtured by self-interest. But the Bedford group was now cognisant of Rockingham's impossible demands and of the virtual royal veto on Grenville. Next time they would make their own bargain.[136]

None of this political activity during the first year of Chatham's ministry had touched upon Ireland, for here his policy initiative had been aborted. Yet Ireland was a matter that came naturally to his attention when he formed his ministry. During the Seven Years War he had, when Southern Secretary, accepted Undertaker power to avoid an Irish crisis in wartime. Now he took up the positive approach formally initiated by the Grenville ministry. The replacement of courtier Lord Hertford by the Earl of Bristol would seem to have been motivated by the professed willingness of Lord Bristol to live in Ireland, which George III himself made a condition of appointment: 'expecting his constant residence while he holds that office', the King specified on 22 August 1766.[137] This intention was soon known in Britain and Ireland. On 7 September Thomas Whately reported to Grenville that 'Lord Bristol is to hold the Lieutenancy for five years, and to reside constantly'.[138] Four days later Edmond Pery was writing of this plan as part of Chatham's imperial scheme. 'I am persuaded he will execute some plan by which the colonies will be better secured to and connected with the mother-country than they are at present. If such a plan shall ever take place, Ireland will not be left out of it. I am the more confirmed in this opinion from the appointment of Lord Bristol to the government of this kingdom, and his resolution of residing there.'[139]

It was not possible, however, to implement this policy immediately, for the Irish Parliament was not due to sit during the winter of 1766–67, and Lord Bristol would not go to Ireland until the summer of 1767. This interval afforded John Ponsonby an opportunity to counter the threat. A propaganda campaign over such dangers as a land tax or a Union failed. Ponsonby then changed tactics and sought to save his patronage by a direct approach to Lord Bristol. In a letter of 23 May 1767 he asked his brother Lord Bessborough to obtain some such concession, but at an interview on 2 June Lord Bristol was adamant. 'He has not the least thoughts of agreeing to what you expect', Bessborough reported to Ponsonby the next day. 'He said that for a long time past the Lords Lieutenant were under the direction and almost command of some few chiefs in Ireland, but that he was determined to be the Chief Governor himself and to break through that old method of proceeding.' Bristol at once reported the interview to George III, and received confirmation of royal support.[140] Yet two months later he resigned without ever taking up his post in Ireland. Bristol was upset when his proposed Chief Secretary, his own brother Augustus Hervey, resigned on 1 July. Later that month the Irish Lord Chancellor died, and the King's refusal to appoint an immediate successor gave Bristol a pretext to resign in August. The prospect of a battle with the Undertakers had lost its appeal, since the support from London would now be that of a weak and divided ministry, not that of the formidable Chatham.[141]

Any relief among the Undertakers at the news of Bristol's resignation promptly turned to dismay. For on 19 August a formidable politician was appointed to carry out the same policy, Lord Townshend. Contemporaries assumed that this choice reflected the influence of his younger brother Charles, even though Lord Townshend himself ascribed it entirely to Lord Bute.[142] For in the summer of 1767 the star of Charles Townshend was in the ascendant. He had in effect replaced the hesitant Conway as Commons Leader. He had formulated and enacted the key policy decisions on America and India. In August his role was acknowledged by a long-desired British peerage for his wife as Baroness of Greenwich, with reversion to their sons. Political speculation in the press, though not in more informed circles, forecast that he would succeed Chatham as Prime Minister.[143] His sudden death from a fever on 4 September therefore stunned contemporaries. 'The opposition expected that the loss of this essential pin would loosen the whole frame', wrote Horace Walpole a few weeks later. Walpole might comment that 'that first eloquence of the world is dumb', and bemoan the loss of 'a man of incomparable parts'; but he shrewdly observed to Conway that 'in a political light, I own I cannot look upon it as a misfortune'.[144] The death of this talented maverick may not have removed a potential Premier, but it paved the way for one who would achieve the political stability the King craved. It was in that sense that 4 September 1767 was the turning point of the first part of George III's reign. The era of Lord North was about to commence.

Notes

1 *Corr. of George III*, I, 368.
2 Malmesbury MSS. Harris Diary, *sub* 23 Ap. 1766.
3 *Corr. of George III*, I, 368.
4 *Bute Letters*, p. 251.
5 Malmesbury MSS. Photocopies B828–9, 851.
6 Langford, *First Rockingham Administration*, p. 281.
7 For fuller detail on this see Brooke, *Chatham Administration*, pp. 6–19;
   Langford, *First Rockingham Administration*, pp. 257–63; and Thomas,
   British Politics and the Stamp Act Crisis, pp. 283–90.
8 BL Add. MSS. 47584, fos 50–1.
9 Malmesbury MSS. Photocopies B829.
10 BL Add. MSS. 47584, fo. 53.
11 Quoted in Black, *Pitt the Elder*, p. 263.
12 *Chesterfield Letters*, VI, 2,752.
13 Peters, *The Elder Pitt*, p. 172.
14 Escott, Thesis, p. 232.
15 *Chesterfield Letters*, VI, 2,753.
16 BL Add. MSS. 47584, fo. 53.
17 Escott, Thesis, p. 231.
18 BL Add. MSS. 47584, fos 54–5.
19 PRO 30/29/1/14, fos 591–2.
20 BL Add. MSS. 47584, fo. 55.
21 BL Add. MSS. 32976, fo. 315.
22 BL Add. MSS. 32976, fo. 223.
23 BL Add. MSS. 32976, fo. 253.
24 BL Add. MSS. 47584, fos 51–2.
25 *Chatham Papers*, III, 15–20.
26 *Chatham Papers*, III, 29–32, 42–3, 46–50, 67–71, 139–43.
27 Scott, *British Foreign Policy*, pp. 109–12.
28 Escott, Thesis, pp. 101–23. Rice, *IHR*, 2 (1980), 386–409.
29 Escott, Thesis, pp. 219–55.
30 Hoffman, *Edmund Burke*, pp. 366–8.
31 *Bedford Journal*, pp. 592–3.
32 Walpole, *Letters*, VII, 73.
33 Williams, Thesis, pp. 44, 51–2, and *passim*.
34 *Corr. of George III*, I, 394, 398. *Chatham Papers*, III, 73.
35 *Grenville Papers*, III, 337–40.
36 *Commons Journals*, XXXI, 6, 9–41.
37 *Chatham Papers*, III, 125–7.

38 BL Add. MSS. 57833, fos 36–8. *Corr of George III*, I, 414–15. *Grenville Papers*, III, 383. Walpole, *Memoirs*, II, 263–4.
39 *Grenville Papers*, III, 382–4. Walpole, *Memoirs*, II, 264–5.
40 *Grenville Papers*, III, 384.
41 *Commons Journals*, XXXI, 15. *Grenville Papers*, III, 343, 386–7. Walpole, *Memoirs*, II, 268–9.
42 *Commons Journals*, XXXI, 23–4. Walpole, *Memoirs*, II, 275.
43 *Chatham Anecdotes*, II, 38–9.
44 Hoffman, *Edmund Burke*, p. 375.
45 BL Add. MSS. 33001, fo. 368.
46 Hoffman, *Edmund Burke*, p. 396.
47 For more detail on the Edgcumbe affair see Brooke, *Chatham Administration*, pp. 53–6.
48 This thought in Langford, *First Rockingham Administration*, pp. 283–4, has been developed by Elofson, *The Rockingham Connection and the Second Founding of the Whig Party*.
49 *Bedford Journal*, p. 596.
50 *Chatham Anecdotes*, II, 41–3.
51 *Barrington-Bernard Corr.*, pp. 119–20. For a similar report by Barrington to Sir Andrew Mitchell in Berlin see *Cavendish Debates*, I, 596 n.
52 BL Add. MSS. 32977, fo. 160.
53 BL Add. MSS. 32978, fos 206–7.
54 *Grenville Papers*, III, 394–5. Walpole, *Memoirs*, II, 286. The Bill passed the Commons without further incident: *Commons Journals*, XXXI, 39–41.
55 *Chatham Anecdotes*, II, 46–9.
56 Fortescue, *British Army*, III, 65–108.
57 BL Egerton MSS. 218, fos 150–1.
58 Bowen, *HJ*, 30 (1987), pp. 910–14.
59 Sutherland, *East India Company*, pp. 138–47.
60 Bowen, Thesis, pp. 279–80.
61 *Grafton Autobiography*, pp. 98, 109.
62 For this debate see three letters (a) E. Burke to C. O'Hara, Hoffman, *Edmund Burke*, p. 374. (b) G. Onslow to Newcastle, BL Add. MSS. 32978, fo. 86. (c) H. Flood to Lord Charlemont, *Chatham Papers*, III, 144 n. For a fuller account see Bowen, Thesis, pp. 298–303.
63 BL Add. MSS. 32978, fos 264, 410; 35607, fo. 332. *Corr. of George III*, I, 425. Walpole, *Memoirs*, II, 287–90.
64 *Chatham Papers*, III, 149–52, 157–8, 168–70, 176–8.
65 *Grafton Autobiography*, pp. 116–17.
66 *Chatham Papers*, III, 196 n, 204–6, 216 n.

67 *Ryder Diary*, p. 334. Walpole, *Memoirs*, II, 302–3. Brooke, *Chatham Administration*, pp. 110–11.
68 *Chesterfield Letters*, VI, 2,798. *Grafton Autobiography*, p. 123. *Corr. of George III*, I, 459–60.
69 Malmesbury MSS. Photocopies B854.
70 BL Add. MSS. 32978, fos 398–403.
71 *Gage Corr.*, II, 47–51. For more detail on ministerial attitudes see Thomas, *British Politics and the Stamp Act Crisis*, pp. 291–9.
72 *Ryder Diary*, p. 331.
73 Thomas, *British Politics and the Stamp Act Crisis*, pp. 344–7.
74 *Grenville Papers*, IV, 211–12.
75 *HMC Stopford Sackville*, I, 120.
76 *Chatham Papers*, III, 224. For a similar analysis by Edmund Burke, who had abstained, deeming the motive factious and the result pernicious, see Hoffman, *Edmund Burke*, p. 389.
77 *Chesterfield Letters*, VI, 2,799.
78 BL Add. MSS. 33001, fos 357–63. The misleading precision of this list had been demonstrated by a comparison with a Rockingham list of earlier in the session. Even for their own supporters they agree on only 77 of 121 on Rockingham's list and 101 on Newcastle's list. Brooke, *Chatham Administration*, pp. 241–3. But for a detailed critique explaining away much of this discrepancy see O'Gorman, *Rise of Party*, pp. 221–2.
79 Malmesbury MSS. Photocopies B858.
80 Bowen, Thesis, pp. 341–2.
81 For this debate see *Ryder Diary*, pp. 333–4; Walpole, *Memoirs*, II, 304–5. Hoffman, *Edmund Burke*, pp. 390–1. BL Add. MSS. 32980, fos 215, 222.
82 *Grenville Papers*, IV, 6–7.
83 BL Add. MSS. 32980, fo. 221.
84 *Ryder Diary*, pp. 334–5. See also Walpole, *Memoirs*, II, 305–7; *Corr. of George III*, I, 464–6. BL Add. MSS. 32980, fo. 248.
85 *Ryder Diary*, pp. 335–6. Walpole, *Memoirs*, II, 309. Hoffman, *Edmund Burke*, p. 304. BL Add. MSS. 32980, fo. 262.
86 Bowen, Thesis, pp. 354–66.
87 BL Add. MSS. 32980, fos 343–4.
88 Bowen, Thesis, pp. 373–80.
89 *Ryder Diary*, pp. 336–8.
90 Walpole, *Memoirs*, II, 315.
91 Hoffman, *Edmund Burke*, p. 397.
92 BL Add. MSS. 32981, fo. 61.
93 BL Add. MSS. 32981, fo. 159.

94 *Ryder Diary*, pp. 338–40. Walpole, *Memoirs*, III, 1–3. BL Add. MSS. 32981, fos 151–5.
95 Walpole, *Memoirs*, III, 8, 11.
96 BL Add. MSS. 32981, fo. 303.
97 *Ryder Diary*, pp. 341–2. BL Add. MSS. 32981, fos 321–3.
98 Bowen, Thesis, pp. 399–406. Sutherland, *East India Company*, pp. 173–4.
99 *Ryder Diary*, p. 350. BL Add. MSS. 32982, fo. 130.
100 BL Add. MSS. 38205, fo. 174.
101 *Ryder Diary*, p. 350.
102 BL Add. MSS. 35608, fo. 19.
103 Walpole, *Memoirs*, III, 36.
104 *Ryder Diary*, pp. 349–51. Bowen, Thesis, pp. 406–8.
105 BL Add. MSS. 35608, fos 8–9.
106 Brooke, *Chatham Administration*, pp. 117–21.
107 BL Add. MSS. 32980, fo. 450.
108 Brooke, *Chatham Administration*, pp. 121–6.
109 BL Add. MSS. 32981, fo. 156.
110 BL Add. MSS. 32981, fo. 34.
111 *Chatham Papers*, III, 213.
112 Thomas, *British Politics and the Stamp Act Crisis*, pp. 308–9.
113 Thomas, *British Politics and the Stamp Act Crisis*, pp. 312–14.
114 *Burke Corr.*, I, 306.
115 BL Add. MSS. 32981, fos 65–6.
116 BL Add. MSS. 32981, fo. 158.
117 BL Add. MSS. 32981, fos 107–14, 137–8. *Bedford Journal*, p. 601. Thomas, *British Politics and the Stamp Act Crisis*, pp. 315–18.
118 *Corr. of George III*, I, 470–1.
119 *Bedford Journal*, p. 602. Walpole, *Letters*, VII, 111.
120 *Chatham Papers*, III, 258, 261–4.
121 BL Add. MSS. 32982, fos 237–8.
122 BL Add. MSS. 32982, fo. 353. *Chatham Papers*, III, 274.
123 Bowen, Thesis, pp. 411–16.
124 *HMC Stopford Sackville*, I, 122–3.
125 BL Add. MSS. 32981, fo. 175; 35608, fo. 145.
126 BL Add. MSS. 32981, fos 193–4.
127 Thomas, *EHR*, 83 (1968), 42–3. Bowen, *Revenue and Reform*, p. 64.
128 Walpole, *Letters*, VII, 105–6.
129 Walpole, *Memoirs*, III, 24.
130 Thomas, *British Politics and the Stamp Act Crisis*, pp. 322–9.
131 For my three accounts of Townshend's American taxation, see Thomas,

EHR, 83 (1968), 33–51; Thomas, *British Politics and the Stamp Act Crisis*, pp. 337–63; and Thomas, *Townshend Duties Crisis*, pp. 18–35.

132 Walpole, *Memoirs*, III, 38–9.
133 For confirmation of Rockingham's belief from a Grenvillite source see Malmesbury MSS. Photocopies A567–72.
134 *Grenville Papers*, IV, 94.
135 *Bedford Journal*, p. 607.
136 Brooke, *Chatham Administration*, pp. 162–217. Lawson, *George Grenville*, pp. 241–3.
137 *Corr of George III*, I, 388–9.
138 *Grenville Papers*, III, 316.
139 Bartlett, Thesis, p. 23.
140 *Corr. Of George III*, I, 484–8.
141 Powell, Thesis, pp. 120–1.
142 Hoffman, *Edmund Burke*, p. 409. In Feb. 1770 journalist John Almon stated that Townshend was Bute's 'own appointment'. *London Museum*, 1770, p. 134. That may have been so, but Townshend was in any case a member of 'the Court party', and Bute's influence had effectively ended a year earlier.
143 *London Evening Post*, 4 July 1767.
144 Walpole, *Letters*, VII, 129, 133.

8

The Chatham ministry II.
Grafton as caretaker (1767–1768):
political re-alignments

'I suppose my Lord North is to succeed poor Charles Townshend. I hear they seem not to be sorry for his loss. They may stand in need of his abilities sooner than they imagine.'[1] The Duke of Newcastle's comment, written only the day after Townshend's death, was grudging testimony to the talents of the young Lord North, now thirty-five years old. Newcastle himself had in 1759 appointed North to the Treasury Board, where for six years he had acquired financial expertise. The contrast between the dazzling and unpredictable Townshend and the sound, reliable North could hardly have been greater. Yet Townshend himself was among those who had discerned the talents of the man now to be his successor.[2] George III at once instructed Grafton to offer the Exchequer to Lord North. The Duke later noted that this decision was 'particularly satisfactory to me, as I knew him to be a man of strict honour: and he was besides the person whom Lord Chatham desired', recalling the abortive attempt to replace Townshend by North in March.[3] North's debating and administrative skills were already so apparent that he had recently sometimes attended cabinet, even though he only held the post of Joint Paymaster General. He was to surpass expectations by creating the permanent administration George III had been seeking since 1760. North became the main prop of government: for nearly fifteen years he was Chancellor of the Exchequer and Commons Leader, replacing Conway at the beginning of 1768; and Prime Minister for over twelve years from January 1770.

In 1767, however, that development lay in the future. The political game continued as before, and the customary pre-sessional moves and hopes manifested themselves in opposition circles. In September the Rockinghamite leadership, intending to revive the combined opposition of the previous session, was belatedly prepared to concede the points that had wrecked the July negotiations, dropping the insistence on including Conway in and excluding Grenville from any future Rockingham administration.[4] But the Bedfordite party was not now interested in planning a ministry for the Marquess, while Grenville, aware that he would not fit into any such arrangement, rejected the idea of opposition for its own sake. When Bedford suggested a united opposition of the three factions, Grenville replied that 'measures alone were what he regarded'.[5] Bedford and Newcastle also suffered from the same vestigial hangover of contemporary convention, the idea that opposition to the King's government needed to be justified; for on 19 November Newcastle made this comment. 'I like the Duke of Bedford's notions of opposition, upon *proper points*, to the present administration'.[6]

The Rockinghamites nevertheless sought to achieve a united opposition vote when Parliament met on 24 November, by an umbrella motion under which all opposition MPs could unite. This was an anodyne amendment by Dowdeswell to the Address, deploring the omission of any measures to promote trade. The tactic failed dismally. In the debate no support came from either Grenville or the Bedfordites, and the amendment was rejected without a vote. Worse was to follow. Grenville had sat simmering with rage, because on the previous day he had been told that at a recent Newmarket race meeting Rockingham had publicly vetoed any alliance with the Grenville family.[7] He also knew of incipient colonial protests against the Townshend duties, and of long-term resistance in America to the trade laws and the Mutiny Act. As soon as Dowdeswell's amendment was rejected Grenville rose to make a virulent attack on the repeal of the Stamp Act: here is a summary of his speech in Newcastle's papers.

> After declaring his sentiments about America, and of the necessity of enforcing (supposed to mean, by some new Act) the superiority of this country over the colonies; that there were persons of contrary sentiments (turning his eyes towards Mr Dowdeswell) whom he would never support in power, or cooperate with, and that he would hold the same distance from them, that he would from those, who opposed the principles of the Revolution.[8]

Bedfordites like Rigby apologised at the time for Grenville's behaviour, and that evening Weymouth told Rockingham that Grenville and the Bedford group were quite distinct parties. Rockinghamite retaliation, led by Edmund Burke, produced two further Parliamentary rows with Grenville over America later that month, and all semblance of opposition unity was destroyed. Lord Chancellor Camden gleefully commented that 'it was impossible for *Stamp Men* and *No Stamp Men* ever to agree'.[9] Misguided Rockinghamite attempts to take the Bedfordites to task for Grenville's behaviour worsened the situation. The Bedford party, aware that the antipathy and rivalry of Grenville and Rockingham was a more divisive and permanent factor than the American question, perceived the futility of opposition in such circumstances. By the end of November they began a negotiation with Grafton to join the ministry.[10] On 2 December Bedford, as a courtesy, informed his old ally Grenville, who made no objection, if the Bedford group maintained the same policy. He said he would never force himself into office, and the two men parted political company on friendly terms, although henceforth their factions were quite separate.[11] Bedford did not wish to break all links with the Grenville party. He therefore soon told Lord Lyttelton that 'the basis of the late treaty with the Duke of Grafton was a supposition that Lord Chatham was politically dead', and that he personally wished to see Grenville 'at the head of the Treasury'.[12] Grenville for his part thought the new arrangement was 'too disjointed to last'.[13]

Grafton welcomed the Bedfordite approach, because it would give him the Parliamentary strength he had sought in the July negotiations, in so far as his intention then was genuine. But George III disliked the Bedford party, because of their involvement in the 1765 coercion of him towards the end of Grenville's ministry, and seemingly also from personal antipathies. Grafton therefore had to promise the King that neither then nor later should they have more than two cabinet posts.[14] That presented no problem, since only two were available. Lord Northington was anxious to retire as Lord President of the Council, and Conway seized the chance to do so as Northern Secretary. They were succeeded respectively by Lords Gower and Weymouth. Bedford wanted no post himself, but why Sandwich, already with ample cabinet experience, was passed over is unclear: he was less than satisfied with the post of Joint Postmaster General.[15] Conway now also gave way to Lord North as Commons Leader, but remained in the cabinet, even though merely Lieutenant-General of Ordnance, a post he had taken when it was vacated in August by Lord Townshend's appointment to Ireland. He held it without salary when Northern Secretary, presumably wanting a suitable post to which he could retreat. This ministerial reshuffle was prolonged by the creation of a new Secretaryship of State for America, to relieve the workload of the Southern Secretary. Shelburne agreed to this, but resisted Grafton's pressure to become American Secretary. The Duke wished to avoid placing a hardliner in that sensitive post, but perforce had to accept a man reputed to be so in Lord Hillsborough, twice President of the Board of Trade, from 1763 to 1765 and in 1766, and so rightly deemed a colonial expert.[16]

Administration must have expected a quiet time when Parliament reassembled in January 1768 after the Christmas recess. The defection of the Bedford group was a body-blow to the opposition, not only in terms of numbers and debating talent, but also because it removed the link between Grenville and Rockingham. The Duke's former Treasury Secretary James West made this wry comment to Newcastle on 21 December. 'Nothing can be done now but Lord Rockingham's shaking hands with Mr Grenville and shewing their joint feeble efforts for another two or three years.'[17] The next general election, moreover, was due by March, and many MPs were absent attending to their re-elections. The ministry, too, apart from financial business, had only one piece of legislation to offer, but it did constitute a hostage to fortune, being a topic likely to revive the alignment of the previous session, another East India Company Dividend Bill.

This had been introduced early, and received a second reading on 16 December 1767 by 128 votes to 41. On 15 January 1768 a motion by William Dowdeswell to refer the Company accounts to a Committee was opposed by new Commons Leader Lord North, William Beckford, and Lord Barrington, who claimed the motive to be delay. Dowdeswell, reminded by North of the previous vote, did not force another.[18] The General Court of the Company this time itself limited its dividend to 10 per cent. That was the rate fixed by the Commons Committee on 22 January, but although the substance of the dispute was over Dowdeswell 'injudiciously' divided the House next day on a postponement motion, being heavily defeated by '120 to poor 25'. James West thought that such a debacle put an end to any opposition. 'It looks as if it would be the last division of the session.'[19] The minority vote went up to 41 for the third reading on 27 January, and included Conway, but the Rockingham party was fighting a lone battle. The Grenville group was abstaining as well as the now ministerial Bedfordites, apparently because of an abortive Grenvillite flirtation with administration. For it was also on 27 January that Lords Temple and Lyttelton had a long discussion with Charles Jenkinson, whom James West, in a version of the King's Friends myth, coupled with Sir Gilbert Elliot as 'the sole governors deputed for national affairs'.[20]

Rockingham therefore did not expect Grenvillite support in the Lords on the Dividend Bill, or to muster more than 20 votes.[21] But by the second reading, on 4 February, the Grenvillite faction was back in open opposition, and both Lyttelton and Temple spoke against the legislation, as did Rockinghamites Richmond, Dartmouth and Hard-wicke. When speaking for the ministry both Shelburne and Grafton, though believed to be at odds with each other, asserted the state's right to the Indian territories, with Grafton even talking of 'the *share* which Parliament might *allot* to the East India Company'. The opposition vote was boosted to 35, as against 73, by a silent phalanx of Bedford peers, led by the Duke, anxious to demonstrate their consistency on that issue.[22] The new Act extended the dividend limitation to 1 February 1769, the date of expiry for the 1767 agreement of government and Company.[23]

The imminence of a general election was a political factor that cut both ways for a ministry. While it reduced the attendance of independent MPs, it was also an opportunity for opposition to raise popular issues that would remind MPs that they soon had to face their electors. Two such came before the Commons early in 1768. William Beckford introduced an Election Bill. Before the Christmas recess he had been saying it would be a Triennial Bill, 'Lord Chatham's favourite', according to James West. But on 19 January 1768, when he gave public notice, he said privately it would be a Bribery Bill, to oblige MPs to swear that they had not secured votes by corrupt means.[24] When leave was given for the Bill on 26 January, Beckford mentioned several instances of bribery, notably one at Oxford. In 1766 the two Oxford MPs were asked by the corporation to pay off the city debt of £5,670, and one of them, Sir Thomas Stapleton, now confirmed this to the House.[25] At least 340 MPs, probably the fullest House of the session, attended on 1 February, when the Oxford MPs produced the incriminating letter, and the Mayor and Aldermen were ordered to attend on 5 February.[26] The corporation members, ten of them, were then found guilty of corruption, and after a long debate over their punishment the House voted in what James West termed 'a very motley' division by 129 to 111 to send them to Newgate Prison. They remained there for five days before being released after a reprimand.[27]

This scandal was freshly in mind when on 3 February Beckford produced his Bribery Bill, increasing penalties for corruption and enacting oaths to be taken by candidates at elections and by MPs before taking their seats in the House.[28] After the second reading on 5 February Dowdeswell and Burke spoke strongly against its committal, because the measure would strike at individual MPs while leaving government corruption unchecked. But a more constructive approach to this problem was adopted by another Rockinghamite, Sir George Savile, who, so West told Newcastle, 'spoke exceptionally well' in arguing for clauses 'to prevent the power of the Crown being employed in bribery against the subject'.[29] The Bribery Bill was under consideration at a time when the impending general election highlighted malpractices. 'Boroughs had been publicly advertised for sale in the newspapers', so Horace Walpole later wrote. But Beckford's Election Bill contained no check on government influence, and on 17 February Dowdeswell therefore announced he would propose a clause to disfranchise revenue officers when the Committee sat two days later.[30] The customs and excise men, being on the government payroll, were deemed to play the key role in so-called 'Treasury boroughs', and to vote in favour of ministerial candidates throughout the country. This idea anticipated a Bill that Dowdeswell would propose in 1770, and foreshadowed the Economical Reform programme that began a decade later. In the Committee on 19 February Beckford's proposals were criticised as too severe, as excluding neighbourly charity, and also for encouraging informers. He stormed out when accused of creating a new crime of perjury. Burke and Dowdesdwell continued to oppose his ideas, but Grenville supported them, 'to flatter the country gentlemen, who can ill afford to combat with great lords, nabobs ... and West Indians', so Horace Walpole thought. When the ministry moved to kill the measure by closing the Committee without a report, Dowdeswell opposed this, because of his intended clause, and voted with Grenville in a minority of 69 to 93.[31]

The opposition, however, had meanwhile taken the opportunity to end the session on a high note. During the last few years there had developed in Cumberland an electoral feud between Sir James Lowther, a son-in-law of Lord Bute, and the Duke of Portland, a Rockinghamite peer. In 1767 Lowther contrived what he must have thought a devastating coup. Sir Fletcher Norton had told him that two parts of Portland's Cumbrian estate, the Forest of Inglewood and the Socage of the Manor of Carlisle, did not form part of the Honour of Penrith granted to the Duke's Bentinck family by William III in 1694. Lowther therefore applied on 9 July 1767 for a lease of them to himself, and, doubtless assisted by his court connections, he obtained a patent on 28 December, despite Portland's objections. The area looked to be decisive in the county constituency, since it contained over three hundred freeholders, who would now be expected to change sides. Portland contrived to keep most of their votes, by offering indemnities and announcing legal proceedings, and Lowther was to lose his election. Whatever the legal niceties, his action was perceived as deploying Crown power against private property, and aroused alarm and consternation both locally and nationally, not least as fuel for the Bute myth.[32]

The Rockingham party resorted to legislation to remedy the injustice inflicted on one of their number, and Sir George Savile on 17 February moved a Nullum Tempus Bill, intending to set a time limit of sixty years for Crown claims to property in other hands. It was a cause the ministry found difficult to fight, and the opposition was in fine fettle. Savile, Charles Yorke, Dowdeswell, and Burke all shone for the Rocking-hamites, while the Marquess conceded that 'Mr G. Grenville spoke well and much better than I have often heard him'. James West told Newcastle 'the administration behaved very poorly'. At first North and Jenkinson objected to the encroachment on the royal prerogative, not a popular line to take with MPs. North then argued that it was too late in the session for such legislation, and Secretary at War Lord Barrington even said he would support the measure in a new session. North avoided a direct vote by moving for next business, carried by the slender majority of twenty, 134 to 114, with, so Horace Walpole later wrote, 'many courtiers voting in the minority'. But Rockingham told Newcastle that 'only two men in office ... voted with us' and that 'Conway kept away'. The episode put the opposition in good heart, with a triumph in prospect early in the new Parliament.[33]

Parliament was dissolved on 11 March 1768, but since it had lasted the full seven years the general election campaigns had long since commenced. Newcastle had told Rockingham in December 1766 that it was 'high time' to be planning for it.[34] The unusually large number of eighty-three constituencies went to the poll, thirty more than in 1761, but that was due to a multitude of local circumstances, not to any great political excitement. A rare mention of political issues occurred in the City of London, where opponents of Barlow Trecothick made much of his role as 'a friend to the colonies', for hostile American responses to the Townshend Duties were now becoming known.[35] If policy matters seldom impinged on the electoral scene, neither was there any clash of administration and opposition. There was less government interference than had been usual under the Duke of Newcastle, for Chatham disapproved of ministerial electioneering in principle, and Grafton was too idle and uninterested, even permitting Newcastle, though in opposition, to nominate candidates for the Treasury boroughs of Rye and Seaford, as he had done for so long. Local electoral alliances bore no necessary relation to national politics, as when Grenvillite Lord

Buckinghamshire supported two Rockinghamites in Norfolk against a sitting Grenvillite member. Although faction leaders sought to match candidates and seats, whether their followers fared well or badly depended on circumstances over which they had little influence. At this election the Grenvillite party of 41 MPs was reduced by ten, with nineteen losses and nine new supporters.[36] The Rockinghamite party, which had dropped to 54 MPs, ended the election with 57.[37]

As usual the new House of Commons would contain over a quarter of new members, this time 167, and the political attitude of most was unknown, a ground for optimism for opposition and concern to administration. When the new Parliament met briefly in May Lord North 'plumed administration on there being between 3 and 400 of the last Parliament in the present', a customary occurrence but a debating-point reminder of that House's support of each successive ministry. James West, reporting this to Newcastle, commented that 'it is more difficult now perhaps than in any part of the Duke of Newcastle's life to form a judgement of this Parliament, when matters of real business and altercation may come on'.[38] A few days later this more considered, and shrewdly accurate, opinion was penned by Sir Matthew Fetherstonhaugh.

> If I can give any guess at Parliamentary Connections, I *do* not think the majority (by far) of the new members stand well disposed towards the present people in power. I hear a great many free censures thrown out, which make me think (if our friends play their cards right) they may make us happy in a better system. But if I might advise, they should hazard no division, but upon a strong and material subject, for as in war so in Parliament, a good blow *staggers* the adversary, but slight skirmishes only serve to strengthen the enemy (who sets out superior), and waste your own forces, who generally desert, upon unsuccessful combats.[39]

What gave the general election significance was the return of John Wilkes for Middlesex. Wilkes, though still an outlaw, returned to Britain early in 1768 from his French exile, aiming to obtain a Parliamentary seat by popular election. He had little to lose in a well-calculated gamble to retrieve his political and financial fortunes. The ministry studiously ignored his presence, not to avoid another gift of martyrdom, but simply because the cabinet was split, the Chathamite part favouring leniency as against the hardline attitude of their colleagues. Wilkes was left free to stand for Parliament, and, after coming last of seven candidates in London, declared his candidature for the metropolitan county of Middlesex. A whirlwind campaign, assisted on election day by mob intimidation of opposing voters, put Wilkes at the top of a low poll, swept to victory by a tide of popular enthusiasm channelled by a superb organisation, as the artisans and shopkeepers of London outvoted the rural gentry.[40]

The cabinet, stunned by this event, in April decided, under pressure from George III, to expel Wilkes. But a pretext was not easy to find, especially after Lord Chief Justice Mansfield revoked the outlawry on 8 June, on a technicality. For although Wilkes was imprisoned for two years after surrendering to justice in April, that was punishment for the libels for which he had already been expelled in 1764. The London area meanwhile was the scene of repeated disorders, celebrations over his election being followed by protests over his incarceration, culminating in a riot of 10 May outside his prison that was quelled by soldiers with seven fatalities, the so-called 'Massacre of St George's Fields'. These political disturbances had a background of social distress produced by a combination of a bitter winter and economic recession, and the propertied class closed ranks in face of this threat. Opposition MPs joined with ministerial supporters to criticise not the deployment of troops but the government failure to maintain order. Lord North replied by blaming the local magistrates.[41]

No Parliamentary action could be taken about Wilkes until November, and the attention of the ministry was directed to more urgent and important matters, the French seizure of Corsica, renewed defiance in the American colonies, and a developing crisis in Ireland. In 1767 Secretaries of State Shelburne and Conway had so neglected Europe because of their concern with imperial matters and internal politics that Britain could not be said to have had a foreign policy at all. Nor did Conway's replacement by Weymouth in January 1768 lead to any improvement. Horace Walpole wrote scathingly of the administration then that 'they endeavoured to doze over all thoughts of the continent'.[42] There was no anticipation in London of France's acquisition of Corsica from Genoa in May 1768, even though French soldiers had since 1764 been assisting Genoa in the suppression of a Corsican nationalist movement under Pasquale Paoli. Only in April did the British ambassador to Paris, Lord Rochford, pick up rumours of French intentions, and, misled by Choiseul, his assessment was that France would not risk a war with Britain. This British failure in timing was crucial. The prior dispatch of a British naval squadron to Corsica would have thrown that decision on Choiseul: and France's naval weakness, and a hostile French public opinion, might well have deterred him from the venture. But after May the decision whether to embark on a war to reverse the French coup lay with Britain.

This international crisis coincided with disorders in London. The British government was pre-occupied, and also divided. Chathamites Shelburne, Camden, and Hawke were alarmed by the new French threat to British naval and commercial interests in the western Mediterranean, but the cabinet majority did not think Corsica worth a war. The official British response was impotent disapproval, conveyed by Shelburne.[43] That he had been overruled in his own department widened the breach with his colleagues. When later in the summer Paoli appealed for help to Britain, where the Corsican cause was popular, he received help not only from private individuals but also secretly from the British government. George III approved this, but firmly told Grafton on 16 September that a war to prevent French military occupation of the island would be both expensive and futile.[44] This aid merely delayed completion of the French conquest until 1769, when Paoli took refuge in Britain.[45] The Corsican episode seemed to confirm the belief of contemporaries at home and abroad that Britain had lost interest in Europe, and statesmen like Panin and Frederick II wrote her off as a continental power.[46] They were so far correct in this assessment in that for the next two years, until the Falkland Islands Crisis, British political attention was focused on America and Wilkes.

Throughout the winter of 1767–68 disturbing news had been arriving from America of opposition to the Townshend duties, first of trade boycotts in most of New England, and then of the publication in colonial newspapers from December 1767 of the serial 'Letters of a Pennsylvania Farmer', written by lawyer John Dickinson of Philadelphia. These explicitly denied the right of Parliament to lay any taxes at all on the colonies, whether internal like the stamp taxes or external like Townshend's port duties. This claim in the *Farmer's Letters* was endorsed by public meetings from Massachusetts to Georgia, and officially by the Massachusetts Circular Letter approved by that colony's assembly on 11 February as an example to be adopted elsewhere. This still conceded that Parliament was the legislature for 'the whole empire', but any tax infringed the rights of 'American subjects' because they were not represented there.[47]

This new constitutional challenge, making clear what had only been implicit in the Stamp Act Crisis, did not become the subject of Parliamentary attention until the end of the year. The ministry meanwhile took stern and effective action to control the situation in

America. Responsibility for this lay with American Secretary Hillsborough, who as soon as he knew on 15 April of the Massachusetts Circular Letter obtained cabinet approval, Shelburne being the sole dissenter, to circularise all governors with an order to prevent any response from their assemblies, and to instruct Governor Bernard of Massachusetts to force withdrawal of the circular. This hardline policy was followed on 8 June by an order to General Gage to send soldiers to Boston to maintain order there. Simultaneously the Admiralty was instructed to send five ships. This action was a response to a plea of 12 February from the American Customs Board, based in that port. This firm action was retrospectively fully justified, by a Boston riot of 10 June when custom officials sought to impound for smuggling a ship owned by John Hancock, a prominent patriot. It was in this atmosphere of excitement that the Massachusetts Assembly on 30 June rejected the ministerial demand for repudiation of its circular, by 92 votes to 17, and was then dissolved by Governor Bernard. Eight colonial assemblies had responded to that circular before Hillsborough's letter reached their governors, and the other four did so by the end of the year. The protest was universal, but the trade boycott to give it teeth was as yet ineffective, since Philadelphia led a widespread refusal to cooperate with Boston, and Gage warned Hillsborough not to be fooled by colonial propaganda in that respect.[48]

Further escalation of the crisis came with news on 19 July of the Boston riot of 10 June. Several cabinet meetings culminated in two policy decisions on 27 July. One was to send Lord Botetourt to Virginia as resident governor, in place of the absentee Sir Jeffrey Amherst. That colony had been to the fore in opposing taxes both in 1765 and 1768, and was perceived to need a firm hand; but Amherst regarded his salary as a pensionary reward for his wartime command in America. The second decision was to dispatch more soldiers to Boston, by now obviously under mob rule in the absence of any military protection for officials there. The ministry was calling the colonial bluff in Boston, where during the summer Sam Adams and other patriots professed defiance, claiming that the government could not even suppress riots in London. In Britain many feared that civil war might ensue, but the colonists attempted no resistance when the soldiers arrived in Boston on 28 September. News of this bloodless coup reached Britain on 4 November, before Parliament met. Grafton, by then officially head of the ministry, would be able to propose colonial conciliation from a position of strength.[49]

The third ongoing major problem, Ireland, would not attract atten-tion at Westminister, being as yet a matter only for King and cabinet. Lord Townshend's 1767 appointment as Lord-Lieutenant was intended to implement the decision of the Grenville cabinet in 1765, that hence-forth Ireland would be directly ruled by a viceroy living in Dublin Castle. That idea was dropped by the Rockingham ministry, but revived by George III and Chatham in 1766. Lord Bristol had let them down, but Lord Townshend, a former army general, was made of sterner stuff. The purpose of his appointment was recalled in 1771 by Lord North, by then Prime Minister, when he promised Townshend full support 'to establish and confirm the measure adopted in 1767, having a Lord Lieutenant constantly resident in Ireland'.[50] And Grafton stated in 1804 that Townshend was appointed 'under the same stipulation for perma-nent residence as Lord Chatham had intended'.[51] Townshend was a courtier, who so strongly shared George III's views on the role of the monarchy that on Bute's resignation in 1763 he had commented to him on 'the insolence of an aristocracy … forging fetters' for the King,[52] an analogy applicable to the Undertakers and Dublin Castle.

Prior to his departure for Ireland Townshend obtained from cabi-net meetings of 7 and 8 October permission for two popular measures, septennial Irish Parliaments and security of tenure for Irish judges.[53] The Judges Tenure Bill was rejected by the Irish Commons after an unacceptable clause was inserted by the British Privy Council against Townshend's advice, one that would allow the British Parliament a voice in the removal of Irish judges: Camden and Conway supported Townshend in a ministerial split on this point.[54] The Septennial Bill was sent over to Britain with the next election specified for 1774. It returned to Ireland as an Octennial Bill, but with the election to be in 1768. Shelburne told Townshend that eight-year intervals would better suit the Irish circumstance of biennial sessions, and that simul-taneous general elections in Britain and Ireland would be avoided.[55] The Octennial Act made the passage of unpopular government meas-ures more difficult, as MPs became more aware of their electors: but the real losers were the shocked Undertakers, who had assumed the Septennial Bill would be rejected as usual. Opposition peer Lord Charlemont recorded John Ponsonby's reaction to the news. 'His countenance fell. He turned pale, and it was visible to every one that some fatal news had been received … Never did I see in one group so many doleful faces, nor to me so laughable a sight.'[56]

The ulterior motive behind the ministry's willingness to accept some such popular demand was the desire to obtain a reciprocal acceptance of an increase in the size of the Irish army from 12,000 to 15,000 men. There were two distinct motives behind this policy. The introduction in 1764 of a rotation of army regiments throughout the British Empire made necessary their equalisation in size, and those in Ireland were smaller than elsewhere. There was also an intention that Ireland should contribute more to imperial defence.[57] To allay Protestant fears about the Catholic majority, the ministry gave an assurance that despite the rotation system there would never be less than 12,000 soldiers in Ireland.[58] But on 19 April 1768, despite the support of many independent MPs, this measure was defeated, by 105 votes to 101, because of the hostility of the Undertakers, displeased by the Octennial Act and by failures to meet their patronage demands. There was also the suspicion that the increase, paid for by Ireland, was intended to enable Britain to deploy more soldiers to control America.[59] This episode convinced Townshend of the need to free Dublin Castle from reliance on the Undertakers, a situation Southern Secretary Shelburne had hitherto been prepared to countenance.[60] The Lord-Lieutenant wrote to warn him on 31 May that 'this is now the crisis of Irish government. If a system is at this time wisely formed and steadily pursued, his Majesty's affairs may hereafter be carried on with ease, with dignity and safety'. Further temporising as in the 1750s would only 'bring the King's authority in Ireland, low as it is, into still greater contempt'.[61] The cabinet was now convinced in principle of the need to humble the Undertakers, but preferred to await events at the meeting of the newly elected Irish Parliament in October 1769 before deciding on a course of action. By then Grafton had been official head of the ministry for a year.

Grafton's formal elevation to the status normally appertaining to his post as First Lord of the Treasury, and one which he had indeed been enjoying unofficially during Chatham's illness, was a consequence of his decision to remove Shelburne from a cabinet wherein he was increasingly isolated from his colleagues. Shelburne's offence was personal behaviour, not disagreement on policy: contrary to much contemporary and historical opinion, he did not oppose the dispatch of soldiers to Boston.[62] When Grafton raised the subject with George III, the King closeted Lord Chancellor Camden and 'very frankly said that Lord Shelburne manifestly still attempted to thwart every measure that originated from you', so he told Grafton. The problem was that Shelburne enjoyed the protection of Chatham, the shadow of whose possible return to health and political dominance still hung over the ministry. That was why George III had sounded out Camden, who agreed that

Shelburne had lost the 'good opinion' of all the 'active members of the cabinet'. The replacement envisaged was Lord Rochford, a professional diplomat rather than politician, currently ambassador to Paris. Camden approved this choice, because 'he could neither be called of the Bedford connection nor adverse to the Earl of Chatham'.[63] Rochford, who arrived in London on 6 September, was summoned by the King. 'His Majesty ordered him to take the Seals. That he is of no party.' So Rochford told Albemarle, who told Newcastle.[64]

Camden, however, now warned Grafton that if Chatham, still Lord Privy Seal, resigned because of Shelburne's dismissal he himself would do the same.[65] This highlighted the delicate problem of removing Shelburne without losing the entire Chathamite part of the administration, as might happen if Chatham himself expressed disapproval. The panic-stricken Grafton, himself, as he said, in 'a similitude of situation', wavered as to whether to take the risk, and in a letter of 2 October threw the decision on the King.[66] George III had no doubt as to what should be done. Shelburne's conduct, especially towards Grafton, had caused 'most of the members of my administration separately' to insist on his removal from office. The King suggested therefore that Grafton should see Lady Chatham beforehand and explain why Shelburne was being dismissed. Grafton did so on 9 October, and explained how Shelburne had 'on every occasion' sought 'to thwart and not to assist His Majesty's government'. But Lady Chatham warned that her husband would not easily accept Shelburne's removal, and the approach produced the very result Grafton and the King had tried to avoid.[67] Chatham, evidently believing that Shelburne had already been dismissed, submitted a letter of resignation on 12 October, ostensibly because of his 'extremely weak and broken state of health', but also pointedly mentioning the removal of Shelburne.[68] Grafton sought to dissuade Chatham, and he mentioned to the King that it was fortunate Shelburne had not yet been removed, since it would be a crucial point whether Chatham resigned on that issue, or whether Shelburne merely followed him out of office. George III himself wrote to urge Chatham to stay so that, when recovered, 'I may have your assistance in resisting the torrents of factions'. He was rewarded for his effort when Chatham gave only ill health as the reason for his resignation.[69] That removed the danger of a general Chathamite exodus from the ministry, especially when Chatham urged Camden not to resign. Grafton spoke to Granby, an enemy of the Bedfords, and Camden persuaded the highly regarded lawyer John Dunning to stay on as Solicitor-General, even though he had

owed that post in January as much to Shelburne as to Camden, and
sat for a Shelburne borough.[70] The only resignations were of Shelburne and his Commons mouthpiece Barré. In the reshuffle Rochford
became Northern Secretary, Weymouth having expressed a wish to
transfer to the Southern Department.[71] Chatham's own post of Lord
Privy Seal was now demoted from cabinet status, after Northington
declined it. Despite applications from Sandwich and from North, on
behalf of Halifax, it was somewhat inexplicably given to Lord Bristol,
who in 1766 had been Chatham's unwise choice as Lord-Lieutenant
of Ireland. The French embassy was given to Lord Harcourt, a
courtier high in favour with the King.

   Grafton had for eighteen months headed the ministry on behalf of
Chatham. He was to do so in his own right for only fifteen months,
and a troubled time he had of it. Leading an administration that was
an uneasy coalition of Chathamites and Bedfordites, colleagues
divided by personal animosities as well as political attitudes, he was to
be confronted, and his ministry eventually destroyed, by the second
John Wilkes case, that of the Middlesex Election.

Notes

1 BL Add. MSS. 32985, fos 14–15.
2 Thomas, *Lord North*, p. 20.
3 *Grafton Autobiography*, pp. 166–8.
4 BL Add. MSS. 32986, fos 58–60.
5 Malmesbury MSS. Photocopies B875–6.
6 BL Add. MSS. 32987, fos 49–50.
7 This incident is well authenticated. BL Add. MSS. 32931, fos 289–92.
   Malmesbury MSS. Photocopies A478. Lawson, *George Grenville*, pp. 249–
   50, 252–3. Brooke, *Chatham Administration*, p. 321.
8 For reports of the debate see Simmons and Thomas, *Proceedings and
   Debates*, II, 518–19.
9 BL Add. MSS. 32987, fo. 149.
10 Thomas, *Townshend Duties Crisis*, pp. 41–5. Brooke, *Chatham Administration*, pp. 315–24.
11 Malmesbury MSS. Photocopies B878–82.
12 BL Add. MSS. 42086, fos 5–8, printed in *Grenville Papers*, IV, 249–53.
13 Malmesbury MSS. Photocopies B882.
14 Grafton MSS. no. 545, quoted Brooke, *Chatham Administration*, p. 330 n.
15 Rodger, *Insatiable Earl*, pp. 114–15.
16 Thomas, *Townshend Duties Crisis*, pp. 45–7. Brooke, *Chatham Administration*, pp. 324–33.

17 BL Add. MSS. 32987, fos 270–1.
18 BL Add. MSS. 32988, fo. 21. *Commons Journals*, XXXI, 482, 505.
19 BL Add. MSS. 32988, fos 58–9. *Commons Journals*, XXXI, 533–4, 538.
20 BL Add. MSS. 32988, fos 74–5, 81–2, 85–6. Hoffman, *Edmund Burke*, p. 423. Lawson, *George Grenville*, pp. 253–4, assumes Grenville opposed the measure.
21 BL Add. MSS. 32988, fos 81–2.
22 BL Add. MSS. 32988, fos 170–3. Walpole, *Memoirs*, III, 111.
23 Bowen, Thesis, pp. 426–30. Brooke, *Chatham Administration*, pp. 336–7.
24 BL Add. MSS. 32988, fo. 48.
25 BL Add. MSS. 32988, fos 85–6. *Commons Journals*, XXXI, 545. Walpole, *Memoirs*, III, 109.
26 BL Add. MSS. 32988, fos 136–7. *Commons Journals*, XXXI, 566–7.
27 BL Add. MSS. 32988, fo. 185. *Commons Journals*, XXXI, 583–4, 597–8. Walpole, *Memoirs*, III, 109.
28 BL Add. MSS. 32988. fo. 152. *Commons Journals*, XXXI, 573.
29 BL Add. MSS. 32988, fos 184–5. Walpole, *Memoirs*, III, 111–12.
30 BL Add. MSS. 32988, fos 355–6. Walpole, *Memoirs*, III, 112.
31 BL Add. MSS. 32988, fo. 381. Walpole, *Memoirs*, III, 113.
32 The whole episode is covered by Bonsall, *Sir James Lowther and Cumberland and Westmorland Elections 1754–1775*, pp. 83–103.
33 BL Add. MSS. 32988, fos 357–8, 369–70. Walpole, *Memoirs*, III, 114–16.
34 BL Add. MSS. 32978, fos 235–41.
35 BL Add. MSS. 32988, fo. 49.
36 Lawson, *George Grenville*, pp. 258–69.
37 O'Gorman, *Rise of Party*, pp. 220–8.
38 BL Add. MSS. 32990, fo. 57.
39 BL Add. MSS. 32990, fo. 107.
40 Thomas, *John Wilkes*, pp. 68–76.
41 Thomas, *John Wilkes*, pp. 76–86.
42 Walpole, *Memoirs*, III, 146.
43 Legg, *British Diplomatic Instructions*, pp. 101–5.
44 *Corr. of George III*, II, 44.
45 For a detailed examination of the Corsica question see Escott, Thesis, pp. 134–218.
46 Scott, *British Foreign Policy*, pp. 112–24.
47 Thomas, *Townshend Duties Crisis*, pp. 76–8.
48 Thomas, *Townshend Duties Crisis*, pp. 81–6.
49 Thomas, *Townshend Duties Crisis*, pp. 86–93.
50 Townshend Letter-Books, 7. North to Townshend, 3 June 1771.
51 *Grafton Autobiography*, p. 157. For a similar opposition assumption see Hoffman, *Edmund Burke*, p. 407. For a challenge to this interpretation

see Bartlett, 'The Townshend Viceroyalty 1767–72', in Bartlett and Hayton, *Penal Era and Golden Age*, pp. 88–112.

52 Namier and Brooke, *House of Commons 1754–1790*, III, 552.

53 BL Add. MSS. 57817, fos 150–3. Powell, Thesis, p. 125. Southern Secretary Shelburne later claimed Townshend had misunderstood and exceeded his authority. *CHOP*, II, 195–200, 212–14, 219–20.

54 *CHOP*, II, 220, 238. Walpole, *Memoirs*, III, 78–80. Powell, Thesis, pp. 131–2.

55 *CHOP*, II, 195, 202, 205.

56 *HMC Charlemont*, I, 26.

57 Shy, *Towards Lexington*, p. 274. McDowell, *Ireland in the Age of Imperialism and Revolution*, p. 218. Bartlett, *EHR*, 96 (1981), 540–1.

58 *CHOP*, II, 214–15.

59 *CHOP*, II, 333–5. Fitzmaurice, *Shelburne*, I, 356–9.

60 *CHOP*, II, 296, 299, 304–5.

61 *CHOP*, II, 345.

62 *Grenville Papers*, IV, 332.

63 *Corr. of George III*, II, 42–3.

64 BL Add. MSS. 32991, fo. 331.

65 *Grafton Autobiography*, p. 214.

66 *Corr. of George III*, II, 47–8.

67 *Corr. of George III*, II, 49–51. *Chatham Papers*, III, 334–7.

68 *Chatham Papers*, III, 338.

69 *Corr. of George III*, II, 53–8.

70 Brooke, *Chatham Administration*, pp. 383–4.

71 Grafton MSS. no. 799.

9

The Grafton ministry (1768–1770):
the Middlesex Election and
the Townshend Duties Crisis

'The King seems to have changed his plan of government. The idea of an unconnected independent Administration is given up, and the Duke of Grafton is declared first Minister, with full confidence and ample powers.'[1] So did Grenvillite William Knox write the epitaph of the Chatham experiment of non-party government. Grafton had already sold the pass by admitting the Bedfords as a group. Chatham's resignation finally removed the shadow hanging over the administration, the possibility that he might return and reverse policy decisions taken in his absence. Grafton, now with full power and responsibility, enjoyed the King's wholehearted support throughout his brief ministry: on 13 October George III told the Duke that he was a man 'in whom I can in the most entire manner rely, and whom I sincerely value as a friend'.[2] Grafton possessed more in the way of ability and character than tradition has accorded him, though the distractions of his private life, women and horse racing, may have contributed to his ministerial failure. But he did not have an easy task. Faced with a divided cabinet and an increasingly united and formidable opposition, he inherited also a difficult policy legacy: the fiasco over Corsica, confrontation with John Wilkes over the Middlesex Election, and the ongoing American crisis. All those issues would at once be raised in the new Parliament, for it was due to meet on 8 November.

Within the cabinet Grafton obtained scant support from the original Chathamite part of his administration. The respective heads of the army and navy, Lord Granby and Sir Edward Hawke, were little interested in politics. Camden and Conway were both indecisive men, the Lord Chancellor unreliable, the latter still sensitive about offending his former Rockinghamite allies. Fortunately for the Duke, his ministry derived strength from the newer recruits. Lord North was emerging as the key figure, doing the financial business as well as leading the Commons. Lord Hillsborough proved an effective American Secretary. Lord Rochford, an experienced diplomat, possessed a safe pair of hands in foreign policy. None of these three had factious connections, and their loyalty was to the King's government. But in the policy clashes that arose over America and Wilkes they tended to side with the hardline Bedford faction, as ever greedy for power and patronage. The ailing Bedford now took a back seat, but Gower was proud and ambitious, Weymouth difficult to control, and Sandwich anxious for a cabinet post.

This discordant element in the ministry was now finally separated from their old Grenvillite allies. The summer of 1768 had witnessed a rapprochement between the Rockingham and Grenville factions. In July Edmund Burke told Alexander Wedderburn that Grenville was 'a most excellent Party man', one on whom reliance could be placed. Grenvillites optimistically detected a Rockinghamite willingness to follow Grenville's lead in the Commons, and thought that Rockingham himself had 'lowered his pretensions', presumably with respect to any future coalition ministry.[3] The threat of a formidable opposition coalition increased when Chatham sought and obtained a reconciliation with his brother-in-law Lord Temple, already allied with Grenville. The *Political Register*, a Grenvillite paper, announced this union on 25 November.[4] It was fortunate for Grafton that Chatham did not recover his health until the following summer.

Although the political omens were black, Grafton got off to a good start in Parliament, because opposition overplayed its hand over Corsica. Newcastle with this topic in mind, had put foreign policy at the top of the agenda for a meeting of the Rockinghamite leadership on 8 June.[5] The Duke was to play no further part in Parliament, for he died on 17 November, aged seventy-five, reputedly £300,000 the poorer for his public career. His political reputation has now been rescued from the tradition of corruption and incompetence, and contemporaries never doubted his personal integrity. 'I knew him to be very good-natured, and his hands to be extremely clean', wrote his old colleague and sometime opponent Lord Chesterfield.[6] That Newcastle had picked out Corsica as a subject to take up suggests that his advice would not have averted the subsequent opposition blunder. In the customarily wide-ranging debate on the Address on 8 November seconder Hans Stanley played down the significance of Corsica. Edmund Burke criticised the administration's lack of alertness, Grenville the feebleness of policy in contrast to his own gunboat diplomacy. Sir Edward Hawke publicly belied his earlier private cabinet opinion by claiming there was little threat to British trade.[7]

Opposition then decided to make Corsica the basis of the first major challenge to government. On 17 November Grenvillite Henry Seymour moved for all relevant papers, in effect asking whether the ministry had any policy. Answer was there none. Commons Leader Lord North countered with the argument that Britain did not want to be seen as the bully of Europe. Grenville replied that such ministerial weakness was dangerous. 'For fear of going to war, you will make a war unavoidable'. Bedfordite Rigby, though in office, scored an irrelevant party point by the claim that Britain's weakness on America had encouraged Choiseul to annex Corsica. The political consensus was that Corsica was not worth a war, and the Parliamentary opposition had clearly made a big mistake by selecting the topic as the subject of the first vote in the new Parliament, for the ministry won by 230 to 84.[8] James Harris noted 'a most motley minority of Rockinghams, Grenvillians, Country Gentlemen, Lord George Sackville's Friends, and even of Lord Bute's'.[9] Horace Walpole, apart from the wrong choice of topic, thought the opposition had magnified its mistake by the wording of the motion.

> When the strength of a new Parliament is not known, methinks it were wise, by a plausible question to draw in as many of the lookers out, at least of the rational, and the well meaning, as possible. In lieu of that, they frame a question that required a very strong opposition stomach to digest ... and thus a fluctuating majority becomes a stable one – for every interested man will now be in a hurry to be the two hundred and thirty-first. It was a great day for the administration, a better for the Duke of Choiseul ... France will look on this vote as a decision not to quarrel for Corsica.[10]

In this fortuitous manner the Grafton ministry was strengthened rather than weakened by the Corsica question, and thereafter Lord Rochford ensured that foreign policy would not again be a focus for political attack. He was a career diplomat, and he stood aloof from the distraction of internal politics, conducting a positive foreign policy while his cabinet colleagues were concerned with Wilkes and America. His aim was to end the diplomatic isolation made starkly obvious by the Corsican crisis, and Russia was now the only possibility, an opportunity enhanced by Turkey's declaration of war, in October 1768, on a Catherine II already concerned about guerrilla warfare in Poland and the revived power of the anti-Russian Hat party in Sweden. This threefold Russian crisis she blamed on Choiseul's machinations, and so Russia looked to Britain for help. But Rochford maintained the British refusal to pay a peacetime subsidy, claiming that Parliament would never endorse it, and offered merely a twenty-year defensive treaty, excluding any colonial war to balance the absence of a 'Turkish clause'. This proposal was scorned in St Petersburg, and even the vital assistance given by Britain to the Russian fleet on its epic voyage in 1769–70 from the Baltic to the eastern Mediterranean, an exploit impossible without repairs and supplies in British ports, failed to produce a more favourable reaction. Yet the episode worsened Britain's relationship with the Bourbon Powers. Choiseul did reject a Spanish suggestion of October 1769 that the Russian fleet should be intercepted, fearing that a general war would result; but British determination to protect the Russian fleet both on its journey and while in the Mediterranean opened the prospect of confrontation even before the Falkland Islands Crisis.[11]

While the Grafton ministry must have anticipated adverse criticism over Corsica, it could invite commendation for the successful military coup in Boston. The cabinet was nevertheless aware of the deeper American problem, the challenge to Parliament's right of taxation. American Secretary Hillsborough understood all too well the legacy bequeathed by Charles Townshend. The American objection to taxation, based on non-representation in Parliament, logically implied an exemption from all legislation. Simple repeal of Townshend's taxes was therefore not an option the cabinet could consider or Parliament would accept. British political attitudes during the Stamp Act Crisis seemed to make that clear, although in both administration and opposition that course of action had its advocates. Yet Hillsborough was among those who soon perceived that the duties Townshend had levied on colonial imports of British manufactured goods might be deemed 'uncommercial', as adversely affecting their sale. Therein lay the path to a solution.[12]

The ministry was not able to give America the attention it deserved. John Wilkes could not afford to languish forgotten in prison, and on 3 November he announced his intention of petitioning Parliament for a redress of his grievances. It was in vain that Grafton sought conciliation rather than confrontation. On 10 and 13 November he sent a message and then a messenger to Wilkes, offering not to expel him from Parliament if he dropped his petition, and even release from prison if he would make a token submission to the King. Wilkes declined this invitation to embrace ignominious obscurity.[13]

But before the Middlesex Election case came to dominate the political landscape the Grafton cabinet contrived to devise an agreed colonial policy. Events in both America and Britain made that possible. The resignation of Chatham gave ministers a free hand to act, without fear of rebuke or overrule. The American problem appeared less intractable, for the colonies this time had so far failed to organise an effective trade boycott, and Boston had quietly succumbed to military occupation. The general mood of the Commons debate of 8 November on the Address, which mostly concerned America, was in favour of moderation, although Lord North, in a phrase later remembered against him, declared himself against repeal of the Townshend taxation 'until he saw America prostrate at his feet'.[14]

During November Grafton formulated an American policy acceptable to both cabinet and Parliament. There would be a series of Parliamentary resolutions condemning the resistance in Massachusetts, followed by an Address asking George III to order Governor Bernard to submit names and evidence concerning any treason committed in the colony during 1768, so that under an old statute of Henry VIII such offenders could be tried in Britain. American Secretary Hillsborough favoured alteration or even forfeiture of the Massachusetts charter, but was outvoted in cabinet. Deeming the policy a meaningless gesture, words not action, he refused to move the Address in the Lords. Public opinion was broadly on his side, for when the policy became known the ministerial failure to exact retribution from Boston or change the Massachusetts charter aroused widespread astonishment. The cabinet decided to refuse repeal of the taxation until the colonies showed a proper submission, but by the end of 1768 the prospect of a repeal in the Parliamentary session of 1770 was being leaked. The Grafton ministry had devised a complete American policy, intended to solve the double problem of British indignation and colonial defiance: apparent initial firmness and subsequent concession, if colonial behaviour allowed Britain to save face.[15] As a compromise it was neither negative nor foolish, for the current situation in America raised hopes that the colonial problem might, with a little encouragement, simply fade away.

The ministerial policy was revealed in the House of Lords on 15 December. It nonplussed the Rockinghamite party, which had been expecting a harder line, and was denounced as 'a paper war' by Lord Temple. Grafton answered the accusation of softness by stating that there would be no repeal of American taxation that session.[16] The resolutions and Address were carried in the Lords without a division, but the Commons was already too busy with Wilkes to consider America until 26 January 1769. Dowdeswell then denounced the proposed use of the Treason Act as unfair, Grenville the whole policy as a sham, echoing his brother when he described it as 'waste paper'. North replied that order had been restored; that refusal to repeal the taxes was a policy decision; and that mention of the Treason Act was a warning to the colonists not to rely with impunity on their own law courts. Barré urged repeal of the Townshend duties, as 'contrary to commercial principles' and because America would not otherwise be quiet. At the end of the debate the Grenvillite party voted for the resolutions, carried by 213 to 80, and against the Address, carried by 155 to 89.[17] In a subsequent debate on 8 February the ministry did not deny the opposition contention that Townshend's duties were unenforceable and harmful to British exports, simply answering that the American denial of Parliament's right of taxation made repeal impossible.[18]

By then Wilkes had long virtually monopolised political attention. The presentation on 14 November of his petition alleging malpractice over the *North Briton* case sparked off a series of Commons proceedings as the House examined the complaints. The ministry was undecided what to do, and on 10 December postponed the hearing until 27 January 1769. On that same day, 10 December, Wilkes finally succeeded in goading the ministry into acting against him, by publishing in the *St. James's Chronicle* two papers relating to the St George's Fields 'Massacre' of 10 May. One was a letter of 17 April by Secretary of State Weymouth reminding local magistrates of the availability of soldiers. The other was a preface alleging this to be proof that the slaughter had been planned. It was this outrageous accusation that provoked Grafton into finally deciding on the expulsion of Wilkes from Parliament. On 15 December he moved a Lords resolution that the comment was 'an insolent, scandalous and seditious libel', the same wording used in 1764 about the *North Briton*. The Commons received this Lords resolution the same day, but postponed consideration of it also to 27 January.[19]

Within the cabinet Camden, Conway, Granby and Hawke, the remnant of the old Chatham ministry, still resisted expulsion; but scruples about expelling Wilkes twice for the same offence could now be overcome by the new alleged seditious libel, and on 22 January 1769 the cabinet decided to proceed. There followed a succession of long and heated Commons debates. The first, on 23 January, was over an opposition motion to reverse the resolution of 24 November 1763 that Parliamentary privilege did not cover seditious libel; the ministry may have been caught unawares, for the attendance was low, but Grenville and his followers voted with administration in a majority of 165 to 71.[20] After the allegations in the petition from Wilkes were all successively rejected as trivial, the House on 2 February voted the Lords resolution of 15 December, by 239 to 136. The stage was set for the expulsion of Wilkes.[21]

The expulsion motion, proposed on 3 February by Lord Barrington, was a composite one, listing libels from 1763 as well as that of 10 December. Opposition speakers denounced as unfair this tactic, evidently designed to maximise support. Wilkes had already been expelled once for that in the *North Briton*, while five years earlier the Commons had ignored the three 'impious and obscene' libels now cited from the *Essay on Woman*. Grenville, who had then been Prime Minister, made that point in a speech deemed his best ever oration. Grenville's opposition to expulsion aroused widespread astonishment, and was not followed by some of his own adherents. More ominous for the ministry was that of Barré, for it reflected the hostility of Chatham, many of whose followers were still in office. Although Lord North defended the ministerial tactic, and pointed out that the libel on Lord Weymouth was a new crime since the election of Wilkes, unease among customary administration supporters was reflected in a lower attendance than in some previous debates, a majority of 219 to 137 for expulsion. Hawke and Granby voted for a measure they had opposed in cabinet but Conway was absent.[22]

In that debate of 3 February Grenville reminded MPs that already public opinion could foresee only two ways the ministry might extricate itself from the trap Wilkes had set, for the common and correct assumption was that he would seek and secure continuous re-election. Either the administration could refuse to issue a new writ, thereby depriving the Middlesex electorate of a representative: or the seat would have to be awarded to a minority candidate. The saga was prolonged by the inability of the ministry to find a candidate bold enough to challenge Wilkes on the public hustings. His first re-election, on 16 February, was unopposed, with reputedly 2,000 freeholders present. Next day the Commons voided this election, after resolving that since he had been expelled he was 'incapable' of election. This was opposed by Dowdeswell, Grenville and Barré, but carried by 235 votes to 89.[23] At the next election, on 16 March, a rival candidate briefly appeared, a saw-mill proprietor Charles Dingley, but no one was willing to propose him. In the Commons debate next day Grenville accepted that the resolution of 17 February made Wilkes inadmissible and the opposition did not force a vote when his election was disallowed.[24] Whether or not the ministry was involved in the Dingley fiasco, it produced a candidate for the third monthly by-election, on 13 April. He was Colonel Henry Luttrell, a young war hero from the Portugal campaign of 1762 and already MP for Bossiney, a seat he vacated only on 11 April. Luttrell attended the election under the protection of a large posse of horsemen, and an orderly poll saw Wilkes defeat him by 1,143 votes to 296.

This return was invalidated the next day, and the ministry called for a Commons examination of the poll on 15 April, when a motion to award the seat to Luttrell produced a lively debate. The government case was that the House of Commons had the power to expel and incapacitate its members, and therefore, as Lord North put it, the freeholders polling for Wilkes had thrown away their votes. Radical MP William Beckford warned that a corrupt majority could expel whoever they wished, an alarmist and improbable scenario. Grenville made another fine speech in his role as guardian of the constitution, distinguishing between a Parliamentary resolution and the law of the land. The House alone had no right to impose a legal disqualification. The ministry won by 197 to 143. Its majority had fallen to 54 as against 82 for the original expulsion. Six supporters on that occasion had changed sides, and a further 27 were absent. The administration was so alarmed at this drop in support that it mustered a large attendance for the next chapter of the story, the hearing of a petition of Middlesex freeholders on 8 May, when the ministry won by 221 votes to 152.[25]

Next day the opposition held a morale-boosting dinner at the Thatched House Tavern, attended by 72 MPs, including Grenville, Rockinghamites Burke and Dowdeswell, Chathamite Barré and City radical Beckford. The Middlesex Election case had united the various opposition factions in a common cause. Altogether 215 MPs had voted with opposition on the issue, and, with Lord Temple correctly calculating their potential strength at a minimum of 200, they looked forward to toppling the Grafton ministry in 1770.[26]

During the early months of 1769 the Parliamentary scene was largely taken up with and public attention engrossed by the furore over Wilkes. But during this very same time the ministry had to pay heed to America and India. American Secretary Hillsborough was so concerned about the lack of any positive policy that on 13 February he submitted to the cabinet a comprehensive list of proposals, major and minor, mostly coercive in attitude. They included suggestions that the Massachusetts Council, recently obstructive to the Governor, should henceforth be appointed by the Crown instead of being elected by the Assembly; and that the refusal of several colonies to comply with the 1765 Mutiny Act should be countered by the threat of quartering soldiers in private houses. But he also put forward the conciliatory suggestion that any colonies making provision for civil government costs should be exempted from the Townshend taxation. Hillsborough invited the comments of George III, who rejected the proposal about the Massachusetts Council because 'altering charters is at all times an odious measure', and declared that obedience should be the criterion for relieving colonies from the taxation.[27] All Hillsborough's ideas were rejected by the cabinet, after objections from Camden, Conway, and Grafton.[28]

The ministry would not endorse coercion of America, but its failure to offer any concession other than the vague prospect of taxation repeal next year, if the colonies should prove quiet and obedient, did not satisfy the lobby of colonial agents, merchants, and other friends of America. An attempt to expedite a decision was therefore made on 19 April, when Thomas Pownall proposed in the Commons a Committee on America. A former governor of Massachusetts, he avowedly sought a consensus solution, and disclaimed any attack on the ministry. What he had in mind was a repeal of the Townshend duties on economic grounds. Not even the Rockinghamite party supported him, and Edmund Burke expressed concern lest a confrontation might develop over America in Britain. 'I never thought America should be beat backwards and forwards as the tennis ball of faction.' Some cynical observers thought the opposition wished the tax to remain, as an embarrassment for ministers. Lord North opposed the motion because of the American trade boycott, and criticised Conway for favouring a declaration of intent. An inconclusive debate, in which no one defended the taxation, and few sought its repeal, ended in the rejection of the motion without a vote.[29]

But the discussion had served a useful purpose, in showing the ministry that there would be strong Parliamentary support for concession. It prepared the way for the cabinet decision of 1 May, when the prospect of other problems impelled ministers to seek a solution to that of America. The Middlesex Election threatened to be an ongoing issue. An international crisis was foreshadowed by Spanish designs on the Falkland Islands. While every political problem might be worsened by the impending recovery at last of Chatham from the ill health of the last few years.

Complete repeal of the Townshend duties was the solution proposed on 1 May by Prime Minister Grafton, and for obvious reasons. It was now known that by January 1769 the duties had raised a mere £11,000, in over a year. Another new factor was the decision of Philadelphia on 10 March to join the hitherto ineffective colonial boycott: expedient action might avert the economic consequence. But the Premier, though supported by Chathamites Camden and Granby and former Rockinghamite Conway, found himself outvoted by five to four over retention of the tea duty. That was favoured by North, Hillsborough, Rochford, and the two Bedfordites, Gower and Weymouth. Grafton later attributed this defeat to the absence of Sir Edward Hawke through an illness that was prolonged for much of May.[30] By such accidents is history made. Since tea was simply a commodity imported from Asia and re-exported to America, that duty was not liable to the same objection as the others, all on British manufactures. Nor was its retention merely symbolic, for it had yielded some three-quarters of that tax revenue to date, and North was to use the money to carry out the Townshend aim of paying colonial salaries. In retrospect this decision to keep the tea tax can be seen as a turning point in the story of the American Revolution, but at the time Grafton may have thought the simultaneous cabinet decision of a public promise that no future taxes would be levied on America to be of more significance. These decisions were made known to the colonies by a circular letter of 13 May, obviously intended to undermine the trade boycott and divide colonial opinion.[31]

India, by comparison with 1767, took up little Parliamentary time or political attention. The ministry was resolved to restrict consideration to financial negotiation with the Company, and to disregard such wider issues as the problem of Indian government and the question of territorial right. By the end of 1768 the ministry and Directorate had negotiated an agreement whereby the government would receive the same payment of £400,000 for another five years, while the Company would be allowed to raise its dividend eventually to 12.5 per cent, by not more than 1 per cent a year. But objections raised in the Court of Proprietors, that while the state revenue was fixed the Company income was uncertain, exposed to the risks of Indian wars and commercial hazards, led to the agreement being rejected there on 13 January 1769 by 248 votes to 207. However the Directorate, by a compromise wording that reflected this concern, persuaded the Court of Proprietors to accept the agreement on 9 February by 290 votes to 250, after a warning that the alternative would be a Parliamentary inquiry.[32] The only important Commons debate on India in 1769 took place on 27 February, over the Company petition containing the already agreed proposals. Lord North urged MPs to discuss only the financial terms and not 'the general state of the East India Company'. But Lord Clive sought to do just that in his maiden speech, asserting the need to reform the Company. His suggestions anticipated much of Lord North's legislation of 1773, notably that Directors should be elected for four or five years, and that there should be a Governor-General and Council in India. Sulivan echoed Clive's concern for reform, but the financial plan was accepted without a vote, and the subsequent Bill passed with little discussion.[33]

Although the ministry suffered no Parliamentary embarrassment in 1769 over the major issues of America and India, it faced such a prospect on two other matters, the Nullum Tempus Bill and the Civil List Debt. The opposition wasted no time in playing its trump card in order to win over the support of new MPs, a motion for a Nullum Tempus Bill being made on 15 November 1768. Proposer Sir George Savile explained to the 'many young members' that a similar act of 1623 had merely safeguarded estates derived from the Crown that had been held for sixty years before that date. He intended 'a moving limitation, to make a sixty years possession, in all future times, a bar against the claims of the Crown'. Lord North rose not to oppose but to reserve his opinion, and support for the principle of the measure was voiced by Secretary at War Lord Barrington, true to his promise in the previous session, and by George Grenville, who linked the Bill with the King's voluntary surrender in 1760 of his hereditary revenue in exchange for a fixed annual income.[34] Such was the evident popularity of the measure that the ministry offered no initial resistance, and early in February 1769 Charles Yorke thought 'there will be no opposition. The Court think it a sweetener to the pill of the Civil List Debt.'[35] No subsequent debate on the Nullum Tempus Bill took place until the House went into Committee on the measure on 24 February. Procedural expert Jeremiah Dyson then complained that there had been no discussion of the principle on the second reading, as was customary, and that then took place. William Beckford opposed the whole measure, on the radical ground that all Crown property belonged to the people, but he found no support for this view. The debate centred on an amendment by Attorney-General De Grey to make the Bill merely retrospective, like that of 1623. Solicitor-General Dunning backed his colleague with the argument that otherwise the Bill would encourage future fraudulent acquisition of

Crown property. Wedderburn replied that ministers ought to welcome the measure as a reason to refuse future applications for Crown
land. It did not reduce any royal prerogative, and would quieten public concern. Moreover, the House of Commons needed to win public
goodwill after the Middlesex Election case. This point was echoed by
Grenville, who declared that he had expected unanimous approval,
because the main objection in the previous session had been that the
Bill then had been brought in to deal with a particular case, Lowther's
action against the Duke of Portland. Now that objection did not exist,
for the eighth clause stipulated that the legislation would not apply to
actions commenced before 1 January 1769. Amid scenes of disorder
the amendment was rejected by 205 votes to 124, the extent of the
ministerial defeat being increased by the deliberate abstention of the
Bedford group for a reason that even Horace Walpole could not surmise. 'We ... beat the administration hollow', wrote the jubilant
George Byng, a Portland adherent, 'ministerial power has not, in this
instance, as yet prevailed.'[36] The Bill passed the Commons on 6 March
and went through the Lords without resistance.[37] Two years later, in
February 1771, the opposition attempted to delete the eighth clause.
In a brief Parliamentary contest, this measure survived two votes by
majorities of twenty-nine and fifteen, but failed in a third division
by ten votes.[38]

In the Nullum Tempus episode Parliamentary sympathy lay with private property as against Crown rights. But the Civil List Debt produced
a vastly different reaction, and the opposition attempt to embarrass the
ministry proved to be a bad miscalculation of Westminster opinion. It
was led by Dowdeswell and Grenville, who, as former Chancellors of
the Exchequer, must have been aware of the true reasons for the royal
deficit.[39] They had advance knowledge of the royal message submitted
to the Commons by Lord North on 28 February 1769, which acknowledged a debt of £513,511, and asked for payment to be made; for on
the previous day they consulted together on draft motions.[40] Opposition MPs sensed an opportunity to score points, even though dispas-
sionate opinion, as voiced by Horace Walpole, reflecting on all the royal
expenses, believed that sum 'could not be thought exorbitant'.[41]
William Beckford promptly suggested that money had been used, by
way of pensions, to influence voting in that House, and commented that
changes of administration were always expensive in compensatory payments to displaced office-holders. He moved for an account of all
payments from 1760 to 1769, and welcomed North's motion to add
those from 1752 to 1760. Dowdeswell, supported by Grenville, said

the accounts should distinguish the responsibility of each Chancellor of the Exchequer. North replied that all of them must share the blame, and urged that, in fairness to creditors, the debt should be paid before any inquiry. The motion for accounts was agreed, but the ministry rejected, by 164 votes to 89, another by Dowdeswell to state the Civil List balance at the time of Newcastle's resignation in May 1762, when, as he knew, it was still in credit.[42]

On the next day, 1 March, Dowdeswell moved an instruction to the impending Committee of Supply that it should not vote money before accounts were examined. Initial reactions in the ensuing debate were not what he had anticipated. Suggestions that the Civil List grant might be inadequate were made by opposition MP Charles Cornwall and by Secretary at War Lord Barrington, while Lord Granby and Charles Jenkinson both said that the 1760 settlement was the cause of the deficit. But Beckford, armed with instructions from his London constituents, demanded an inquiry first, even adopting the radical stance that 'the Crown is trustee for the people'. So did Lord George Sackville, claiming that the recent vote on the Nullum Tempus Bill showed that House to be 'the friend of liberty and the constitution, and the true friend of the people'. Edmund Burke declared that it would be 'a downright mockery of Parliamentary proceedings' if the Committee of Supply paid the debt without accounts. But this time the ministry had whipped up a large attendance, and Dowdeswell's motion was defeated by 248 votes to 135. In the ensuing Committee of Supply North gave an accurate account of Civil List expenditure, and said that George III had made the 1760 agreement 'before he had had time to form a judgement what his expenses would be'. His motion to discharge the debt was agreed without debate.[43]

Next day Dowdeswell moved to recommit the resolution, arguing that MPs 'ought to derive our information, not from … the minister, but from the accounts themselves', and even claimed that 'there has been blame somewhere'. Grenville spoke at length, objecting to two of the arguments being deployed as reasons for immediate payment, the plight of royal creditors and 'disrespect to the Crown'. As ever Grenville appealed to the country gentlemen, urging a return to 'the good old Parliamentary law: let us examine before we give'. He also pointed out that many of the expenses during the 1760s had been non-recurrent, and that £800,000 should now be sufficient. North complimented Grenville on his financial skill, but could not promise there would never be a future deficit. The House agreed without a vote that the debt be promptly paid.[44] There were two debates in the

Lords. Rockingham spoke in both, and together with Grenvillite peers Temple, Lyttelton and Suffolk, put forward the same demand for prior accounts. The ministry won the only vote by 60 to 26.[45]

During the Parliamentary session of 1768–69 circumstances had provided the opposition factions with topics over which they could unite to attack the ministry. This cooperation gave rise to rumours of a formal agreement, as Lord Buckinghamshire reported to Grenville on 20 March. 'The news of yesterday was, that an alliance, offensive and defensive, had been concluded between you and Lord Rockingham, through the mediation of the Earl of Chatham: this, men in office give a degree of credit to.'[46] Such reports prematurely anticipated the return of Chatham to the political arena, and were otherwise unfounded. For, in contrast to 1767, opposition politicians in 1769, doubtless aware of the insuperable difficulties over both America and possession of the Treasury, made no attempt to plan future ministries. And despite the ostentatious display of unity at the Thatched House dinner of 9 May, they embarked separately on the nationwide campaign of protest about the Middlesex Election that engrossed most political attention during the remainder of 1769.

This petitioning movement was not spontaneous, for the lead was invariably undertaken by Parliamentary politicians and London radicals. It made an uncertain start, for, as Burke and Wedderburn later lamented, 'there was not time after the meeting at the Thatched House to concert the proper proceedings in the several counties'.[47] Many MPs and peers, too, entertained constitutional scruples about petitioning the King over the behaviour of Parliament. Prime Minister Grafton expressed this opinion strongly, taking the line that the petitions were 'innovations of a dangerous tendency, injurious to Parliament, and dangerous to the constitution', and had to be dissuaded by Lord Chancellor Camden from instigating prosecutions.[48]

The initiative for the first petitions came from members of the newly formed Bill of Rights Society and fellow radicals. That Society, founded in February to support Wilkes, included men like John Horne who took a wide view of radical objectives.[49] The petitions from Middlesex in May and London in June therefore comprised general attacks on the ministry. Radicals active in petitioning outside the metropolitan area included Henry Cruger in Bristol, William Beckford in Wiltshire, John Sawbridge in Kent, and John Glynn in Devonshire and Cornwall. Rockinghamite politicians were the other main driving force behind the petitioning movement. They strove to be more moderate in tone, confining the grievance to the Middlesex Election decision, as Dowdeswell did in his native Worcestershire. Yorkshire was so slow to act that the ministry spread rumours that Rockingham was against a petition:[50] but the county petition eventually weighed in with 11,000 signatures. Later petitions, led by Westminster, boldly asked the King for a dissolution of Parliament. Among those that followed this line were Buckinghamshire, at the instigation of Lord Temple, Cavendish-dominated Derbyshire, and Somerset. Geographically the movement did not extend to Scotland or Wales, and was strongest in the north-East of England, and in the South-West, where the cider tax controversy had created a recent tradition of petitioning. Altogether some 15 counties petitioned. Nascent moves in at least another five were discouraged or deterred by ministerial supporters, Grafton himself intervening in Norfolk and Essex, and Bedford in Bedfordshire. About a dozen boroughs also petitioned, but the total number of petitions, which is unknown, was clearly no more than about thirty, with a total of 60,000 signatures.[51] The Parliamentary opposition intended these petitions to provide a basis for a renewed attack on the Grafton ministry when the new session began in January 1770. But that veteran politician Lord Chesterfield opined in August that the campaign might prove counter-productive. 'Another thing will be of use to the administration, which is, that factious and seditious spirit that has appeared of late, in petitions, associations, etc., which shocks all sober thinking people.'[52]

A more potent threat to the ministry was the return of Chatham to an active political career. By April Chatham's recovery of health was virtually complete, and on 29 April Lord Granby visited him, only to discover his hostility to ministerial policy and his personal animosity towards Grafton, whom he refused to meet.[53] This antipathy preceded the Duke's marriage to Bedford's niece on 24 June, which Chatham wrongly deemed a political alliance. Grafton was wary of being captured by the Bedfords, and aware of the King's personal dislike of that faction, and of their seemingly insatiable desire for office. From the moment of their accession to the ministry in December 1767 the Bedfords sought to replace Lord Townshend by Sandwich as Lord-Lieutenant of Ireland, an office that would not breach their royal quota of two cabinet posts. George III backed Townshend, but the issue did not die even when in January 1769 Townshend appointed Lord Bute's son-in-law Sir George Macartney as his Chief Secretary. For on 6 June the King rejected a tentative suggestion of Grafton that Lord Sandwich be appointed Irish viceroy, because 'Lord Chancellor, Lord Granby and others in less superior stations who are already jealous of the weight the Bedfords have in administration would be much hurt'.[54]

A visit to Chatham by Camden early in July confirmed his hostility to the Prime Minister, who in turn naturally resented the attitude of the man who had left him to carry the burden of high office. Matters came to a head on 7 July, when Chatham, adhering to his own strict constitutional ideas, had a private audience with the King. He there criticised ministerial policy, for not ignoring Wilkes into political oblivion, and for according too great importance to the East India Company, whose General Courts were behaving like 'little Parliaments'.[55] Afterwards Chatham lingered outside the royal closet, being cool to Grafton and the Bedfords, civil to Conway, and cordial to Granby.[56] Thereafter there was no contact between Grafton and Chatham, whose return to the political scene posed a clear threat to the unity and consequent survival of the ministry. That became even more obvious when Chatham sought to construct an opposition alliance.

Early in August Temple and Chatham visited Grenville, who afterwards informed his ally James Harris that 'there was perfect harmony between him and the two Earls … there was no looking back, particularly as to America'; and all condemned the expulsion of Wilkes as unconstitutional.[57] 'The re-union of the triumvirate', would, so Lord Chesterfield commented to General Irwin on 6 August, 'alarm the administration, but still I think they will hold it out another year, by certain ways and means, which the payment of the civil debts will enable them to put into practice, and you will know, that the votes in both the chaste Houses of Parliament, are counted, not weighed'.[58] Chesterfield's cynical forecast was to prove wrong, even though Chatham failed in his attempt to assume leadership of the Parliamentary opposition. Oblivious of the lessons of 1766, he displayed delusions of grandeur, approaching individual Rockinghamites like Portland, Burke and Albemarle, until negative responses brought the realisation that he would have to deal with the party as a whole.[59] The Rockinghamites saw the opposition as distinct factions, and Rockingham's own preference now was for Grenville as an unthreatening ally. 'The use of him in the House of Commons would be of service … and *the personal ill footing he is and has long been on in the closet* all coincide to make him the more safe for us'. Chatham, by contrast, constituted a rival and a threat to party unity. 'A negotiation for an arrangement, thrown into Lord Chatham's Hands', would, the Marquess commented to Burke on 15 October, '*if executed*, produce another edition of a court patched up administration', as in 1766.[60]

For there was a clash of ideology as well as personality between Chatham and Rockingham. Although Chatham was now prepared to play the game of opposition, his political attitude was at variance with the Rockinghamite concept of party, which was reaffirmed at a leadership conclave at Wentworth early in November. There, in the absence of its author, approval was given to Edmund Burke's draft of his pamphlet *Thoughts on the Cause of the Present Discontents*, much of which was concerned to justify party politics.[61] The Rockinghamite view was that party was an essential weapon to fight the power of the Crown, and the Marquess wrote in that vein to Charles Yorke on 4 November. 'The Ministers may declaim against *faction*, but the general cry of the nation will bestow that epithet upon them, and with a steady perseverance I think we may yet see a thorough overturn to that ruinous and dangerous system on which most administrations have been formed for the last eight years.'[62]

In a conversation with Lord Temple on 23 November Burke took the same line, as he reported to Rockingham. 'I told him that I believed, no union could be formed of any effect or credit, which was not compacted upon this great principle, "that the King's men must be utterly destroyed as a Corps" – to which he assented very heartily.'[63] Lord Temple may have been an anti-establishment figure, but Chatham was not, and his personal and political record in 1766 made the Rockinghamites suspicious of a repeat performance, if any offer was made by the Crown. Rockingham in any case had no intention of playing second fiddle to either Grenville or Chatham in a ministerial coalition. At the end of 1769 the opposition was poised to strike, united in their resolve to topple the Grafton ministry, but had no plan as to its replacement.

The Rockingham and Grenville factions had failed to bring down the ministry in the previous session, but Chatham was a new factor in the political equation. His role would be twofold: to launch a Parliamentary onslaught, and to subvert the ministry by detaching his adherents. He had already announced the points of attack in November. 'Corsica for foreign affairs; America for home policy; the Right of Election as a constitutional principle.'[64] As the meeting of Parliament drew near, Chatham exerted pressure on his former followers within the ministry. Granby was the first major recruit: he was won over by Chatham at an interview on 26 November, despite his dislike of Temple and Grenville.[65] Camden, with his open criticism of the policy on Wilkes, had seemed the most likely catch, although after Grafton dined him and George III closeted him in mid-December opposition thought his allegiance still in doubt.[66] But his sovereign and ministerial colleagues anticipated his desertion. Grafton found himself under pressure to replace Camden by Charles Yorke, who

with characteristic family prudence had not committed himself to an
opinion on the Middlesex Election, and now seemed likely to achieve
his long-held ambition of becoming Lord Chancellor, like his father.
While Grafton was enjoying his Christmas holiday at his Euston
home, Gower and Weymouth arrived with a message to that effect
from George III. But although the King told Grafton that he was 'now
emancipated from the chains of Lord Chatham and the burden of the
Chancellor',[67] the Duke, with residual Chathamite loyalty, refused to
dismiss Camden, who was still Lord Chancellor when Parliament met
on 9 January 1770.[68]

The power struggle that would then erupt at Westminister was
expected also to resolve the situation in Ireland, where the autumn
meeting of the Dublin Parliament had revealed an open confrontation
between the Grafton ministry and the Undertakers: for it was generally assumed that the overthrow of the ministry would mean a return
to power of John Ponsonby's friends in the Rockingham party. The
cabinet, so divided over Wilkes and America between Chathamites
and Bedfordites, was at one over Ireland. It had been for reasons of
patronage not policy that the Bedfords sought to displace Townshend.
They favoured British control over Ireland just as much as over America, and in July 1769 the Bedfordite Southern Secretary Weymouth
promised Townshend patronage support against the Undertakers.[69]
Townshend was confident of success, making an analogy between the
fragility of Undertaker power and that of the Whig aristocracy in
Britain. 'Do you think Mr Ponsonby's friends will gang to their
destruction', he observed to Macartney on 28 June. 'It is ridiculous to
suppose it, as if this their *minority* were of hardier stuff than the late
Duke of Newcastle's followers', recalling the desertions of that fallen
Prime Minister in 1762.[70]

John Ponsonby and Lord Shannon refused to promise support for
the augmentation of the army when the Irish Parliament met in October, but many of their followers voted in the majority for it, thereby
confirming Townshend's prognosis.[71] Irish MP Charles O'Hara had
earlier commented to Edmund Burke that 'some people suppose that
a vigorous opposition was wished for, as it will authorise a good deal
of turning out'. O'Hara realised that Townshend, with Bedfordite
encouragement, was seeking a confrontation with the Undertakers.
'His modes of business come entirely from the Gang; their friends are
his ... No retreat held out to Ponsonby and his friends.'[72]

Ponsonby and Lord Shannon continued to act in opposition, and
a final showdown was precipitated when on 21 November their

factions defeated an Irish Money Bill by 94 votes to 71, because it had originated in the Privy Council not the Commons: that reason opened up a disputed interpretation of Poyning's Law, a challenge that could not be ignored by the British government. George III reacted with anger, recalling how in 1761 the Undertakers had supported the Lord Lieutenant in a similar confrontation. In a letter of 29 November to Prime Minister Grafton the King suggested that a cabinet be at once called to instruct Townshend to prorogue the Irish Parliament. That would follow the only precedent, one of 1692.[73] The cabinet unanimously agreed on a punitive prorogation: later, indeed, Lord Chancellor Camden, to Chathamite embarrassment, was widely deemed to have been the instigator.[74] Next day Southern Secretary Weymouth, who may possibly have put the idea in the King's head when forwarding Townshend's report to him, duly sent the Lord-Lieutenant the appropriate instruction.[75]

There is reason to believe that Townshend himself was unhappy about such a draconian response: in the consequent British House of Commons debate of 3 May 1770 his friend Lord George Sackville stated that 'Lord Townshend sent home for instructions ... Report says, he wished the prorogation had not been insisted on'.[76] The Viceroy postponed it until 26 December, so as to allow the passage of finance measures in another form. In this interval the Undertakers justified the as yet secret ministerial decision by continued Parliamentary recalcitrance, behaviour explained perhaps by the expectation of a change of ministry in Britain. Townshend meanwhile prepared his attack on the Undertakers, sending detailed proposals to Weymouth in 'a most secret' letter of 23 December. Speaker John Ponsonby should be removed from his patronage power base of the Revenue Board, and Lord Shannon dismissed as Master-General of the Ordnance. Other holders of offices and pensions who had engaged in Parliamentary opposition should suffer the same fate, a long list being named. Furthermore, to signify royal disapproval of their behaviour, Shannon, Ponsonby, and five other opponents should be removed from the Irish Privy Council.[77] Since 1768 Townshend had also been advocating an administrative reform, the division of the Irish Revenue Board into separate Boards of Customs and Excise. This was first conceived primarily as a scheme to transfer Ponsonby's patronage to the Lord-Lieutenant, but greater efficiency was also an important motive. Although not mentioned in the letter of 23 December, this plan had already been placed on the ministerial agenda.[78] Whether Townshend would triumph or suffer ignominious dismissal by friends of the

Undertakers was dependent on the outcome of the imminent battle for power in Britain.

Notes

1 *Grenville Papers*, IV, 395.
2 *Corr. of George III*, II, 56. Diarist James Harris noted this explanation on 30 Nov. 'That Lord Bute recommended him.' Malmesbury MSS. Photocopies B909.
3 BL Add. MSS. 42086, fos 60–3, printed in *Grenville Papers*, IV, 308–12.
4 *Chatham Papers*, IV, 349 n.
5 Escott, Thesis, p. 194.
6 *Chesterfield Letters*, VI, 2,873.
7 BL Egerton MSS. 215, fos 92–134.
8 *Cavendish Debates*, I, 52–61.
9 BL Add. MSS. 35608, fo. 290.
10 Walpole, *Letters*, VII, 239.
11 Scott, *British Foreign Policy*, pp. 131–5. Tracy, *Navies*, pp. 73–5.
12 Thomas, *Townshend Duties Crisis*, pp. 95–6.
13 Thomas, *John Wilkes*, pp. 90–1.
14 *Trumbull Papers*, p. 303. For the debate see Simmons and Thomas, *Proceedings and Debates*, III, 3–13. It is described in Thomas, *Townshend Duties Crisis*, pp. 104–7.
15 Thomas, *Townshend Duties Crisis*, pp. 107–11.
16 Simmons and Thomas, *Proceedings and Debates*, III, 47–50.
17 Simmons and Thomas, *Proceedings and Debates*, III, 64–83.
18 Simmons and Thomas, *Proceedings and Debates*, III, 87–112.
19 Thomas, *John Wilkes*, pp. 91–3.
20 BL Add. MSS. 35608, fo. 324.
21 Thomas, *John Wilkes*, pp. 93–5.
22 Thomas, *John Wilkes*, pp. 96–8.
23 BL Add. MSS. 35608, fo. 338. *Commons Journals*, XXXII, 228.
24 BL Add. MSS. 35608, fo. 348.
25 Thomas, *John Wilkes*, pp. 97–103.
26 *Chatham Papers*, III, 359–61.
27 *Corr. of George III*, II, 82–5.
28 Thomas, *Townshend Duties Crisis*, pp. 126–31.
29 Simmons and Thomas, *Proceedings and Debates*, III, 147–60. Thomas, *Townshend Duties Crisis*, pp. 133–5.
30 Mackay, *Admiral Hawke*, p. 318. *Grafton Autobiography*, pp. 228–9.
31 Thomas, *Townshend Duties Crisis*, pp. 137–41.

32 Bowen, Thesis, pp. 430–47. Sutherland, *East India Company*, pp. 184–7.

33 For the debate of 27 Feb. 1769 see BL Egerton MSS. 218, fos 94–182.

34 *Cavendish Debates*, I, 50–2.

35 BL Add. MSS. 35362, fo. 237.

36 *HMC Kenyon*, p. 501. For the debate see *Cavendish Debates*, I, 240–51. Walpole, *Memoirs*, III, 225–6.

37 *Commons Journals*, XXXII, 58, 72, 98, 245, 271, 289, 327. For the Act see *Statutes at Large*, VII, 27–9.

38 BL Add. MSS. 35609, fos 321–2. *Cavendish Debates*, II, 265–72, 313–21, 324–36. Walpole, *Memoirs*, IV, 181–2.

39 For them see Reitan, *HJ*, 9 (1966), 324–5, and Brooke, *King George* III, pp. 202–3, 206–8.

40 *Grenville Papers*, IV, 411–12.

41 Walpole, *Memoirs*, III, 227.

42 *Cavendish Debates*, I, 262–78.

43 *Cavendish Debates*, I, 278–90.

44 *Cavendish Debates*, I, 290–307.

45 Walpole, *Memoirs*, III, 228–30. After 1769 the Civil List costs averaged nearly £890,000, and North in 1777 had to ask payment of over £600,000 arrears. The grant was then raised to £900,000. Reitan, *HJ*, 9 (1966), 325–6. By then the revenue sacrificed in 1760 amounted to £1 million. Brooke, *King George III*, p. 204.

46 *Grenville Papers*, IV, 412–13.

47 *Grenville Papers*, IV, 444.

48 *Grafton Autobiography*, pp. 238–41.

49 Davies, Thesis, is a full account of the Society.

50 *Burke Corr.*, II, 51–2.

51 Rudé, *Wilkes and Liberty*, pp. 105–34. This account is corrected and supplemented, less sympathetically, by Hamer, Thesis, pp. 100–25.

52 *Chesterfield Letters*, VI, 2,887.

53 *Chatham Papers*, III, 335–7.

54 Grafton MSS. no. 535.

55 *Grafton Autobiography*, pp. 236–7.

56 Walpole, *Memoirs*, III, 249.

57 Malmesbury MSS. Photocopies B973.

58 *Chesterfield Letters*, VI, 2,887.

59 Hamer, Thesis, pp. 129–32.

60 *Burke Corr.*, II, 93.

61 For the background and text see *Writings and Speeches of Edmund Burke*, II, 241–323.

62 BL Add. MSS. 35430, fo. 156.

63 *Burke Corr.*, II, 113.
64 *Burke Corr.*, II, 112.
65 *Chatham Papers*, III, 364 n.
66 *Grenville Papers*, IV, 477–8.
67 Grafton MSS. no. 540.
68 *Grafton Autobiography*, pp. 245–6.
69 CHOP, II, 484–5.
70 *Macartney Papers*, p. 33.
71 CHOP, II, 519, 523.
72 Hoffman, *Edmund Burke*, pp. 456–7. 'The Gang' were 'the Bloomsbury Gang', a contemporary name for the Bedford group.
73 Grafton MSS. no. 539. For a draft see *Corr. of George III*, II, 60–1.
74 *Macartney Papers*, p. 100.
75 CHOP, II, 527.
76 *Cavendish Debates*, I, 558.
77 *Macartney Papers*, pp. 49–53. Summary in CHOP, II, 544–8.
78 *Macartney Papers*, pp. xix–xxi.

10

George III, Lord North and the defeat of 'faction' (1770)

The political contest at the beginning of 1770 marked the culmination of the events of the first decade of George III's reign. The King's opponents pitted the power of the House of Commons against that of the Crown, but circumstances tipped the balance in favour of the monarchy. The success of Lord North enabled George III to defy 'faction' and make good his royal claim to have a Prime Minister of his own choice.

When Parliament met on 9 January neither the eve-of-session meetings nor the debates on the Address presaged a change of administration. If 80 opposition MPs mustered at the Thatched House, 179 met at the ministerial Cockpit.[1] In the Commons Grenville's constitutional scruples prevented him from trying to amend the Address, but Dowdeswell did so after Chatham had sent Temple to express his concern that otherwise no debate would develop.[2] The amendment asked the House to take into consideration 'the cause of the unhappy discontent which prevailed in every part of his Majesty's dominions'. The ensuing debate, as befitted this wording, ranged widely over Ireland, America, Corsica, the Civil List, as well, of course, as the Middlesex Election. Attorney-General De Grey and Bedfordite Rigby both pointed out that only a minority of counties and a few boroughs had petitioned. Grenville responded with the claim of 60,000 signatures. Ominous for the ministry was the behaviour of Chathamites still in office. Granby recanted his voting on the Middlesex Election, and Solicitor-General Dunning spoke for the amendment, but Hawke's son supported the ministry. Thomas Townshend, however, though voting in opposition, said that he had refused to sign a petition because of the adverse reflection on that House. That reaction to popular pressure, anticipated by Chesterfield in the summer, and a widespread feeling that the amendment was too sweeping a condemnation, contributed to a ministerial triumph by 254 votes to 138 when the debate ended after midnight.[3]

In the Lords Chatham moved a similar amendment, with more emphasis on the Middlesex Election. Camden, though Lord Chancellor, spoke strongly for it, making certain his dismissal, for the King sharply commented that 'the Great Seal never was before in opposition'.[4] So did Temple, Lyttelton, and Shelburne, but the Rockinghamite peers remained silent, presumably reflecting jealous disapproval of Chatham's lead. Lord Mansfield declared the Commons decision to be no business of the Lords. The ministry had the better of the debate, in the opinion of Horace Walpole, with Chatham being savaged for lack of precision and logic by courtier Denbigh and by Sandwich, and won the division by 89 votes to 36, eleven proxies being then added to the majority.[5] 'Vociferous has shot his bolt', wrote John Robinson, soon to become Treasury Secretary, 'and will probably come no more this session'.[6] The King prematurely congratulated Grafton on his Parliamentary success, and complimented him on being 'one man of my own age on whose resolution, abilities, and attachment I can rely on'.[7] For a few days this government optimism appeared to be justified. Apart from Camden, Granby and Dunning, the Chathamite haemorrhage seemed small, and by no means fatal: one Irish Vice-Treasurer, three Lords of the Bedchamber, and two Lords of the Admiralty, but not Sir Edward Hawke. The ministry, too, was afforded a lull in the Parliamentary battle. The lack of a Lord Chancellor provided a reason to adjourn the Lords until 22 January, and the House of Commons also did no important business before that date because of the illness and resignation of Speaker Sir John Cust.

Grafton sought to take advantage of this respite by patching up the ministry, and offered Charles Yorke the Lord Chancellorship on 13 January. He declined after consulting his family and Rockingham;[8] but was then bullied into changing his mind by George III on 17 January, with the threat that he would never again have the opportunity. Yorke's already poor health collapsed under the nervous strain, and he died of an internal disorder on 19 January, not by suicide as was widely rumoured at the time. Since Grafton shared that belief, the shock shattered his morale, and he now contemplated resignation.[9] George III persuaded him instead to postpone that problem by putting the Lord Chancellorship into commission, and Lord Mansfield agreed to act as Speaker in the Lords. Bedford, Gower and Weymouth pressed Grafton to continue, and so did Conway, who also suggested an approach to the Rockinghamite party. George III, believing that that would mean a dissolution of Parliament as demanded in some petitions, refused to entertain the idea. A month earlier the King had taken out insurance against Grafton's resignation by an invitation to Lord North on 20 December to take the Treasury in the event of a vacancy.[10] The Chancellor of the Exchequer was now twice closeted by George III, who also sent Gower and Weymouth on 23 January to press North. The same day the King wrote to North. 'You must easily see that if you do not accept I have no peer at present in my service that I could consent to place in the Duke of Grafton's employment.'[11]

The King was then briefly faced with the prospect of two Premiers instead of none. Before the appointment of North was finalised, Grafton on 25 January told George III that he might continue, for he hoped Attorney-General De Grey would agree to be Lord Chancellor. Grafton's continuance in office was implied by discussion with the King of various other ministerial changes. George III welcomed this news, commenting on 26 January on 'the excellence of your conduct over any of your predecessors since I have mounted the throne.'[12] But that same day Grafton must have finally decided on resignation, after failing to persuade the Attorney-General to become Lord Chancellor.[13] For, in a letter timed at 9.50 a.m. on 27 January, the King informed Grafton, 'I have seen Lord North, who in the most handsome manner feels he cannot refuse upon this unfortunate occasion coming to my assistance, though not without much reluctance'.[14]

These discussions were conducted against a background of Parliamentary debates. On 22 January the Commons elected a Speaker, the ministerial candidate Sir Fletcher Norton being voted into the Chair by 237 votes as against 121 for a last-minute and unwilling opposition nominee Thomas Townshend.[15] The same day the opposition launched an attack in the Lords, for Chatham persuaded and his own friends shamed the normally mute Rockingham to move for a Committee on the State of the Nation, to examine public grievances. The aim was to provide a forum for Chatham to make a general attack on the ministry. Chatham said himself that he did not know what would take its place, a tacit admission that Rockingham would not cede the Treasury to Grenville.[16] The Lords fixed 24 January for the Committee, but postponed it then until 2 February because of the illness of both Chatham and Rockingham.[17] By that date there had been a change of ministry.

In the Commons on 25 January, in a Committee on the State of the Nation, Dowdeswell moved that in election cases the House was bound to judge according to the law of the land, a proposition

equally impossible for the ministry to reject in principle or to accept
in the context of the Middlesex Election. Since the House was in
Committee the normal evasive device of the previous question could
not be deployed, and great indignation was manifested when ministerialist Lord Clare proposed to end the Committee forthwith.
Diarist Henry Cavendish witnessed how the dilemma produced
'some confusion among the gentlemen on the Treasury Bench', for
the ministry's procedural expert, Jeremiah Dyson, nursing a grievance over a pension, had refused to attend. After several urgent
appeals he sent a form of wording for North to move, to the effect
that the resolution of 17 February 1769 declaring that Wilkes having
been expelled was 'incapable' of election was 'agreeable to the law
of the land'. This device of joining together two propositions
was denounced as unfair by opposition speakers, notably Grenville,
Wedderburn, Sackville, Burke, and Lord Granby. Administration
spokesmen claimed that the right of the House to expel and disqual-
ify MPs was part of the law. When the Commons voted nearly three
hours after midnight the amendment was carried by 224 to 180.
Cavendish noted that 'the minority seemed not a little pleased
with their numbers in the division, which were greater than they
had had upon any other question during the present Parliament'.[18]
Analysis of a minority voting list shows what had happened. Twenty-
six more MPs had voted in opposition, sixteen of whom had previously voted for administration, a turnaround of forty-two votes
in a division. The Chathamite connection directly explained the
behaviour of about half this number, and perhaps also of some
independent MPs.[19]

There is no direct reference in Grafton's memoirs to the Parliamentary situation, but that it was more than the difficulty of recon-
structing the ministry that drove him to resign can be seen from his
letter of explanation to the Lord-Lieutenant of Ireland on 30 January.
The death of Charles Yorke and the 'inability' to find a Lord Chancellor, he wrote, 'made it unwarrantable for me to stand for the
adviser of measures to be discussed only in another place, where I
could give no open support'.[20] The opinion of contemporaries and
historians has been that the collapse of the ministerial position in the
Commons precipitated his fall, and he knew of that vote before his
resignation. What was certainly true was that the sharp drop in the
ministerial majority jeopardised Lord North's chance of survival as
Prime Minister. Lord Mansfield forecast that the new 'ministry would
be beat in the House of Commons two to one'.[21]

Grafton's resignation was kept secret for some days, to prevent any mass exodus from the administration, with so many posts still unfilled. North meanwhile busied himself to secure a majority, as when on 29 January he summoned to his house five Court Party MPs, and, as Sir Gilbert Elliot took note, 'stated the resignation, lamented it, mentioned the Duke's reasons, the desire of the King that he (Lord North) should accept as opposition so combined, that no breach could be made there'. Elliot commented that Grafton's resignation 'so unexpected, and so near the last division, ... might possibly cause a great defection'.[22]

News of Grafton's resignation broke on 30 January. 'The present plan appears to be a trial, with Lord North at the head of the Treasury', was how MP John Calcraft informed his leader Chatham. 'But I have reason to think the court not resolved on this measure, and have some thoughts of sounding your Lordship or other heads of opposition.' The opposition leaders were astonished not to have been summoned, assuming, as Lady Chatham put it, that Grafton's resignation must mean the 'ministry breaking up'.[23] Courtier Elliot noted the next day. 'Opposition disconcerted with the resignation, mortified that not sent to, their own measures and arrangements not settled, expected and hoped we should propose to adjourn, but it was better determined on our part not to lose a moment but to go on boldly.'[24] North wrong-footed his opponents by the gamble of risking an immediate Parliamentary confrontation in the major Commons debate already scheduled for 31 January. Southern Secretary Weymouth wrote that day that 'the most experienced politicians could not guess' the outcome of recent events. 'It was necessary to wait the fate of two or three questions in the House of Commons before a conjecture could be made about Lord North's situation.'[25]

'If the Court should be beaten, the King would be at the mercy of the Opposition.' So did Horace Walpole set the scene for the Commons debate of 31 January 1770, in another meeting of the Committee on the State of the Nation.[26] The opposition sought North's immediate defeat. Dowdeswell put forward a motion even more difficult to counter than his previous one of 25 January. 'That by the law of the land and the known and established law and custom of Parliament no person eligible of common right to serve in Parliament can be incapacitated by any vote, or resolution of this House, but by Act of Parliament only.' Office-holder Lord Clare at once conceded that 'there is certainly no act of Parliament, upon which Mr Wilkes's incapacity is founded'. That eminent lawyer William Blackstone, shortly to leave Parliament for the Bench, argued that the House had acted by exercising judicial rather than legislative power, but ended by admitting that he would have to support Dowdeswell's proposition. Other ministerial lawyers like George Hay and Charles Ambler reiterated the argument that incapacity was the consequence of expulsion, and North took up that point. He also declared the motion to be irregular, since it did not relate to any current business, a reason for him this time to deploy the procedural weapon deemed improper on 25 January, the evasive motion to 'leave the Chair'. Grenvillite Alexander Wedderburn denounced this as a mean device, reminding MPs that it was equivalent to a negative. The debate became heated. Chathamite Barré waxed sarcastic on North's claim that he had taken office out of a sense of duty, not from ambition, jibing that he was not only First Lord of the Treasury and Chancellor of the Exchequer, but also Lord Chancellor, Commander-in-Chief, and two Lords of the Admiralty. Thereby Barré reminded undecided voters of the widespread lack of confidence in North's prospects. The Premier 'replied not only with spirit but good-humour', Walpole recorded, 'and evidently had the advantage, though it was obvious how much weight the personal presence of a First Minister in the House of Commons carried with it'.

The House, diarist Henry Cavendish noted, later became 'so impatient and noisy' that the debate could not continue. North's motion to leave the Chair was carried by a majority of forty, 226 to 186, greater, Walpole thought, 'by some fifteen or twenty' than the most optimistic ministerial forecast. Opposition journalist John Almon attributed the result to the unfair use of 'Parliamentary craft to prevent the putting a question … By this means the question was lost, as several of the majority had owned the truth of the proposition, and must have voted for it'. Another reason was that perennial weakness of opposition, failure to muster every supporter: for, although their total had risen only by 6, they claimed 21 new voters.[27]

The opposition believed the game was still on, but George III thought it virtually over. He commented to North that the majority of 40 was 'a very favourable auspice on your taking the lead in administration … Believe me, a little spirit will soon restore a degree of order in my service'.[28] The King knew the morale boost to government supporters of the visible presence in the Commons of a Prime Minister determined to stand his ground, and North's gifts of Parliamentary skills and financial expertise were exactly what a Premier needed. North himself already commanded personal liking and respect in the House. And the hardline attitude he had taken on

Wilkes and America would consolidate behind him not only the Court
Party but conservative opinion generally. For former Tory squires like
Sir Roger Newdigate and Sir John Glynne there was the added attraction that North was not a Whig faction leader in the mould of Fox,
Grenville, Bedford, Newcastle, Rockingham or even Pitt. In that
sense, too, North was the Prime Minister George III had been seeking
since 1760. When accused in a Commons debate of 5 February of
lacking political support, North scorned the notion of party. 'If by
friends and acquaintances is meant a little knot of men who are always
to be of the same opinion; in that point of view, I certainly have no
friends and acquaintances.'[29] North was for George III the antidote to
the poison of faction politics the King had been fighting all his reign.

The success of 31 January enabled North to complete his ministerial reconstruction. At the end of the year North, when seeking to
recruit the followers of the then recently deceased Grenville, claimed
that his intention to bring in that former Premier had met the King's
disapproval, and not only because George III feared the appearance
of surrender to the opposition and the displacement of many of his
own 'friends'. For 'his Majesty had conceived a dislike (he Lord North
could not tell why) against Mr Grenville, whom he liked less than any
man, Lord Chatham excepted'.[30] As it was, instead of major political
surgery, only minor changes were implemented. The vacancies caused
by the resignations of Treasurer of the Navy Lord Howe and Irish
Vice-Treasurer Lord Cornwallis, were filled respectively by Sir Gilbert
Elliot and Welbore Ellis. All the three vacancies on the Admiralty
Board were also filled up, one by young Charles James Fox, and most
other lesser offices. The cabinet was drastically reduced in size from
ten to six, for Camden, Granby, and Grafton were not replaced, and
Conway was no longer willing to attend.[31] Although North's uncle
Lord Halifax became Lord Privy Seal, he did not enter the cabinet,
which now comprised North, Southern Secretary Weymouth, North-
ern Secretary Rochford, American Secretary Hillsborough, Lord
President Gower, and political nonentity Hawke at the Admiralty.

The opposition still aspired to bring down the ministry, but committed the tactical blunder of not forcing another major Commons
debate for nearly a fortnight. Their next attack was the postponed
Rockingham motion of 2 February in the Lords, where the safe
administration majority meant that only prestige was at stake. The
contrast in political atmosphere between the two Houses of Parliament served to emphasise Chatham's mistake in taking a peerage:
would North have survived if Pitt had been in the Commons on 31

January? Rockingham repeated Dowdeswell's motion of 25 January, and the debate continued until two hours after midnight, an almost unprecedented duration for the Lords. Although the minority was a large one for that House, 47 against 96, the debate was a triumph for administration, with Bedfordite sarcasm and invective scoring heavily against the prolixity of Chatham and the diffidence of Rockingham. Grafton spoke for the ministry, and North wrote to thank him for this act of 'friendship'.[32] Administration rammed home its victory by a motion condemning any Lords resolution on a Commons decision as unconstitutional, despite Chatham's objection that the Lords had a duty to defend the people's liberties.[33] The House of Lords was seldom a happy hunting ground for opposition in the later eighteenth century, and the next attack there, delayed by a Chatham illness, did not take place until 2 March, on the state of the navy. A rambling speech by Chatham was derided by Grafton as 'only the effects of a distempered mind, brooding over its own discontent', before the ministry won by 70 to 38.[34]

By then the Commons battle was over. Not until 12 February did the opposition launch the next major attack there, when, in another Committee on the State of the Nation, Dowdeswell, reviving an idea he had raised in 1768 on Beckford's Bribery Bill, moved for the electoral disfranchisement of revenue officers, those thousands of voters on the government payroll. A key proposal in the Economical Reform campaign of a decade later, it was a popular topic, attracting a recorded attendance at the division of 454 MPs, the fullest House for six years. Grenvillite Harris thought it 'a rather tedious debate, full of that patriotic common-place which nobody believes that talks it, nor anyone else but a few dupes in the provinces'.[35] The disbursement of what Dowdeswell calculated at £600,000 in salaries was, he said, equivalent to the bribery of electors that was forbidden by law. Cornwall MP Sir John Molesworth, whose county was full of Parliamentary boroughs and revenue officers, spoke warmly for the proposal. Administration speakers sarcastically expressed delight at having finished at last with the Middlesex Election. Colonel George Onslow, one of the former Newcastle Whigs who had stayed on in office in 1766, sought to arouse Whig prejudices against the motion by describing Dowdeswell as 'a moderate Tory', thereby reminding MPs of the Tory or country party antecedents of the motion. Barré retorted that the objection seemed to be that it 'strikes deep at the faction who call themselves the King's Friends; those who, in their different capacities, vote for every administration'. When both Dowdeswell and

Grenville pledged themselves to the measure if again in office, North commented that they could not think much of their own prospects.[36]

The motion failed by a majority of 75 votes, 263 to 188, but there were opposition suspicions that a ministerial bench of thirty MPs was accidentally counted twice.[37] Whether or not the rise in ministerial support was due to such a mistake, it delighted George III, who commented to North that 'as the question proposed by Mr Dowdeswell was well calculated to catch many persons I think it has been rejected by a very handsome majority'.[38] Contemporaries were astonished that the squirearchy supported government on such a popular topic. Radical journalist John Almon appended this comment to his report. 'We are not surprised at the Court carrying the question, but a good deal so, that the *country gentlemen*, who have so long been exclaiming against the undue influence of the Crown, should join with them in this vote.'[39] Horace Walpole pointed to the revival of an ancient political tradition when he wrote that 'the old artillery of the Court, the Tories, were played against the proposal'.[40] The Tory wheel had turned full circle, from 'country' back again to 'court'.

Thomas Allan, London agent of the Irish Lord-Lieutenant, reported to Dublin that 'this division, I think, adds permanency to the ministry'.[41] The opposition then compounded the disaster of this defeat when Grenville, in the face of both logic and Parliamentary precedent, sought to insist on his right to divide a complex motion. The occasion was the report on 16 February of Dowdeswell's motion of 25 January as modified by North. The fiery new Speaker Sir Fletcher Norton played his part in discomforting the opposition, both then and on 19 February, when the ministry won a division on that point by 243 votes to 174, and then confirmed North's amendment by 237 to 159.[42] Allan deemed this 'a decent majority, besides a list of 28 who from illness or being obliged to be in the country, could not attend. I think this concludes matters for the minority for this session'.[43]

It did not, for the opposition believed it had not polled its full strength. 'We rather gain than lose', John Calcraft now assured Chatham, explaining the fall in the opposition vote by 'sickness, loss of relations, idleness and the Ridotto ... Had not these accidents interfered, we should have turned 200, which we have strength to do'.[44] Subsequent events did not bear out this optimism. Grenville made one more attack, a motion on 28 February for the Civil List account of the year to 5 January 1770, following the presentation to the House on 12 January of the accounts from 1752 to 1769 ordered in the previous session. That was flogging a dead horse, the more so because those accounts showed that the deficit lacked the sinister implications of secret bribery. The ministerial majority was 262 to 165, and Thomas Allan wrote: 'last night they [the opposition] got the *coup de grâce* by a majority of 97'.[45] A year later North, reflecting on this Parliamentary battle to James Harris, thought the opposition had overplayed its hand, binding court and country MPs together in support of his ministry. 'That the violence of the questions kept people together, for fear of dismissal and of the expense of a general election.'[46]

North's rise to power had been to many so unexpected that he was widely believed to be a caretaker Premier, or a figurehead for either the Bedford group or the mythical 'King's Friends'. On 2 February even Grenville told his political associates that 'Lord North was the Ostensible Minister, but no more – that the majority in the House consisted of the old Torys, of the King's Friends (as usually so called) and of the Bedford party ... that these last were the real Ministers'.[47] That notion was short-lived. By early April it was common knowledge that 'there is no great harmony between the Bedfords and the Premier', who 'brought in Lord Halifax without consulting them'.[48] The Bedford party, with the Duke ailing, was beginning to disintegrate, as Gower and Weymouth became intent on their own personal ambitions, while Sandwich and Rigby gravitated to North's orbit.

The myth of 'the King's Friends', as a secret ruling cabal, was, by contrast, a constant backdrop to the North ministry. James Harris wrote on 18 February, 'I hear Lord North is not so much controlled by Bloomsbury [the Duke of Bedford's residence] as by Carleton House [residence of the Princess Dowager of Wales], and the Junto there, Elliot, Morton and Jenkinson'.[49] Already Thomas Townshend had declared in the House of Commons on 5 February, 'I see the administration placed in the hands of men who are ready to do most of the midnight cabinet work we have heard of'.[50] A fuller exposition of this idea was given to the House on 2 April by Barré. Here is Thomas Allan's report of his speech:

> The noble lord thinks he is minister. I tell him he is not. My friend near to me (Mr Dowdeswell) thought he was minister. He found he was not. A right honourable gentleman at the end of this bench (Mr Grenville) thought he was minister. He found he was not. I will tell them all who is minister; a junto at Carlton House, and they consist of (pointing to each as he named them) Mr Stuart Mackenzie, Sir Gilbert Elliot, Mr Jenkinson and Mr Samuel Martin. With them every point is settled and the mandate issued to your lordship.

Almon's report has Jeremiah Dyson not Martin as the fourth member of the alleged 'cabinet of Carleton House', and recorded Dowdeswell, Grenville, and North as all denying being governed by secret influence while in office.[51] There never was any such 'inner cabinet', dictating policy with North as a puppet, though such an idea long survived in the popular imagination. But the designation 'King's Friends' confusingly also had a wider connotation, that of the Court Party in Parliament, as when Barré so described such men in the debate of 12 February. This was not a new phenomenon, but its existence was highlighted in the 1760s by the frequent changes of ministry. As Grenville said on 1 July 1770, 'those called *King's men* had been with him as minister, and every minister since'.[52] They were not a sinister novelty of George III's reign, but a permanent feature of the political scene throughout the century.

Lord North was to be Prime Minister for 12 years. Later in 1770 his already comfortable position in Parliament was strengthened by mortality and defections among his leading opponents. Death deprived Chatham of both William Beckford, his most valuable link with the City of London, and Lord Granby, on 21 June and 18 October respectively. These events left Chatham 'without troops or generals', so Horace Walpole wrote in exaggeration.[53] Shelburne, Camden and Barré still carried the flag for a party that, with Chatham himself inclined to temporary political retirement, often was known as 'the Shelburnes'. A greater blow to opposition was the death of George Grenville on 13 November, the first day of the new Parliamentary session. For this resulted in the political retirement of his brother Lord Temple;[54] and in the defection to administration of much of his following. As early as 16 November North told George III that he thought there was 'an opening to acquire not only Mr Wedderburn, but all Mr Grenville's friends'. By the end of the month he had seen Lord Suffolk, whose rank gave him the best claim to be the group leader in the absence of Temple.[55] The former Grenvillites negotiated individually with North, regarding the party as dissolved. Lord Hyde observed to James Harris on 11 December, 'Now Mr Grenville was dead, that his friends of principal rank looked upon themselves as disengaged, and at their liberty'.[56] Suffolk was soon to become Lord Privy Seal, and Wedderburn Solicitor-General, while James Harris and Thomas Whately were also among those who took office. The faction dissolved as others, notably Lord Clive and Henry Seymour, remained in opposition. From three parties opposition was in effect reduced to barely more than one, and the Rockinghamite sense of

isolation is conveyed in this comment by Dowdeswell to Burke on 8
February 1771. 'The Bedfords deserted us; so have the Grenvilles;
and the Chathams would do the same.'[57]

Despite frequent rumours, and several flirtations with administration, Chatham was never again to be in office. But his followers,
though in opposition, acted as a distinctive political grouping, often
disagreeing with the much larger Rockingham party on both constitutional issues, as the rights of juries in 1771 and the Royal Family
Marriage Act of 1772, and imperial matters, the East India Company
in 1773 and usually over America thereafter. It was a coalition of two
separate factions that eventually replaced Lord North in administration in 1782, not the 'Whig party' of legend.

Lord North's establishment in power altered the character of British
politics. In the 1770s this came to centre on the ministerial making of
policies, and no longer, as in the 1760s, on the planning of new administrations by King and opposition alike. The end of political instability
made it possible for Prime Minister Lord North, as early as the first
quarter of 1770, to carry out policies for Ireland and America that both
achieved short-term success. Even the imperturbable North felt the
strain of conducting so much business: in a letter of 14 April to the
Lord-Lieutenant of Ireland he complained of 'the whirlwind in which
I have lived since the resignation of the Duke of Grafton'.[58]

Ireland had been accorded priority as soon as North believed that
he was safe in office. Townshend's opponents were encouraged by
the news of Grafton's resignation in January 1770, but Lord North's
successful establishment in power soon dashed their hopes. The new
Premier was too busy ensuring his political victory to pay heed to matters of policy, Irish or American, for some weeks; but on 20 February
Weymouth was able to reassure Townshend that there would be no
change when the cabinet considered Ireland the next day.[59] The cabinet then endorsed virtually all of Townshend's proposals concerning
the Undertakers, but North would not yet commit himself to the
administrative proposals. Weymouth promptly informed Townshend:
the time of 'temporising' was over.[60] Townshend at once sent out
letters of dismissal from their offices to Lord Shannon and Speaker
John Ponsonby, on 6 March. This vigorous action, he reported to
Weymouth, gave the lie to opposition claims that the 'English government either would not or dared not remove a person of the
Speaker's imagined consequence'.[61] Shannon was also among those
removed from the Irish Privy Council, but Townshend allowed

Ponsonby to remain, since it was customary for the Speaker to be a member. Townshend, more attuned than his predecessors to public opinion, reported that there had been no hostile reaction to the fall of the Undertakers, but admitted that the prorogation of the Irish Parliament was widely unpopular. He therefore launched a press campaign, blaming it on the misbehaviour of the Undertakers and other opponents of Dublin Castle. This propaganda, he claimed, brought about a change in the public mood, assisting his efforts to recruit Parliamentary support. But he still thought it too risky to meet Parliament, and in April asked and obtained permission to wait until the next usual meeting time of October 1771.[62]

In Britain the attack on the Undertakers was generally approved, as Townshend's London agent Thomas Allan reported to his Chief Secretary Sir George Macartney on 29 March.

> I wished to hear fully the opinion of all parties on his Excellency's transactions in Ireland, and have the satisfaction to find they are extremely approved of here. Our adherence to the same maxims, and executed with the same spirit, will ever make the residence of a Lord Lieutenant easy and agreeable. We are told Lord Shannon says he has played for a deep stake and has lost it ... As for the Speaker, he falls as much unpitied and as deservedly, as ever man did. I do believe that they had strong assurances from some here that spirited measures would not take place.[63]

Since the royal prerogative to appoint and dismiss office-holders was universally accepted, no open Parliamentary attack in Britain could be made on that subject. The prorogation of the Irish Parliament was quite another matter, but it was difficult for the three opposition groups to mount a concerted critique of ministerial policy. It was Grenville's ministry that had officially launched the plan of a resident viceroy, and Chatham's administration that had implemented it, with Camden widely being deemed the adviser of the prorogation. Allan reported to Macartney on 13 March that 'it is now said the opposition will not take any notice of what has passed in Ireland this winter'.[64] Allan overlooked the ministerial record, and close connections to the Undertakers, of the Rockingham party. On 3 May Lord Shannon's own brother, Rockinghamite Boyle Walsingham, moved for copies of correspondence with the Lord-Lieutenant to ascertain where the blame for the prorogation lay.[65] He was seconded by Constantine Phipps, who neatly linked the topic to wider imperial issues by stating that no MP could doubt the right of the House to examine

ministerial behaviour in every part of the King's dominions, a contention no minister could dispute. Phipps denounced the prorogation
as 'founded upon unconstitutional principles'. Lord North promptly
denied the premiss of the motion. 'There is no blame … It was the
duty of His Majesty's servants, in that situation, to advise … that prorogation.' It signified the Crown's displeasure at the challenge to
Poyning's Law. George Grenville seized the opportunity to make an
indirect reference to America. 'I agree … that it is the duty of every
Minister to preserve entire the constitutional authority of Great
Britain over every part of the subjects of this Empire. I wish I could
say that had been done.' But the administration was behaving in
Ireland as Charles II had done in England, taking money and then
proroguing Parliament. Edmund Burke denied that the Irish House of
Commons had broken Poyning's Law. It had simply exercised its right
to reject a Bill. He and Chathamite Dunning were among speakers
who attacked the impolicy and dishonesty of accepting taxes and then
proroguing Parliament. What would happen next time? Throughout
a long and complex debate not one speaker mentioned the dismissal
of the Undertakers. The ministry triumphed at the division, by 178
votes to a mere 66.

The main Commons debate on America had taken place two
months earlier, for the ministry needed to obtain Parliamentary
approval for the policy agreed upon by the Grafton cabinet on 1 May
1769, the repeal of all Charles Townshend's revenue duties except
that on tea. This would be retained as both a symbol and the most
lucrative source of income. The cabinet had now shed all the four
members who had then favoured repeal of the tea duty also, and the
decision to retain it was not an issue there, being confirmed on 2
March, only three days before the date fixed for a Commons debate
on America.

North on 5 March took the line that it would be foolish to retain
bad taxes, the Townshend duties on British manufactures, simply
because of anger at American behaviour. The colonial trade boycott
he brushed aside as ineffective, for any apparent concession under
coercion would be unpopular with MPs. North then proposed repeal
of all but the tea duty. Thomas Pownall moved to add that also, since
it gave smugglers an advantage. These rival contentions, of course,
concealed the underlying argument as to how much conciliation
should be extended to America. The ensuing debate was confused.
Some MPs were so undecided as to abstain from voting. The followers of Rockingham and Chatham were for complete repeal, as was

Conway. The Grenville party would vote for no concession, and left before the end of the debate. Some administration supporters who felt the same way were spared the embarrassment of a vote on North's motion after the amendment was defeated by 204 votes to 142.[66] Events turned out as the ministry hoped. 1770 saw a gradual breakdown of the colonial trade boycott, as a result of this token concession of cancelling unremunerative duties. By the end of the year the North ministry could deem the American crisis to be at an end.

Other policies pursued by Lord North in the earlier 1770s were also to enjoy success, notably his management of the national finances and his settlement of the problems of the East India Company.[67] North, as a personable man, able minister, and skilful politician, fulfilled the expectations of George III. But for the War of American Independence the King might have enjoyed two decades of political tranquility before the storm of the French Revolution broke over Europe. For by 1770 the King had succeeded in his political objective, the assertion of the royal power to appoint ministers in disregard of the political connections in Parliament.

That was what George III had set out to achieve. Confusingly to more modern eyes, policy was not the King's chief criterion in selecting his ministers. Personal prejudice was the key to their choice and removal. Grenville in 1765 was aggrieved at his dismissal, for his policies had met with both success and royal approval. Antipathy towards Grenville and his colleagues was why George III replaced them by men whose political views were less congenial to the King's mind. Grenville soon came to suspect a royal veto on his return to office, but even Lord North did not know of this until he recommended Grenville for a post in 1770. By contrast, the King's correspondence with the Duke of Grafton reveals a personal affinity with a man who, for all his political defects, he would have preferred to retain as his Premier instead of appointing North in 1770. Above all it was William Pitt whose political fortunes fluctuated in accordance with the King's view of him. Royal dislike at the beginning of his reign was soon replaced by a desire to appoint him as Premier because of his professed disapproval of party politics: but by 1770 he was the politician most detested by George III.

To reverse a cant phrase of the time, the King chose 'men not measures'. Politics were conducted by George III on a highly personal basis. Conscious of his own rectitude, he ascribed base motives to those who opposed the Crown. Hence his frequent use of the pejorative word 'factions', with the connotation of self-interested combinations acting against the interests of the state. In 1770 Edmund Burke produced a famous justification of party in his pamphlet *Thoughts on the Cause of the Present Discontents*. It was, however, one party, not a system of party politics, that Burke had in mind. For in the opinion of the Rockingham group there then existed only one party, their own, and a number of factions. One motive behind the pamphlet, as Burke observed to Rockingham on 29 October 1769, was to show how different 'the party ... as well as the persons who compose it are from the Bedfords, and Grenvilles, and other knots, who are combined for no public purpose; but only as a means of furthering with joint strength, their private and individual advantage'.[68] By a nice irony Edmund Burke, whose political analysis of the period formed much of the basis of the historical writing that so denounced George III, here found some common ground with that King; the difference was that his monarch included the Rockingham party among the factions.

George III's conception of politics struck an old-fashioned but still popular chord. At the moment of crisis in 1770 men of both 'court' and 'country' outlook supported the Crown against the factions. Lord North that year correctly deemed it a political advantage to disparage party in theory and practice. The power of the monarchy, in the sense that George III wished to exercise it, was not yet curtailed by party politics in Parliament. Factions might be the embryos of parties, but their very multiplicity in the 1760s afforded the King room for manoeuvre, and some active and able men, like Lord North himself, were not faction leaders at all. Still less did public opinion impact on the levers of power. In this respect the decade did witness the first signs of a more permanent development than the ephemeral phenomena, riots over food shortages and demonstrations over naval victories and defeats, sometimes prematurely described by historians as the public opinion factor in politics. The expansion of the press, and the first stirrings of political radicalism in the Wilkite movement, were portents of the future, but no more than that. By 1770 George III had made good the royal claim to appoint ministers, and for a long while yet only national disasters like the defeat in the American War would enable Parliamentary politicians to challenge that power with success.

Notes

1   *Chatham Papers*, III, 390.
2   *Chatham Papers*, III, 388–9.

3 BL Egerton MSS. 3711, pp. 1–61 (Henry Cavendish's Parliamentary Diary). A minority list is printed in Almon, *Debates*, VIII, 175–7.

4 Grafton MSS. no. 541.

5 Walpole, *Memoirs*, IV, 23–5. *Chatham Papers*, III, 368–88. *London Museum*, 1770, pp. 120–1.

6 BL Add. MSS. 38206, fo. 195.

7 Grafton MSS. no. 541.

8 Grafton MSS. no. 544.

9 *Grafton Autobiography*, p. 249. One early rumour was that Yorke killed himself by cutting his arm. *Macartney Papers*, p. 83.

10 Thomas, *Lord North*, p. 33.

11 *Corr. of George III*, II, 126. For these negotiations see Hamer, Thesis, pp. 153–4.

12 Grafton MSS. no. 545.

13 *Grafton Autobiography*, p. 249.

14 Grafton MSS. no. 546.

15 BL Egerton MSS. 3711, pp. 66–81.

16 Walpole, *Memoirs*, IV, 39–40. For a report of Chatham's speech, see *Chatham Papers*, III, 400–9.

17 *Chatham Papers*, III, 408–10.

18 BL Egerton MSS. 3711, pp. 106–73 (Cavendish Diary).

19 Thomas, *PH*, 12 (1993), 246–7.

20 *Macartney Papers*, p. 54.

21 Malmesbury MSS. Photocopies A759.

22 *Macartney Papers*, pp. 84, 93. Elliot, *Border Elliots*, pp. 406–7.

23 *Chatham Papers*, III, 412–13.

24 Elliot, *Border Elliots*, p. 407.

25 *HMC Townshend*, p. 407.

26 Walpole, *Memoirs*, IV, 60–1.

27 BL Egerton MSS. 3711, pp. 173–246 (Cavendish Diary). Walpole, *Memoirs*, IV, 50–1. Almon, *Debates*, VIII, 223–4. *Macartney Papers*, pp. 83–5.

28 *Corr. of George III*, II, 128.

29 *Cavendish Debates*, I, 439.

30 Malmesbury MSS. Photocopies A759–60.

31 Walpole, *Memoirs*, IV, 37–8.

32 Grafton MSS. no. 474.

33 Walpole, *Memoirs*, IV, 58–9. *Chatham Papers*, III, 415–20. *Bedford Journal*, p. 623. *London Museum*, 1770, pp. 139–45, 186–7, 190–2.

34 *Chatham Papers*, III, 420–3. *Bedford Journal*, p. 623.

35 *Malmesbury Letters*, I, 192.

36 *Cavendish Debates*, I, 442–58. Walpole, *Memoirs*, IV, 60.

37 Thomas, *House of Commons*, pp. 279–80.
38 *Corr. of George III*, II, 129.
39 Almon, *Debates*, VIII, 231.
40 Walpole, *Memoirs*, IV, 60.
41 *Macartney Papers*, p. 88.
42 *Cavendish Debates*, I, 458–75.
43 *Macartney Papers*, p. 92.
44 PRO 30/8/25, fo. 35.
45 *Cavendish Debates*, I, 479–83. *Macartney Papers*, p. 95.
46 Malmesbury MSS. Photocopies B21–2.
47 Malmesbury MSS. Photocopies B990.
48 *Macartney Papers*, pp. 109, 113.
49 Malmesbury MSS. Photocopies B992. The Carlton House reference is an implication of Bute's continuing influence. The MPs named were John Morton, Charles Jenkinson and Sir Gilbert Elliot.
50 *Cavendish Debates*, I, 438.
51 *Macartney Papers*, p. 116. *London Museum*, 1770, pp. 271–3. This contemporary accusation against North was rather different from the one made by nineteenth-century Whig historians, namely that George III ruled himself, using North as a dummy Prime Minister.
52 Malmesbury MSS. Photocopies B996.
53 Walpole, *Letters*, VII, 418.
54 Malmesbury MSS. Photocopies A770–1.
55 *Corr. of George III*, II, 171, 174.
56 Malmesbury MSS. Photocopies A767.
57 Quoted in Escott, Thesis, p. 447.
58 Townshend Letter-Books, 7. North to Townshend, 14 Apr. 1770.
59 Townshend Letter-Books, 7. Weymouth to Townshend, 20 Feb. 1770.
60 *Macartney Papers*, pp. 54–7. Summary in *CHOP*, III, 11–12.
61 *Macartney Papers*, pp. 57–9. Summary in *CHOP*, III, 17–19.
62 *CHOP*, III, 14–15, 23, 27–9, 30, 31–2.
63 *Macartney Papers*, p. 105.
64 *Macartney Papers*, p. 100.
65 For this debate see the Parliamentary Diary of Henry Cavendish, BL Egerton MSS. 222, fos 64–108, from which all quotations are taken. It is partly and inaccurately printed in *Cavendish Debates*, I, 552–60.
66 Simmons and Thomas, *Proceedings and Debates*, III, 209–42.
67 Thomas, *Lord North*, pp. 55–8, 61–7.
68 *Burke Corr.*, II, 101.

11

Conclusion: factions or parties?

The old concept of a two-party system of Whigs and Tories does not survive detailed knowledge of mid-eighteenth-century politics.[1] By 1760 less than one hundred MPs could be deemed Tories even by a generous definition, and in the ensuing decade they split asunder, being variously attached to the Court or to factions, or remaining independent of all connections. The ministry at George III's accession was a coalition of all the Whig groups, but soon fell apart. The next five ministries were all reshuffles of the Whig pack, and none entailed a complete change of cabinet membership. It was this fluid political situation that gave George III the leverage to exercise the significant power that lay with the Crown. In doing so he acted in accord with much contemporary opinion. Many thought with the King when he used 'faction' and 'party' as pejorative words. For men of both 'court' and 'country' outlook they possessed the connotation of self-interested combinations acting against the interests of the state. In 1770 Lord North clearly deemed it a political advantage to disparage party in theory and practice. In that sense his establishment as Prime Minister that year did mark the victory of George III in his battle with the 'factions'.

By 1763 the disintegration into faction was apparent. Pitt and his friends had left the administration in 1761, and Newcastle led out the 'old Whig corps' in 1762: it was to be merely one, albeit the largest and most permanent, of the four main Parliamentary factions. The ministerial negotiations of 1763 resulted in an alignment of the old Bedford and new Grenville groups in government, and those headed by Pitt and Newcastle in opposition. Two years later the Newcastle group took office under Rockingham, with the initial tacit support of Pitt, while the Grenville and Bedford factions went into opposition.

1766 saw an end to any lingering notion of a Whig party that included both Pitt and Rockingham when Pitt, now Lord Chatham, replaced Rockingham in office. That there were four distinct political factions was recognised in contemporary speculations and negotiations during 1766, for they envisaged the possibility of any of the Rockingham, Grenville and Bedford groups becoming ministerial partners with Chatham. In 1767 the Bedford-Grenville alliance ended when the Bedfords joined the Chatham group in office. This last combination was also the basis of the Grafton ministry at the end of the 1760s, facing opposition from the factions of Rockingham and Grenville. The North ministry, in so far as it related to this decade of faction, was based on the remnants of the Bedford and Grenville groups, which began to disintegrate after the deaths of their leaders: and was confronted by the other two, one headed by Rockingham, and the second often by Shelburne, as deputy for Chatham. This last faction survived under him after Chatham's death in 1778 until it dissolved in the political convolutions of 1782–84 that brought to power Chatham's son, William Pitt the Younger.

The Rockingham party has conventionally been seen as a quite different kind of political entity from the other more ephemeral groups that existed only in the lifetime of a leader. It is usually perceived as the link in personnel and principles between the ruling Whig party of George II's reign and the opposition Whig party of Charles James Fox. Nor is this idea simply the invention of later historians. Newcastle and Rockingham men were wont to assert that they were 'the Whig Party', to the annoyance of other politicians like Grenville and Bedford whose claims to a Whig pedigree were equally valid. In terms of personnel the Rockinghamite claim to be a link in Whig party history is weaker than is often supposed. The two haemorrhages of placemen in 1762 and careerists in 1766 meant that in the 1770s Lord North, in terms of his Parliamentary support, was more the heir of Newcastle than Rockingham himself. On policy the continuity or otherwise of attitude is difficult to establish, for the major problems of America, India, and Ireland were new issues of the 1760s. It might seem that the older Whig tradition of opposition to government power in Stuart times, rather than the actual role of ruling party in the earlier Georgian era, had been revived in the Rockinghamite attitude to those questions of empire: but in each instance the behaviour was explained by specific motives. American policy stemmed from the conviction that the colonies were worth more to Britain in terms of trade than taxation. Attitudes to Ireland were influenced by the many personal and political links with the Undertakers. A belief in the sanctity of charters – and here there was a reminder of Whig attitudes in the later seventeenth century – was the spur to defence of the East India Company from ministerial interference.

Such considerations open up the wider question of how far a party veneer of policy identification can be superimposed on the factions. Some correlations can be established, but the arguments must not be unduly pressed. That policies were based on prejudices and pragmatism was characteristic of an age when ideology did not predetermine attitudes. Policy-making was usually a response to circumstances, but once political opinions had been adopted, the much-vaunted contemporary virtue of 'consistency' obliged politicians to repeat a similar stance if the same topic recurred later. That happened over America. Any politicians in office during the earlier 1760s would probably have taxed and otherwise sought to control the American colonies. The Grenville and Bedford groups happened to be then in government. It might well have been their opponents, who did not at the time challenge colonial taxation and other measures.[2] They did so subsequently, on news of American resistance, Rockingham on grounds of expediency and Pitt out of principle. But it is too facile to suggest simply that circumstances made policies. If the alignments had been reversed, Grenville and Bedford would not have championed the American cause. Grenville was a man obsessed with financial probity and legal authority, principles that determined his political behaviour. Even the Bedford group was something more than a band of politicians cynically united to increase their bargaining power – often their depiction by both contemporaries and historians. The Bedfordites were characterised by hardline attitudes, whether to American colonists, Wilkite radicals or Spitalsfield silk weavers: the consequent unpopularity incurred by the Duke seemed to provoke riots wherever he went![3] Chatham, by contrast, was governed on both America and India by his imperial vision. That led him into difficulty over America, since his desire for popularity in the colonies clashed with his view of America as a subordinate part of the British Empire. On India he held strongly the opinion that the state should claim and benefit from the territories acquired by the East India Company.

Foreign policy also distinguished the factions. The Bedford group was Francophile and pacifist for the most part, though in 1770 Weymouth proved to be the most bellicose cabinet member. Grenville was Francophobe, suspicious of Bourbon intentions, but content to rely on the navy rather than foreign alliances. The Newcastle-Rockingham party passively clung to the traditional Whig idea of an Austrian alliance; but in practice supported Chatham's positive pursuit of the chimera of a Prussian alliance. These policy differences over what to do in Europe came to nothing, for no ally could be obtained. But they reinforce the overall impression that in one sense an embryonic party system did exist, if changes of ministry might lead to alterations of policy.

That argument cannot be pushed further. The British political scene between the accession of George III and the outbreak of the American War was a time when the two sides in Parliament were 'administration' and 'opposition'. That terminology was the usual language of debate.[4] Within that simple political context there existed distinct factions, but the political scene was in detail far more complex than that depicted in the broad strokes of this study. Some individual politicians, conspicuously Charles Townshend, occasionally changed their allegiance. A few such as Lord North professed none. Even the major factions were loosely constructed, with leaders like Grenville all too well aware that they must nurse their connections, and issue requests not summonses for Parliamentary attendance. Formal 'whipping' was a facility available only to the ministry of the day, for it was respectable for the King's government to ask for support.[5] Independent Sir Roger Newdigate hastened to London from Warwickshire in 1770 to answer a summons from Lord North. But the line between the Court Party and such supportive independents was a fine distinction. Many MPs who deemed themselves independent asked government for favours, as when Sir John Glynne requested and obtained an army commission for his son in 1763.[6]

The concept of independence implied a choice of supporting or opposing government to be made on each and every occasion, and almost every Parliamentarian liked to think he had that option. Any examination of the mid-Georgian political system must take its start from the notion that Parliament comprised 558 MPs and some 200 peers, without the easy classification of a party system. Analysis of these men into categories of placemen, political groups, and independents was both tentative and arbitrary. Compilation of lists was the stuff of politics for George III's ministers and their opponents.

Notes

1 For a recent attempt to maintain its validity, see Hill, *British Parliamentary Parties*, pp. 90–128.

2 Thomas, *British Politics and the Stamp Act Crisis*, pp. 112–14.

3 See, for example, *Bedford Papers*, II, 278–9; *Bedford Journal*, pp. 620–1.
4 Thomas, *House of Commons*, p. 210.
5 Thomas, *House of Commons*, pp. 110–19.
6 Thomas, *PH*, 17 (1998), 344.

Bibliography

Primary sources

Manuscripts

British Library [cited as BL]
Egerton MSS. 215-63, 3711: The Parliamentary Diary of Henry Cavendish :
    1768–1774
Add[itional] MSS. 29131-94: Warren Hastings Papers
Add. MSS. 32679-3201: Newcastle Papers
Add. MSS. 35349-6278: Hardwicke Papers
Add. MSS. 36796-7: Bute Papers
Add. MSS. 38190-489: Liverpool Papers
Add. MSS. 42083-8: Grenville Papers
Add. MSS. 47584: Journal of Lord Villiers 1760–66
Add. MSS. 51318-2254: Holland House Papers
Add. MSS. 57804-37: Grenville Papers

Public Record Office
PRO 30/8: Chatham Papers
PRO 30/29: Granville Papers
PRO 30/47: Egremont Papers

In other repositories or in private possession
Bute MSS. (Cardiff group). In the possession of the Marquess of Bute.
Grafton MSS. Bury St Edmunds and West Suffolk County Record Office. (By
    permission of the Duke of Grafton.)
Letter-Books of George Grenville (Stowe MSS.). Henry E. Huntingdon
    Library.

Malmesbury MSS. Photocopies and Transcripts: Harris Diary;Series A and B. Hampshire County Record Office. (By permission of the Earl of Malmesbury.)

Letter-Books of Lord Townshend. William L. Clements Library.

Printed sources

Official and Parliamentary sources

British Diplomatic Instructions 1689–1789. Vol. VII. France 1745–1789 (ed. L.G.W. Legg, Camden 3rd Series, XLIX, London, 1934). Cited as Legg, *British Diplomatic Instuctions.*

Calendar of Home Office Papers … 1760 to 1775 (4 vols, 1878–99). Cited as CHOP.

Journals of the House of Commons.

Journals of the House of Lords.

Statutes at Large (1776).

Almon, J., *The Debates and Proceedings of the British House of Commons from 1743 to 1774* (11 vols, London, 1766–75). Cited as Almon, *Debates.*

Almon, J., *The Parliamentary Register … 1774 to 1780* (17 vols, London, 1775–80).

Wright, J., ed. *Sir Henry Cavendish's Debates of the House of Commons during the Thirteenth Parliament of Great Britain* (2 vols., London 1841–43). Cited as *Cavendish Debates.*

'The Parliamentary Diaries of Nathaniel Ryder 1764–1767' (ed. P.D.G. Thomas, *Camden Miscellany XXIII*, London 1969), pp. 229–351. Cited as *Ryder Diary.*

Simmons, R.C. and Thomas, P.D.G., eds, *Proceedings and Debates of the British Parliaments Respecting North America, 1754–1783.* (6 vols, New York, 1982–86). Cited as Simmons and Thomas, *Proceedings and Debates.*

Contemporary correspondence and memoirs

Reports of the Historical Manuscripts Commission. Cited as HMC.

Charlemont MSS. I, 1745-83 (1891).

Kenyon MSS (1894).

Lonsdale MSS. (1893).

Onslow MSS (1895).

Stopford Sackville MSS. (2 vols, 1904, 1910).

Townshend MSS. (1887).

Memoirs of John Almon, bookseller of Picadilly (London, 1790). Cited as Almon, *Memoirs.*

The Barrington-Bernard Correspondence and Illustrative Matter 1760–1770
   (ed. E. Channing and A.C. Coolidge, Cambridge, Mass., 1912).

*Correspondence of John, fourth Duke of Bedford, selected from the originals
   at Woburn Abbey, with an introduction by Lord John Russell* (3 vols, London, 1842–46). Cited as *Bedford Papers*.

'Private Journal of John, Fourth Duke of Bedford ... 19 October 1766 ... to
   ... 28 December 1770.' *Sir Henry Cavendish's Debates of the House of
   Commons during the Thirteenth Parliament of Great Britain* (ed. J. Wright,
   2 vols, London, 1841–43), I, 591–631. Cited as *Bedford Journal*.

The Correspondence of Edmund Burke, vol. I (ed. T.W. Copeland, 1958); II
   (ed. L.S. Sutherland, 1960), Cambridge. Cited as *Burke Corr.*

The Writings and Speeches of Edmund Burke, vol. II, *Party, Parliament and the
   American Crisis, 1766–1774* (ed. P. Langford, Oxford, 1981).

Letters from George III to Lord Bute 1756–1766 (ed. R. Sedgwick, London,
   1939). Cited as *Bute Letters*.

Selections from the Family Papers preserved at Caldwell (ed. W. Mure, 2 vols,
   Glasgow, 1854).

*Anecdotes of the Life of ... the Right Honourable William Pitt, Earl of
   Chatham ... 1736 to 1778* (ed. J. Almon, 3 vols, London, 1810 edition).
   Cited as *Chatham Anecdotes*.

Correspondence of William Pitt, earl of Chatham (ed. W.S. Taylor and J.H.
   Pringle, 4 vols, London, 1838–40). Cited as *Chatham Papers*.

The Letters of Philip Dormer Stanhope, 4th Earl of Chesterfield (ed. B. Dobrée,
   6 vols, London, 1932). Cited as *Chesterfield Letters*.

'Letters of Dennys De Berdt, 1757–1770', *Transactions of the Colonial Society of Massachusetts*, 13 (1910–11), 293–461. Cited as *De Berdt Letters*.

*The Devonshire Diary. William Cavendish Fourth Duke of Devonshire. Mem-
   oranda on State of Affairs 1759–1762* (ed. P.D. Brown and K.W. Schweizer,
   Camden Fourth Series, vol. 27, London, 1982).

The Political Journal of George Budd Dodington (ed. J. Carswell and L.A.
   Dralle, Oxford, 1965). Cited as *Dodington Diary*.

The Papers of Benjamin Franklin, XIX–XXII (ed. W.B. Willcox, New Haven,
   1975–82).

*The Correspondence of General Thomas Gage with the Secretaries of State,
   and with the War Office and the Treasury 1763–1775* (ed. C.E. Carter, 2
   vols, New Haven, 1931–33). Cited as *Gage Corr.*

The Correspondence of King George the Third from 1760 to December 1783 (ed.
   Sir John Fortescue, 6 vols, London, 1927–28). Cited as *Corr. of George III.*

*Autobiography and Political Correspondence of Augustus Henry, Third Duke
   of Grafton* (ed. Sir William R. Anson, London, 1896). Cited as *Grafton
   Autobiography*.

The Grenville Papers: being the correspondence of Richard Grenville, Earl Temple, K.G., and the Right Honourable George Grenville, their friends and contemporaries (ed.W. J. Smith, 4 vols, London, 1852–53). Cited as *Grenville Papers.*

Additional Grenville Papers, 1763–1765 (ed. J. Tomlinson, Manchester, 1962).

The Harcourt Papers (ed. E.W. Harcourt, 15 vols, Oxford, 1880–1905).

The Hawke Papers: A Selection 1743–1771 (ed. R.F. Mackay, vol. 129, Navy Records Society, London, 1990).

The Diary and Letters of His Excellency Thomas Hutchinson, Esq. (ed. P.O. Hutchinson, 2 vols, London, 1883–86). Cited as *Hutchinson Diary.*

The Jenkinson Papers 1760–1766 (ed. N.S. Jucker, London, 1949).

The Letters of Junius (ed. J. Cannon, Oxford, 1978).

'Leicester House Politics, 1750–1760' (ed. A.N. Newman, *Camden Miscellany XXIII*, London, 1969), pp. 85–228. Cited as *Leicester House Politics.*

Memoirs and Correspondence of George, Lord Lyttelton from 1734 to 1773 (ed. R. Phillimore, 2 vols, London, 1845). Cited as *Lyttelton Memoirs.*

Macartney in Ireland 1768–1772. A Calendar of the Chief Secretaryship Papers of Sir George Macartney (ed. T. Bartlett, Belfast, 1978). Cited as *Macartney Papers.*

A Series of Letters of the First Earl of Malmesbury, His Family and Friends from 1745 to 1820 (ed. Earl of Malmesbury, 2 vols, London, 1870). Cited as *Malmesbury Letters.*

The Parliamentary Papers of John Robinson 1774–1784 (ed. W.T. Laprade, Camden 3rd Series XXXIII, London, 1922).

Memoirs of the Marquis of Rockingham and his Contemporaries (ed. G. Thomas, Earl of Albemarle, 2 vols, London, 1852). Cited as *Rockingham Memoirs.*

The Fourth Earl of Sandwich: Diplomatic Correspondence 1763–1765 (ed. F. Spencer, Manchester, 1961).

'Letters of William Samuel Johnson to the Governors of Connecticut', *Trumbull Papers. Collections of Massachusetts Historical Society*, 5th Series, 9 (1885), 211–490. Cited as *Trumbull Papers.*

The Memoirs and Speeches of James, 2nd Earl Waldegrave 1742–1763 (ed. J.C.D. Clark, Cambridge, 1988). Cited as *Waldegrave Memoirs.*

The Letters of Horace Walpole, Fourth Earl of Orford (ed. Mrs P. Toynbee, 16 vols, Oxford, 1905). Cited as Walpole, *Letters.*

Horace Walpole, *Memoirs of the Reign of King George the Third* (ed. G.F.R. Barker, 4 vols, London, 1894). Cited as Walpole, *Memoirs.*

The Last Journals of Horace Walpole, during the Reign of George III from 1771–1783 (ed. A.F. Stewart, 2 vols, London, 1910).

Contemporary periodicals
Gazetteer
Gentleman's Magazine
London Chronicle
London Evening Post
London Museum
Morning Chronicle
North Briton
Public Advertiser
St James's Chronicle

Secondary sources

Books

Barker, H., *Newspapers, Politics and Public Opinion in Late Eighteenth-Century England* (Oxford, 1998).

Bartlett, T. and Hayton, D., eds, *Penal Era and Golden Age: Essays in Irish History 1650–1800* (Belfast, 1979).

Black, J., ed., *Knights Errant and True Englishmen* (Edinburgh, 1989).

Black, J., *Pitt the Elder* (Cambridge, 1992).

Bonsall, B., *Sir James Lowther and Cumberland and Westmorland Elections 1754–1775* (Manchester, 1960).

Bowen, H.V., *Revenue and Reform: The Indian Problem in British Politics 1757–1773* (Cambridge, 1991).

Brewer, J., *Party Ideology and Popular Politics at the Accession of George III* (Cambridge, 1976).

Brooke, J., *The Chatham Administration 1766–1768* (London, 1956).

Brooke, J., *King George III* (London, 1972).

Brown, P., *The Chathamites* (London, 1967).

Cannon, J., *Parliamentary Reform 1640–1832* (Cambridge, 1973).

Cannon, J., *Aristocratic Century: The Peerage of Eighteenth-Century England* (Cambridge, 1984).

Cannon, J., ed., *The Whig Ascendancy. Colloquies on Hanoverian England* (London, 1981).

Christie, I.R., *Wilkes, Wyvill and Reform: The Parliamentary Reform Movement in British Politics 1760–1785* (London, 1962).

Christie, I.R., *Myth and Reality in late Eighteenth Century British Politics and other Papers* (London, 1970).

Clark, J.C.D., *The Dynamics of Change. The Crisis of the 1750s and English Party Systems* (Cambridge, 1982).

Cronne, H.A., Moody, T.W. and Quinn, D.B., eds, *Essays in British and Irish History in Honour of J.E. Todd* (London, 1949).

Elliot, G.F.S., *The Border Elliots and the Family of Minto* (Edinburgh, 1897).

Elofson, W.M., *The Rockingham Connection and the Second Founding of the Whig Party, 1768–1773* (Montreal, 1996).

Fitzmaurice, Lord, *Life of William Earl of Shelburne, afterwards First Marquess of Lansdowne* (London, 2 vols, 1912).

Fortescue, J.W., *A History of the British Army, vol. III 1763–1793* (London, 1911).

Haig, R.L., *The Gazetteer 1735–1797: A Study in the Eighteenth Century English Newspaper* (Carbondale, Ill., 1960).

Hill, B.W., *British Parliamentary Parties 1742–1832* (London, 1985).

Hoffman, R.J.S., *Edmund Burke. New York Agent, with his Letters to the New York Assembly* (Philadelphia, 1956).

Hoffman, R.J.S., *The Marquis. A Study of Lord Rockingham 1730–1782* (New York, 1973).

Johnson, A.S., *A Prologue to Revolution. The Political Career of George Grenville (1712–1770)* (Lanham, Md., 1997).

Johnston, E.M., *Great Britain and Ireland 1760–1800* (Edinburgh, 1963).

Jones, C., ed., *A Pillar of the Constitution. The House of Lords in British Politics, 1640–1784* (London, 1989).

Labaree, B.W., *The Boston Tea Party* (New York, 1964).

Langford, P., *The First Rockingham Administration 1765–1766* (London, 1973).

Lawson, P., *George Grenville. A Political Life* (Oxford, 1984).

Maccoby, S., *English Radicalism 1762–1785: The Origins* (London, 1955).

McDowell, R.B., *Ireland in the Age of Imperialism and Revolution 1760–1801* (Oxford, 1979).

Mackay, R.F., *Admiral Hawke* (Oxford, 1973).

McKelvey, J.L., *George III and Lord Bute: The Leicester House Years* (Durham, N.C., 1973).

Middleton, R., *The Bells of Victory. The Pitt-Newcastle Ministry and the Conduct of the Seven Years' War 1757–1762* (Cambridge, 1985).

Morgan, E.S. and Morgan, H.M., *The Stamp Act Crisis* (Chapel Hill, 1953).

Namier, Sir Lewis, *The Structure of Politics at the Accession of George III* (2nd edn, London, 1957).

Namier, Sir Lewis, *England in the Age of the American Revolution* (2nd edn, London, 1961).

Namier, Sir Lewis, *Crossroads of Power. Essays on England in the Eighteenth Century* (London, 1962).

Namier, Sir Lewis and Brooke, J., *Charles Townshend* (London, 1964).

Namier, Sir Lewis and Brooke, J., eds, *The House of Commons 1754–1790: The History of Parliament* (London, 3 vols, 1964).

Newman, A., *The World Turned Inside Out: New Views on George II* (Leicester, 1988).

Norris, J., *Shelburne and Reform* (London, 1963).

O'Gorman, F., *The Rise of Party in England: The Rockingham Whigs 1760–82* (London, 1975).

O'Gorman, F., *Voters, Patrons and Parties: The Unreformed Electorate of Hanoverian England 1734–1832* (Oxford, 1989).

Olson, A.G., *The Radical Duke. The Career and Correspondence of Charles Lennox Third Duke of Richmond* (London, 1961).

Olson, A.G., *Making the Empire Work: London and American Interest Groups 1690–1790* (Cambridge, Mass., 1992).

Pares, R., *King George III and the Politicians* (Oxford, 1953).

Penson, L.M., *The Colonial Agents of the British West Indies* (London, 1924).

Peters, M., *Pitt and Popularity. The Patriot Minister and London Opinion during the Seven Years War* (Oxford, 1980).

Peters, M., *The Elder Pitt* (London, 1998).

Rashed, Z.E., *The Peace of Paris, 1763* (Liverpool, 1951).

Rea, R.R., *The English Press in Politics 1760–1774* (Lincoln, Nebr., 1963).

Roberts, M., *Splendid Isolation 1763–1780* (Reading, 1970).

Roberts, M., *Macartney in Russia* (London, 1974).

Roberts, M., *British Diplomacy and Swedish Politics 1758–1773* (London, 1980).

Roberts, R. and Kynaston, D., eds, *The Bank of England: Money, Power and Influence 1694–1994* (Oxford, 1995).

Rodger, N.A.M., *The Insatiable Earl. A Life of John Montagu, 4th Earl of Sandwich* (London, 1993).

Rogers, N., *Crowd, Culture and Politics in Georgian Britain* (Oxford, 1998).

Rudé, G., *Wilkes and Liberty: A Social Study of 1763 to 1774* (Oxford, 1962).

Schweizer, K.W., ed., *Lord Bute: Essays in Re-interpretation* (Leicester, 1988).

Scott, H.M., *British Foreign Policy in the Age of the American Revolution* (Oxford, 1990).

Shelton, W.J., *English Hunger and Industrial Disorders: A Study of Social Conflict During the First Decade of George III's Reign* (London, 1973).

Shy, J., *Towards Lexington. The Role of the British Army in the Coming of the American Revolution* (Princeton, 1965).

Sosin, J.M., *Agents and Merchants: British Colonial Policy and the Origins of the American Revolution 1763–1775* (Lincoln, Nebr., 1965).

Sutherland, L.S., *The East India Company in Eighteenth-Century Politics* (Oxford, 1952).

Taylor, S., Connors, R. and Jones, C., eds, *Hanoverian Britain and Empire: Essays in Memory of Philip Lawson* (Woodbridge, 1998).

Thomas, P.D.G., *The House of Commons in the Eighteenth Century* (Oxford, 1971).

Thomas, P.D.G., *British Politics and the Stamp Act Crisis: The First Phase of the American Revolution 1763–1767* (Oxford, 1975).

Thomas, P.D.G., *Lord North* (London, 1976).

Thomas, P.D.G., *The Townshend Duties Crisis: The Second Phase of the American Revolution 1767–1773* (Oxford, 1987).

Thomas, P.D.G., *Tea Party to Independence: The Third Phase of the American Revolution 1773–1776* (Oxford, 1991).

Thomas, P.D.G., *John Wilkes: A Friend to Liberty* (Oxford, 1996).

Thomas, P.D.G., *Politics in Eighteenth-Century Wales* (Cardiff, 1998).

Tracy, N., *Navies, Deterrence, and American Independence* (Vancouver, 1988).

Whiteman, A., Bromley, J.S. and Dickson, P.M.G., eds, *Statesmen, Scholars and Merchants. Essays in Eighteenth Century History presented to Dame Lucy Sutherland* (Oxford, 1973).

Whitworth, R., *Field Marshal Lord Ligonier: A Story of the British Army 1702–1770* (Oxford, 1958).

Wiggin, R., *The Faction of Cousins: A Political Account of the Grenvilles 1733–1763* (New Haven, 1958).

Williams, B., *The Life of William Pitt Earl of Chatham* (London, 2 vols, 1913–14).

Wilson, K., *The Sense of the People. Politics, Culture and Imperialism in England, 1715–1785* (Cambridge, 1995).

Winstanley, D.A., *Personal and Party Government 1760–1766* (Cambridge, 1910).

Winstanley, D.A., *Lord Chatham and the Whig Opposition* (Cambridge, 1912).

Yorke, P.C., *The Life and Correspondence of Philip Yorke, Earl of Hardwicke, Lord High Chancellor of Great Britain* (Cambridge, 3 vols, 1913).

Essays and articles

Anderson, M.S., 'Great Britain and the Russian Fleet, 1769–70', *Slavonic and East European Review*, 31 (1951–52), 148–63.

Anderson, M.S., 'Great Britain and the Russo-Turkish War of 1768–74', *English Historical Review* [EHR], 69 (1954), 39–58.

Bartlett, T., 'The Townshend Viceroyalty 1767–72', in Bartlett and Hayton, eds, *Penal Era and Golden Age*, pp. 88–112.

Bartlett, T., 'The Augmentation of the Army in Ireland 1767–1769', *EHR*, 96

(1981), 540–59.

Black, J., 'Anglo-French Relations 1763–1775', *Francia*, 18 (1991), 99–114.

Bowen, H.V., 'Lord Clive and Speculation in East India Company Stock, 1766', *Historical Journal [HJ]*, 30 (1987), 905–20.

Bowen, H.V., 'A Question of Sovereignty? The Bengal Land Revenue Issue, 1765–67', *Journal of Imperial and Commonwealth History [JICH]*, 16 (1988), 155–76.

Bowen, H.V., 'The "Little Parliament": The General Court of the East India Company 1750–1784', *HJ*, 34 (1991), 857–72.

Bowen, H.V., 'The Bank of England During the Long Eighteenth Century, 1694–1820', in Roberts and Kynaston, eds, *The Bank of England*, pp. 1–18.

Bowen, H.V., 'British Conceptions of Global Empire 1756–83', *JICH*, 26 (1998), 1–27.

Brewer, J., 'The Misfortunes of Lord Bute: A Case-Study of Eighteenth-Century Political Argument and Public Opinion', *HJ*, 16 (1973), 3–43.

Bullion, J., 'Securing the Peace: Lord Bute, the plan for the Army, and the Origins of the American Revolution', in Schweizer, ed., *Lord Bute*, pp. 17–39.

Bullion, J., '"George, Be a King!". The Relationship between Princess Augusta and George III', in Taylor, Connors and Jones, eds, *Hanoverian Britain and Empire*, pp. 177–97.

Chaffin, R.C., 'The Townshend Acts of 1767', *William and Mary Quarterly [WMQ]*, 27 (1970), 90–121.

Christie, I.R., 'The Cabinet During the Grenville Ministry', *EHR*, 73 (1958), 86–92.

Christie, I.R., 'Was There a "New Toryism" in the Earlier Part of George III's Reign', *Journal of British Studies*, 5 (1965–66), 60–76.

Christie, I.R., 'George III and the Historians – Thirty Years On', *History*, 71 (1986), 205–21.

Christie, I.R., 'Party in Politics in the Age of Lord North's Administration', *Parliamentary History [PH]*, 6 (1987), 47–68.

Dippel, H., 'Prussia's English Policy after the Seven Years War', *Central European History*, 4 (1971), 195–214.

Ditchfield, G.M., 'The House of Lords in the Age of the American Revolution', in Jones, ed., *Pillar of the Constitution*, pp. 199–246.

Elofson, W.M., 'The Rockingham Whigs and the Country Tradition', *PH*, 8 (1989), 90–115.

Grant, W.L., 'Canada versus Guadeloupe: An Episode of the Seven Years War', *American Historical Review [AHR]*, 17 (1911–12), 735–43.

Greene, J.P., 'The Seven Years War and the American Revolution: The Causal Relationship Reconsidered', *JICH*, 8 (1980), 85–105.

Hughes, E., 'Lord North's Correspondence 1766–1783', *EHR*, 62 (1947), 218–38.

Jarrett, D., 'The Regency Crisis of 1765', *EHR*, 85 (1970), 282–315.

Johnston, E.M, 'The Career and Correspondence of Thomas Allan c. 1725–98', *Irish Historical Studies [IHS]*, 10 (1956–57), 298–324.

Langford, P., 'Old Whigs, Old Tories and the American Revolution', *JICH*, 8 (1980), 106–30.

Lawson, P., 'Grenville and America: The Years of Opposition 1765–70', *WMQ*, 37 (1980), 561–76.

Lawson, P., 'Parliament and the First East India Inquiry 1767', *PH*, 1 (1983), 99–114.

Lawson, P., 'Parliament, Corn and the Constitution: The Embargo Crisis of 1766', *PH*, 5 (1986), 17–37.

Lenman, B. and Lawson, P., 'Robert Clive, the "Black Jagir", and British Politics', *HJ*, 26 (1983), 801–29.

Macalpine, I. and Hunter, R., 'A Clinical Reassessment of the "Insanity" of George III and some of its Historical Implications', *Bulletin of the Institute of Historical Research [BIHR]*, 40 (1967), 166–85.

McCahill, M.W., 'The House of Lords in the 1760s', in Jones, ed., *Pillar of the Constitution*, pp. 165–98.

McCracken, J.L., 'The Irish Vice-Royalty 1760–1773', in Cronne, Moody and Quinn, eds, *Essays in British and Irish History*, pp. 152–68.

Olson, A.G., 'The Duke of Richmond's Memorandum, 1–7 July 1766', *EHR*, 75 (1960), 475–82.

Olson, A.G., 'The London Mercantile Lobby and the Coming of the American Revolution', *Journal of American History*, 69 (1982), 21–44.

O'Shaughnessy, A.J., 'The Formation of a Commercial Lobby: The West Indies Interest, British Colonial Policy and the American Revolution', *HJ*, 40 (1997), 71–95.

Owen, J.B., 'George II Reconsidered', in Whiteman, Bromley and Dickson, eds, *Statesmen, Scholars and Merchants*, pp. 113–34.

Penson, L.M., 'The London West India Interest in the Eighteenth Century', *EHR*, 36 (1921), 373–92.

Peters, M., 'The *Monitor* and the Constitution, 1755–1765: New Light on the Ideological Origins of English Radicalism', *EHR*, 86 (1971), 206–27.

Powell, M.J., 'The Reform of the Undertaker System: Anglo-Irish Politics, 1750–67', *IHS*, 31 (1998), 19–36.

Reitan, E.A., 'The Civil List in Eighteenth-Century British Politics: Parliamentary Supremacy versus the Independence of the Crown', *HJ*, 9 (1966), 318–37.

Reitan, E.A., 'The Civil List, 1761–77. Problems of Finance and Administration', *BIHR*, 47 (1974), 186–201.

Rice, G.W., 'Great Britain, the Manila Ransom and the First Falkland Islands Dispute with Spain, 1766', *International History Review* [*IHR*], 2 (1980), 386–409.

Schweizer, K.W., 'Lord Bute and William Pitt's Resignation in 1761', *Canadian Journal of History* [*CJH*], 8 (1973), 111–25.

Schweizer, K.W., 'Lord Bute, Newcastle, Prussia and the Hague Overtures: A Re–Examination', *Albion*, 9 (1977), 72–97.

Schweizer, K.W., 'The Non-Renewal of the Anglo-Prussian Subsidy Treaty, 1761–1762: A Historical Revision', *CJH*, 13 (1978), 383–98.

Schweizer, K.W., 'The Bedford Motion and the House of Lords Debate 5 February 1762', *PH*, 5 (1986), 107–23.

Schweizer, K.W., 'Lord Bute, William Pitt and the Peace Negotiations with France, April–September 1761', in Schweizer, ed., *Lord Bute*, pp. 41–55.

Schweizer, K.W., 'Israel Mauduit: Pamphleteering and Foreign Policy in the Age of the Elder Pitt', in Taylor, Connors and Jones, eds, *Hanoverian Britain and Empire*, pp. 198–209.

Schweizer, K.W. and Leonard, C.S., 'Britain, Prussia, Russia and the Galitzin Letter: A Re-assessment', *HJ*, 26 (1983), 531–56.

Scott, H.M., 'The Importance of Bourbon Naval Reconstruction to the Strategy of Choiseul after the Seven Years War', *IHR*, (1979), 17–35.

Scott, H.M., '"The True Principles of the Revolution": The Duke of Newcastle and the Idea of the Old System', in Black, ed., *Knights Errant and True Englishmen*, pp. 55–91.

Spencer, F., 'The Anglo-Prussian Breach of 1762: An Historical Revision', *History*, 41 (1956), 100–12.

Taylor, R.J., 'Israel Mauduit', *New England Quarterly*, 24 (1951), 208–30.

Thomas, P.D.G., 'The Beginning of Parliamentary Reporting in Newspapers, 1768–1774', *EHR*, 74 (1959), 623–36.

Thomas, P.D.G., 'Charles Townshend and American Taxation in 1767', *EHR*, 83 (1968), 33–51.

Thomas, P.D.G., 'George III and the American Revolution', *History*, 70 (1985), 16–31.

Thomas, P.D.G., 'Thoughts on the British Constitution by George III in 1760', *BIHR*, 60 (1987), 361–3.

Thomas, P.D.G., 'The House of Commons and the Middlesex Elections of 1768–1769', *PH*, 12 (1993), 233–48.

Thomas, P.D.G., 'A Mid-Eighteen-Century Tory: From Country Party to Courtier and Comedian. Sir John Glynne of Hawarden (1713–1777)', *PH*, 17 (1998), 343–53.

Watson, D.H., 'The Rise of the Opposition at Wildman's Club', *BIHR*, 44 (1971), 55–77.

Williams, T., 'The Cabinet in the Eighteenth Century', *History*, 22 (1937–38), 240–52.

Woodland, P., 'Extra-Parliamentary Political Organisation in the Making: Benjamin Heath and the Opposition to the 1763 Cider Excise', *PH*, 4 (1985), 115–36.

Woodland, P., 'Political Atomization and Regional Interests in the 1761 Parliament: The Impact of the Cider Debates 1763–1766', *PH*, 8 (1989), 63–89.

Woodland, P., 'The House of Lords, the City of London, and Political Controversy in the Mid-1760s: The Opposition to the Cider Excise Further Considered', *PH*, 11 (1992), 57–87.

Unpublished university theses

Bartlett, T., 'The Townshend Viceroyalty 1767–72' (Ph.D., Belfast, 1976).

Bowen, H.V., 'British Politics and the East India Company, 1766–1773' (Ph.D., Wales, 1986).

Breeze, H.P., 'The North Ministry and Ireland, 1770–1782' (Ph.D., Wales, 1993).

Davies, N.C., 'The Bill of Rights Society and the Origins of Radicalism in Britain' (MA, Wales, 1986).

Durrant, P., 'A Political Life of Augustus Henry Fitzroy, Third Duke of Grafton, 1735–1811' (Ph.D., Manchester, 1978).

Escott, M.M., 'Britain's Relations with France and Spain, 1763–1771' (Ph.D., Wales, 1988).

Hamer, M.T., 'From the Grafton Administration to the Ministry of North 1768–1772' (Ph.D., Cambridge, 1970).

Hardy, A., 'The Duke of Newcastle and his Friends in Opposition 1762–1765' (MA, Manchester, 1956).

Jones, D.E., 'The Political Career of William Wildman, 2nd Viscount Barrington 1717–1793' (Ph.D., Wales, 1991).

Lawson, P., 'Faction in Politics: George Grenville and his Followers 1765–70' (Ph.D., Wales, 1980).

Lowe, W.C., 'Politics in the House of Lords 1760–1775' (Ph.D., Emory, 1975).

Nicholas, J.D., 'Lord Bute's Ministry 1762–1763' (Ph.D., Wales, 1987).

Powell, M.J., 'An Early Imperial Problem: Britain and Ireland 1750–1783' (Ph.D., Wales, 1997).

Prior, D., 'The Career of Robert, 1st Baron Clive, with special Reference to his Political and Administrative Career' (M.Phil., Wales, 1993).

Rees, A.J., 'The Practice and Procedure of the House of Lords 1714–1784' (Ph.D., Wales, 1987).

Rees, S.E., 'The Political Career of Wills Hill, Earl of Hillsborough (1718–1793) with Particular Reference to his American Policy' (Ph.D., Wales, 1977).

Thomas, J.P., 'The British Empire and the Press 1763–1774' (D.Phil., Oxford, 1982).

Tomlinson, J.R.G., 'The Grenville Papers 1763–1765' (MA, Manchester, 1956).

Williams, D.E., 'English Hunger Riots in 1766' (Ph.D., Wales, 1978).

Index